GOVERNMENT'S END

GOVERNMENT'S END

Why Washington Stopped Working

JONATHAN RAUCH

PUBLICAFFAIRS

New York

Printed in the United States of America.

Portions of this work were originally published in different form in the April
25, 1992, September 5, 1992, August 7, 1993, and September 7, 1996, issues of
National Journal.

Book design and composition by Mark McGarry, Texas Type & Book Works
Set in Fairfield

Library of Congress Cataloging-in-Publication Data
Rauch, Jonathan, 1960–
Government's end : why Washington stopped working / Jonathan Rauch.
— [Rev. ed.]
p.   cm.
Rev. ed. of: Demosclerosis. ©   1994.
Includes bibliographical references (p.   ) and index.
ISBN 1–891620–49–5 (pbk.)
1. Pressure groups—United States. 2. Entitlement spending—United States.
3. Government spending policy—United States. 4. United States—Politics and
government.   I. Rauch, Jonathan. 1960–   Demosclerosis.   II. Title.
JK1118.R4   1999
324'.4'0973—dc21   99–41893
                                                                                    CIP

To the memory of Mancur Olson,

teacher

Contents

1

The Trap

BETWEEN the time when the results became clear and the moment when the new president-elect emerged to acknowledge his victory, two long hours passed. A crowd of fifty thousand stood waiting for their man in front of the Old State House in Little Rock, Arkansas, shivering in bitterly cold weather that, being unseasonable, caught people in their shirtsleeves. Millions of citizens elsewhere waited, too. Younger people could barely remember a Democratic presidency and wondered how the first Democratic president-elect in sixteen years would sound. Their elders wondered whether the new man would show that he had learned from his Democratic predecessors' mistakes.

At 11:22 P.M. central time, on November 3, 1992, Bill Clinton finally emerged, looking exhausted but happy. He had made history, and he knew it. His speech was short and began with thank-yous for the crowd, the family, the voters, the running mate. Then came what was, in effect, the first substantive statement of the Clinton years. He announced that he would "face problems too long ignored," and that people needed to be brought together "so that our diversity can be a source of strength." Then he said: "I think perhaps the most important thing that we understand here in the heartland of Arkansas is the need to reform the political system, to reduce the influence of special interests and give more influence back to the kind of people that are in this crowd tonight by the tens of thousands. And I will work . . . to do that."

Campaigning against special interests—railing against them and deploring them and promising to break them—is a venerable American tradition. In 1948, President Harry Truman cried out from his railway car that his campaign was "a crusade of the people against the special interests," and the people cheered. In private, twenty years earlier, Calvin Coolidge warned his successor, Herbert Hoover, about the armies of interested parties who would be coming to see him. "You have to stand, every day, three or four hours of visitors," Coolidge said. "Nine-tenths of them want something they ought not to have. If you keep dead still, they will run down in three or four minutes. If you even cough or smile, they will start up all over again." Long before Coolidge, James Madison thought hard about how to contain the undue influence of what he called "faction," by which he meant "a number of citizens . . . who are united and actuated by some common impulse of passion, or of interest, adverse to the rights of other citizens, or to the permanent and aggregate interests of the community." If he had known the term "special interest," no doubt he would have used it.

The curious thing is that ever since Coolidge's day, and especially since Truman's, interest-group activity has increased. The more the public complained and the more the politicians promised change, the more the lobbies seemed to thrive and the more powerful they seemed to become. And so the president-elect stood there in 1992, promising "to reduce the influence of special interests," as so many had promised before him.

Some years earlier, another young politician began a crusade against "special interests." Like Bill Clinton, he set out to transform government into something more effective, more forward-looking, more responsive. He was as determined as Bill Clinton, and also as bright (which was saying something). His name was David Stockman, and in those years, in the mid-1970s, he worked as executive director of the House Republican Conference, where his boss was a rather obscure moderate Republican named John Anderson. In 1975, out of the blue, Stockman announced himself to the world with a brilliant and provocative article that opened a new conservative front in the war against big government.

"The vast increase in federal social welfare outlays," wrote Stockman in *The Public Interest* magazine, "has created in its wake a political maintenance system based in no small part on the cooptation and incorporation of Congress itself." Conservatives and liberals alike channeled social spending, not to those who most needed it or to the places where it would do the most good, but to all 435 congressional districts, in a rain of political manna. The maxims of real-world social spending included "Don't close the money sluice no matter how outmoded the program" and—a concise formulation of political utilitarianism—"The greatest goodies for the greatest number." Urban-aid programs and housing programs and education programs had become for the 1970s what dams and bridges had been for the 1930s and 1940s. As a consequence, "what may have been the bright promise of the Great Society has been transformed into a flabby hodge-podge, funded without policy consistency or rigor, that increasingly looks like a great social pork barrel."

Stockman soon went on to become a Republican congressman in his own right, and so fiercely did his intellect and ambition burn on Capitol Hill that the new Republican president, Ronald Reagan, chose him to be the administration's budget director after the 1980 election. From that post, Stockman became general of the campaign he had sketched in his article. He was the chief ideologue and strategist for what amounted to the first reformist conservative administration since the New Deal. As the Reagan administration began, he said: "We have to show that we are willing to attack powerful clients with weak claims. I think that's critical to our success—both political and economic success."

What happened was not what Stockman had in mind. Within five years Stockman had retired from the Reagan administration and from politics, embittered and disappointed. "In 1986," he wrote in the late months of that year in a postscript to his angry book *The Triumph of Politics*, "the federal government again spent 24 percent of the GNP, compared to a pre-1980 norm of about 20 percent. Why? Because the White House has no semblance of a program or political will to spend any less." The powerful clients, he said, had won. After his book was published, little was heard from Stockman.

At about the same time, however, another reformer stood before a small group of conservative activists and explained to the frustrated audience how, despite Ronald Reagan's failure, the fight against entrenched government could yet be won. I happened to be there that night and was fascinated by the peculiar but compelling visitor. Newt Gingrich talked grandly and abstractly and seemed as eccentric as his name. Yet his magnetism was apparent, and his unruly intelligence dazzling. The problem until then, he explained, had been failure to think "outside the box." Whereupon he drew a box: a matrix of dots, three by three. He reminded his audience of the old puzzle: Connect all of these dots by drawing only four lines. The trick is that you can't solve the puzzle unless you draw lines that extend beyond the boundaries of the matrix. But if you break out of bounds, he said, you *can* solve it.

In 1995, he got his chance. When he became speaker of the House, Gingrich was determined to do from Capitol Hill what David Stockman had tried to do from the White House. The result, to Gingrich's credit, included two landmark reforms of recalcitrant and dysfunctional federal programs: farm subsidies and welfare. Elsewhere, however, Gingrich's failure was complete and comprehensive. Indeed, for his party it proved catastrophic. By 1999, Gingrich was a memory.

The contours of Gingrich's assault on Washington were different from those of Stockman's assault, and both differed sharply from Bill Clinton's attempts to change things, most notably the health-care reform effort of 1993 and 1994. Yet the fate of all three reformers was more or less the same. Washington remained much as it had been before. ("Only more so," a wag might add.) Stockman retired denouncing his own failure; Gingrich was unceremoniously dumped by his party. Clinton met, in some respects, the saddest fate of all: He entered office as a reformer, promising a new dynamism in government; he left office as a manager whose domestic policy traded in microscopic initiatives. In a sense, the man who stood on the steps of the Old State House that night in 1992, who promised to "reduce the influence of special interests and give more influence back to the kind of people that are in this crowd tonight," packed up and left town long before Bill Clinton did. As Clinton left the stage, no viable reform movement, conservative or liberal or anything else, remained on the field.

No doubt the future would bring more reformers, more cries to take up arms against "special interests" and return government "to the people." Nonetheless, the twenty or so years that began with Ronald Reagan's election shed a cold and brilliant light on what it is that government's would-be reformers, of whatever stripe, are up against. Change is as easy to promise as ever. But it has grown a good deal harder to deliver. Politicians like Stockman and Clinton and Gingrich and their successors and *their* successors cannot hope to keep their promises to reform the sprawling establishment of Washington, or to "reduce the influence of special interests," until they unriddle the paradoxes of a political malady whose perverse dynamics undermine government and enrage voters.

Why does the "special-interest" sector grow year after year, despite the politicians' promises and the public's disgust? Why does this sector feed on its own growth, with no limits in sight?

Why is it that, despite America's extraordinary wealth and the advent of all kinds of new problem-solving technology, the American government's capacity to solve large problems appears to have diminished sharply since the 1960s? Why has government ceased, for the most part, to be a creative force?

Why does "getting things done" in the short run often make problem solving more difficult for the government in the long run? Why does the constant commotion of activity in Washington stymie rather than advance the effectiveness of government as a whole?

Why are many liberals and Democrats, with their greater proclivity to use government to right wrongs and correct flaws, paralyzing the very government that they believe they are championing? Why are many conservatives, with their blame-the-liberals rhetoric, actually feeding the "big government" that they constantly decry?

Why was Bill Clinton's election-night rhetoric, which promised to reinvigorate the system by reducing the influence of "them" (the special interests) and increasing the influence of "us" (the American people), a cause rather than a cure of the problem he sought to solve?

Why is it that the body politic demands "change" in the abstract but recoils from it in the particular? Why did three waves of determined reform fail, each more spectacularly than the last?

If politicians and the public do not understand the answers to those questions, they will not have a chance.

"The clear mandate of this election," Clinton remarked a few days after winning in 1992, "was an end of politics as usual, an end to the gridlock in Washington, an end to finger-pointing and blame." Alas, his attack on "special interests" was not particularly encouraging, because it implied that the problem was "them." Wrong. The problem is us.

Sighs and Moans

For me, the first inkling that something malign was happening came in February 1985, only a few months after I arrived in Washington. Having just left my job with a newspaper in the

South to become a reporter for *National Journal*, I wandered into the Senate press gallery and beheld the tall, gangly figure of Senator Alan Simpson. The Wyoming Republican was doing what's known as "holding the floor" while the majority and minority leaders worked behind the scenes on some compromise or other. In this case, holding the floor consisted of haranguing an almost entirely empty chamber (and this was before television came to the Senate). I sat down in the gallery, at first listening idly and then becoming absorbed. To this day, I have never witnessed another political speech like that one.

Simpson was complaining about the partisan games that go on in the Capitol. "Out there in the American public," he said, "are people who are watching us go through this, trying to see who can hook the anchor on the Democrats or who can hook the anchor on the Republicans, who look upon that as a childish activity." Well, that was certainly true, but it was hardly new. Simpson went on, however, to talk about the political uses of fear.

"We are frozen in place," he mused. "We are frozen in place because there are enough of us who get a coterie of people and interest groups and media about us and say they are going to do a number on this issue or are going to do this or that." He talked about a veterans' lobbyist he knew. "We have had some very earthy discussions, the two of us. He is a delightful, pleasant guy. But the emphasis was to get the two million members; and you do that . . . just like we do things here—by juicing up the troops. . . . What happened to us was we got a $200 billion deficit by juicing up the troops." And then he said: "One of the things . . . that we do here so beautifully . . . is the use of fear, raw fear. You can do a lot with raw fear. You can do a lot with raw fear with people who do like nuclear power or do not like it. You can do a lot with raw fear with farmers. You can do a lot with raw fear with uranium workers. You can do a lot with raw fear with oil and gas workers. You can do a lot with raw fear with veterans. You can do a lot with raw fear with Social Security recipients.

"And that is what we do beautifully here in this place, because

I guess we really are all impelled by a raw fear—and that raw fear is, I would guess, a fear of what the electorate will do to us, and, of course, maybe that is the primal raw fear in this place."

Simpson's speech was more than just an oration; it was an outburst. The striking thing about it, besides its candor, was the level of frustration it exposed. At that point, "gridlock" had yet to become a political cliché. The same party controlled the Senate and the White House (though not the House) under an extraordinarily popular president. Yet here was rhetoric of stagnation and defeat: "We are frozen in place." Simpson's complaint went deeper than the parties or personalities in the White House or the Congress, deeper even than the difficulty of getting things done. The founders, after all, intended that personalities clash and that getting things done be difficult: better safe than sorry. Simpson's complaint seemed to be that individuals and groups had become adept at mobilizing fear to achieve political goals. His tone suggested the pain of one who is in a trap and does not understand why he can't get out.

In May 1985, three months after Alan Simpson's speech, one Democratic representative from Texas, a former banker and high school teacher named Marvin Leath, rose in the House to propose a budget package that would have significantly reduced the deficit. In those days, the deficit was so large that it threatened to spiral out of control. In his package, Leath included most of what the experts agreed needed to be done: reductions in Ronald Reagan's defense buildup, some increases in taxes, and the abolition of one year's cost-of-living increase in Social Security payments. This last provision was especially courageous, because a Democrat proposing to dock Social Security was like a hemophiliac volunteering for a sword fight. On the House floor, Leath gave a gutsy speech that deserved to be remembered, though it wasn't: "As you could most certainly expect," he said, "conservatives are pointing fingers and telling liberals, 'It's your fault. All the years of massive social and domestic spending are responsible for these deficits. Let's gore your ox, and we can solve the problem.' And just as certainly, as you might also expect, liberals are pointing fingers and telling conservatives, 'It's *your* fault. These massive defense buildups and these massive tax cuts are responsible for these deficits. Let's gore your ox, and we can solve the problem.'

"The . . . truth is, we all know who is to blame. Democrats and Republicans are to blame. Liberals and conservatives and all in between are to blame. The people are to blame for believing all the garbage they get bombarded with through the mail raising money from both parties and a thousand special-interest lobbies who circle this Capitol in their Mercedes automobiles after leaving their million-dollar homes in northern Virginia."

Here again, as in Simpson's speech, were the undertones of rage and entrapment. Politicians have a poor image, but anyone who knows them knows that by and large they are hardworking people who want only the best for their country. They do not want to make things worse; they want to make them better. Yet increasingly they feel that they *cannot* make things better. Increasingly they play the blame game without wanting to but without understanding why they play it or how to escape. They wonder why the swelling crowds of aides and lobbyists and campaign consultants seem not to empower them but to hem them in. And in all of those feelings, they mirror the feelings of the people who elect them.

Many people in Washington admired Leath's budget package, because it made good sense. Practically everyone admired Leath, who stood up and told the truth and stuck his neck out. Practically everyone voted against him, too. His package was defeated, 372 to 56. In 1990, disgusted with his and Congress's inability to solve problems, Leath announced that he would not seek reelection to a seventh term. He became a lobbyist.

For thirty years, the American public has increasingly expressed feelings of frustration and entrapment similar to Alan Simpson's and Marvin Leath's. In 1958, around three-fourths of the people said they trusted the government in Washington to "do what's right" always or most of the time. After the assassination of John F. Kennedy, a long decline of confidence began. By about 1980, the trust level had fallen by more than half, and, apart from a temporary excursion upward during the Reagan years, it has stayed in the 20 to 30 percent range (depending on which poll you look at) ever since. Americans' mistrust of their government's capacity to "do the right thing" ranks among the largest and most consequential political changes of the twentieth century. Other data tell the same story of disillusionment. Two-thirds of Americans, solid majorities of Democrats and Republicans alike, say that the government creates more problems than it solves, rather than vice versa. By more than two to one, people say that abuses by the federal government are a bigger problem than abuses by big business, and that "big government" is a greater threat to the country in the future than "big business" or "big labor." Between the early 1950s and the early 1990s, the proportion of people saying that government wastes "a lot" of their tax money rose from fewer than half to 75 percent. By the time the 1980s came, politicians routinely campaigned against "Washington" and "government," even as voters demanded more from both places. People felt they deserved more, yet they felt they received less, and they didn't understand why. The more they struggled, the more they felt beset.

Red Herrings

The easiest way to refer to government's problems is as "special-interest gridlock." That description isn't completely wrong, but it is far enough off target to be badly misleading.

For one thing, the "gridlock" metaphor implies that nothing gets done. It implies, in other words, that the problem is lack of governmental motion or lack of activity. One of the main goals of this book is to refocus attention away from the quantity of motion in Washington and toward the effectiveness of results. The central issue is not "Why does Washington get so little done?" It is "Why has Washington's activity become so ineffective at solving problems?"

In Washington, after all, things always get done. Despite the talk of gridlock, the government reliably passes scads of laws and scads more regulations and, by any objective measure, gets a lot done. Even the do-nothing, "gridlocked" days of George Bush were in fact neither do-nothing nor really gridlocked. Those years saw passage of the sweeping Clean Air Act and other environmental measures, the equally sweeping Americans with Disabilities Act, new money for child care, a major highway bill, and much else besides. In just the field of civil rights, during the supposedly gridlocked Bush period the government enacted, among other new programs and laws, the Civil Rights Act of 1991, the Voting Rights Language Assistance Act, the Civil Liberties Act Amendments of 1992, the Minority Farmers Rights Act, the Japanese American Redress Entitlement Program, the antiredlining provisions of the banking-reform law, the Hate Crimes Statistics Act, and the aforementioned Americans with Disabilities Act. According to congressional figures, the number and page count of laws enacted during "gridlock" remained well in line with the post-1970 norm.

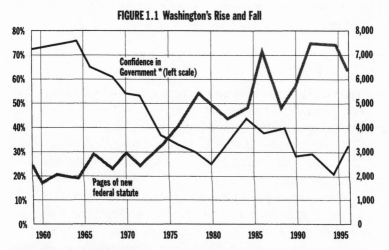

FIGURE 1.1 Washington's Rise and Fall

*Percentage of respondents saying they trust the government in Washington to do what is right just about always or most of the time.

SOURCES: University of Michigan National Election Studies; Norman J. Ornstein, Thomas E. Mann, and Michael J. Malbin, *Vital Statistics on Congress, 1997–1998* (*Congressional Quarterly*, 1998).

In fact, if you look at the record, simple gridlock *can't* be the problem. Figure 1.1 shows two basic indicators plotted against each other: people's confidence in the government, as measured by their responses to that classic "trust in government" question, and pages of new laws enacted by each Congress. Though I would not want to make any sophisticated social-science claims for this chart, it certainly rules out the standard gridlock hypothesis in which people are unhappy because the wheels in Washington are spinning too slowly: Over almost forty years, the more activity Washington generated, the *less* happy people were. So "getting more done," however desirable or undesirable it may be on its own account, cannot go to the root of the problem.

The question is not the quantity of activity but how effectively a given amount of activity solves problems "on net." That phrase "on net"—meaning "on balance," after the wins and losses are tallied up—is important. In life, every solution creates at least some new problems. The trick is always to find solutions that create fewer problems than they solve. In the classic example, if you kill a fly with a flyswatter, you come out ahead on net. If you kill a fly with a cannon, you create more problems than you solve. To the extent that an institution can reliably solve more problems than it creates, it has problem-solving capacity.

Problem-solving capacity is precisely what seems to have been shrinking for the federal government. Political activity has become a kind of flailing that creates frenzy but does little good, or even makes problems worse. Wheels spin and gears mesh, but the car goes nowhere, or goes everywhere at once, or shakes itself to pieces. More problems seem to be created than solved.

The other trouble with the term "special-interest gridlock" is its implication that a few fat cats manipulate the system for their own narrow advantage. The fact is that the American system of governance today is much less at the mercy of any narrow, manipulative few than at any time in the past. The era of the backroom bosses who called the shots, of the rich patrons who could buy the system, is over. The Leath budget was not defeated by any cigar-chomping industrialist with an interest in protecting his western mining interests. It was defeated by a coalition of interests representing virtually everybody. The American Association of Retired Persons alone boasts well over 30 million members, or one of every six adult Americans; because most of us have aged relatives, most of us are among the group's indirect clients; because we all grow old, each one of us is among the group's potential members. If you add the farmers and veterans and oil workers and all the others whom Simpson mentioned and Leath took on, you see there is no longer anything particularly special about "special interests." Today everyone is organized, and everyone is part of an interest group. We have met the special interests, and they are us.

If, however, the interests are no longer special, they are not quite general, either. And here is a puzzle. Conventional wisdom has suggested that as more Americans got organized, and as the process was opened up to more groups and classes than ever before, the claims of all of those competing interests would be weighed and mediated in the political process, producing a more balanced and satisfactory result than the fat-cat system had ever done. But that is not what has happened. The public today is less happy than before, and problems seem less likely to be solved.

It is possible to cook up all kinds of ad hoc explanations for what went wrong. Many have some truth in them. But most of them are ultimately unsatisfying.

A standard complaint has been lack of leadership. But that diagnosis does not explain enough. There is little evidence that the people are electing poorer leaders now than in the past, that a worse class of person runs for public office, or that human leadership capacity has deteriorated over time. Some politicians are fools and rogues, but many more are bright, hardworking, and honest. In times of crisis—the debate over whether to authorize war in the Persian Gulf in 1991, for instance—the system still can and does rise to the challenge magnificently. At exceptional moments, leadership can still be found in abundance, even in the rank and file of politicians. Marvin Leath's ill-fated 1985 budget proposal was only one example.

I know an antigovernment activist who said he became physically ill just looking at the edifices of big government in Washington. For me, the effect is always the opposite. As many times as I have been in the United States Capitol, I can't enter it or even look up at the great dome without catching my breath a little in awe. And I have known and watched enough of the people who work there to reject another popular hypothesis, namely, that politics is dominated by jellyfish and Neanderthals. Today's politicians include a few genuine reactionaries, but also a quantity and range of activists whose commitment and talent yield nothing to the abolitionists of 150 years ago or the Progressives of a century ago or the labor left of fifty years ago. Moreover, today's activists hold positions of power, whereas in the 1950s and 1960s they were mostly locked out by the powerful old men who controlled Congress. If the government is becoming unable to solve problems, that is not because it is filling up with weaklings and reactionaries. The change has to be on the *system* level. And, to judge by the frustration and bewilderment expressed by Simpson and Leath and others, the problem must be of a sort that is not transparent to the people within the system.

Some people, mainly liberals, would say that the public was brainwashed by Ronald Reagan and other Washington-bashing conservatives into hating government, and that the result has been to render government ineffective. Yet the decline in confidence began well before Ronald Reagan and his conservatives came to town. The wave of disgust with government brought Jimmy Carter into office before it swept Reagan to power. Moreover, these days you would have to be brainwashed *not* to have doubts, or worse, about government. Even among thoughtful observers who were no fans of the Reaganites, the feeling has grown that government really is, as Bill Clinton himself once said, "in the way."

The growing influence of money in politics is often held up as the problem. That may be a problem, but there is nothing remotely new in it. There is more money in politics today than before, but money by itself need not lead to stultification. If the money is wielded by a few powerful interests who agree on what to do, then money greases the skids and things get done. Anyway, blaming money begs the real question: *Why* is there more money in politics? Why does political activity devour a growing share of the country's resources? The rising expenditure on politics is itself as much a symptom as a cause of whatever is wrong.

Some liberals complain that the problem is the power of corporate lobbying to block changes that are in the public interest. Here many of the same reservations apply. There was no lack of corporate influence in the days of Andrew Carnegie and J. P. Morgan, and those magnates were unable to stymie the trust-busters. Corporate influence is nothing new. What is new is the proliferation of nonbusiness activist groups, many of them representing what they believe to be the public interest. Some of them, such as the environmental groups, have large amounts of money and wield enough power to push through, for instance, the massive Clean Air Act of 1990, which most corporations would happily have done without. Ask a business lobbyist if he feels he can control what government does, and he will look at you with incredulity.

Still another diagnosis in recent years blamed recurrent episodes of divided control of the government, in which Republicans held the White House and Democrats held the Congress. Unquestionably, divided control can make the process stickier. However, Democrats held both branches under Carter and had plenty of problems; Republicans held effective control of both branches in 1981, and rather than defeating the interest groups, they rolled over for them, handing out tax breaks as party favors. Divided control did not prevent the Nixon administration from making a profound mark on the government and its domestic policy, whereas united Democratic control did Bill

Clinton little good in 1993 and 1994, when he was thwarted repeatedly on Capitol Hill and barely managed to pass his first budget. If divided control was the crucial problem, then matters should have improved, not worsened, after Democrats assumed control of both branches in 1992. Instead, the public wound up angrier than ever, and back swung the government to divided control in 1994, this time with a Democrat in the White House and Republicans running Congress. If experience since the 1970s is any indication, there is more to the story than who controls which branch of government. Moreover, a number of countries with parliamentary systems, under which the ruling party or coalition always controls the whole government, have had "special-interest gridlock" problems comparable to our own. In France, much as in America, opinion polls have found that a record share of the public (82 percent, in one 1993 poll) was dissatisfied with the way the country was being governed. In Japan, decades of single-party control turned government ministries into special-interest protectorates, so that crucial economic and social reforms were blocked for much too long, to the point of dragging down the entire economy.

"Publics all across the industrial world don't know what to do about modern government," writes the public-opinion expert Everett Carll Ladd. "They see no alternative to its playing a large role, but they are increasingly frustrated as they see it malperforming and increasingly doubtful that it can be made to work better." When Robert Putnam, Susan Pharr, and Russell Dalton compared survey data that were gathered over the last few decades in a variety of industrialized countries, they found that, as *The Economist* reported in 1999, "in most of the mature democracies, the results show a pattern of disillusionment with politicians." In eleven of twelve countries surveyed, people's confidence in politicians had fallen (the Netherlands was the exception). In eleven out of fourteen countries, confidence in the national parliament (or Congress) had declined, "with especially sharp falls in Canada, Germany, Britain, Sweden, and the United

States." In eighteen of twenty wealthy countries examined by Martin Wattenberg, of the University of California at Irvine, voter turnout had declined—by a median amount of 10 percent—since the early 1950s. Whatever has happened does not seem to be wholly peculiar to the American system of government.

Deeper Currents

Over the course of several years, I have come to believe that ad hoc explanations based on personalities or political parties are too superficial to explain what has happened. I have come to suspect that the conventional wisdom is backward: The worrisome thing is not so much that American society is in the grip of its gridlocked government, but that American government is in the grip of powerful and broad changes in American society. Alan Simpson and Marvin Leath, without quite understanding how, were squeezed by tectonic forces that are very deep and very difficult to resist and that, importantly, are *directional*. That is, the situation, if left unattended, tends to get worse.

This book is about the side effects of the postwar style of politics, a style that emphasizes interest-group activism and redistributive programs. Because the book emphasizes the darker side of the pressure groups and the programs, it may be most congenial to conservatives, who have always resented programs that take money out of some pockets and put it into others. I hope, though, that nonconservatives will also think hard about what follows, since the argument itself is neither partisan nor ideological. To understand government's debilitation and see that it is a serious problem, you don't need to believe that government is evil and all programs should be abolished. Far from it. Redistributive programs are in use everywhere, and should be. Aid to the unemployed provides security against the most bruising trauma of capitalism; aid to the elderly provides security in old age; aid to students can help open doors and raise incomes; aid to veterans repays a public debt to those who serve. All of those goals are worthy, and all of those programs serve real social purposes. The problem is understanding and then minimizing the groups' and programs' cumulative side effects, which turn out to be both nasty and inherent.

By definition, the power of government to solve problems comes from its ability to reassign resources, whether by taxing, spending, regulating, or simply passing laws. But that very ability energizes countless investors and entrepreneurs and ordinary Americans to go digging for gold by lobbying government. In time, a whole industry—large, sophisticated, professional, and to a considerable extent self-serving—emerges and then assumes a life of its own. This industry is a drain on the productive economy, and there appears to be no natural limit to its growth. As it grows, the steady accumulation of subsidies and benefits, each defended in perpetuity by a professional interest group, calcifies government. Washington loses its capacity to experiment and adapt and so becomes increasingly prone to failure.

Moreover, as the client groups proliferate and professionalize, government becomes less coherent and more difficult for politicians and voters to control. Like the virus that mutates to stay ahead of the latest drugs, programs change, but they do so in ways that preserve their existence and keep their clients happy, rather than in ways that solve any particular social problem with any particular degree of effectiveness. If the business of America is business, the business of government programs and their clients is to *stay* in business. And after a while, as the programs and the clients and their political protectors adapt to nourish and protect each other, government and its universe of groups reach a turning point—or, perhaps more accurately, a point from which there is no turning back. That point has arrived. After a 150-year period of relative modesty and quiescence, and then a fifty-year period of high ambition and rapid expansion, government has become what it is and will remain: a large, incoherent, often incomprehensible mass that is solicitous of its clients but impervious to any broad, coherent program of reform. *And this evolution cannot be reversed.*

That is what I mean by "government's end." Not that government is over; obviously, it is not. In a way, in fact, I mean just the opposite. I mean "end" in a sense more akin to "destination," although certainly no one intended to wind up here. Government has evolved to a steady-state condition from which it cannot be dislodged by any tolerable amount of political brute force. What you see now in Washington is basically what you will get for a very long time to come, even though many people, in fact probably a majority of people, may both wish and vote for something quite different.

If I am right, this diagnosis is, of itself, not necessarily either good or bad. It is certainly not anybody's first choice, but whether it is a crisis or merely a less-than-ideal fact of life depends, like so many other less-than-ideal facts of life, on how well we cope with it. Unfortunately, the political system has had a hard time adjusting, no doubt because the reality of government's condition cuts sharply across the rhetoric of politicians and the expectations of political activists. The public and even some politicians and activists are growing gradually, if grudgingly, more accepting of the natural limits on government's ability to change society. Not even the most liberal Democrats talk anymore of nationalizing great industries or of providing guaranteed incomes for everybody. Beyond that adjustment, however, lies another, which is subtler and may be harder. The public needs to begin accepting the natural limits on *society's* ability to change *government*.

In spring 1994, this book—more aptly, this book's predecessor—was first published under the title *Demosclerosis*. Shortly thereafter came Clinton's dramatic attempt to overhaul the country's health care system, and after that came Gingrich's even more dramatic attempt to overhaul everything. Those events showed that what I call "demosclerosis" held, if anything, an even more powerful grip on Washington than I originally thought. They raised a further question, too. If the ideas of demosclerosis are right, what happens next? The first version of this book focused mainly on the mechanisms of sclerosis. In this revised version, I've taken the opportunity to think about the lessons of the failed reforms, about the possible routes to better success, and about ways in which the country can develop a more productive and less pathological relationship with its government. The new title reflects this edition's larger compass.

No, "government's end" doesn't mean that change can never occur. It does mean that there are some principles we will need to understand about the malady that grips our government:

It is inherent. Democracies are necessarily vulnerable to what I call demosclerosis (though not uniquely vulnerable). The problem is encoded in democracy's DNA.

It is progressive. The disease is gradual, but its effect is cumulative. Resisting it requires constant effort and attention. You can't coast or relax.

It is cunning. Far from being easy to defeat, the syndrome exploits the voters' knee-jerk attempts to fight it. It ensnares the unwary in a trap baited with attractive subsidies and well-meaning programs, and it wraps itself in the language of fairness. It revels in hyperbolic political promises of "revolution" and in rhetorical attacks on "special interests," and turns such tactics to its advantage.

It is not someone else's fault. At government's end, political scapegoating of the customary sort ("Liberals did it!" "Conservatives did it!" "Business did it!" "Labor did it!" "Republicans did it!" "Democrats did it!") is obsolete. The problem is not any kind of "them." It is not the political group you most despise, whichever that may be. The problem is in the system, and you and I and everyone else, however innocent or virtuous we may believe ourselves to be, are deeply implicated.

I am not saying that nothing can be done. Far from it. I am saying that the voters will continue to be frustrated and ineffective until they understand what has gone wrong, and learn how to treat the syndrome rather than just shaking their fists at it. In the last two chapters of the book, I try to sketch the sorts of reforms that can be the foundation for a new and, I think, much more productive entente between Washington and the public. Highest of all the reforms on that list are the ones we will need to make inside our own heads. America's government has grown up, and, in a way, I'm trying to suggest how the citizenry can grow up with it.

Tocqueville's Ghost

A century and a half ago, Alexis de Tocqueville came to America and concluded that democracy's Achilles' heel was tyranny of the majority. "The majority in the United States has immense actual power and a power of opinion which is almost as great," he said. "If freedom is ever lost in America, that will be due to the omnipotence of the majority driving the minorities to desperation and forcing them to appeal to physical force." But democracy, here and elsewhere, has not succumbed to majoritarian tyranny. In fact, America has probably done a better job protecting minorities than any other society in history.

A hundred years after Tocqueville, many people worried that democracy's vulnerability lay in its lack of resolve in the face of totalitarianism. Dictators, after all, could make decisions almost instantaneously, while democratic institutions dithered and deliberated. That fear, too, was misplaced. American democracy saw the dictators to their graves. It saw the Cold War through in a display of consistency and resolve that history can hardly match. Dithering democracies turned out to be much better than dictatorships at finding and correcting their mistakes before the mistakes became cataclysms. Nothing that follows in this book is meant to imply otherwise.

Today it appears that democracy's truer vulnerability lies closer to home — in the democratic public's tendency to form ever more groups clamoring for ever more goodies and perks and then defending them to the death. This drift may now represent the most serious single challenge to the long-term vitality of democratic government. One reason democracy didn't succumb to majoritarian tyranny or to the dictators' resolve was that people became worried about both threats and so managed to defeat them. The current threat is more insidious. It operates quietly and slowly from within. It is a crisis of American collective appetites, one in which well-meaning people and dedicated groups interact to produce collective stalemate.

This book is not an apocalyptic tirade. It is not about the imminent death of American civilization or democracy or prosperity; I believe in no such thing. It is, rather, a diagnosis and a warning. A nation of expectant whiners and angry blamers cannot hope to break out of the trap that I am about to describe.

2

Mr. Olson's Planet

IN THE MID-1950s, a young American traveling in Europe was struck by an economic oddity. The United Kingdom had won two great wars and enjoyed all the splendors of empire, yet it suffered from economic anemia—so much so that people came to speak of the "British disease." Germany had been defeated in two wars and then was broken in half, yet West Germany was booming—so much so that people came to speak of the German "economic miracle." Why would two European economies, of roughly comparable size, with well-educated populaces and with similar technological bases, perform so differently?

That question led the young man to ponder a broader one. Why do stable societies seem to wind down over time? Great Britain was only the most recent example of a society that emerged rapidly, flowered brilliantly, and then sank into torpor and decay. Germany, on the other hand, had suffered cataclysmic destabilization, yet was full of vigor. Most explanations resorted to specific events like wars, spun vague theories about culture, or resorted to clichés about countries' becoming "tired" or "lazy" or "old," as though countries were people. The young American, still fresh out of university and on his way to a career in economics, was unsatisfied. There ought to be a more systematic answer, a regular mechanism to explain a regular pattern. He turned the problem over in his mind for decades. In 1982, he proposed a striking solution.

The Logician of Collective Action

Mancur Olson was born in 1932, sixty miles north of Fargo, North Dakota, on a farm by the Red River, which forms the border with Minnesota. His forebears migrated from Norway, but the peculiar first name was not Norwegian. It was passed down from his father and probably came from the Arabic name Mansur, meaning "victorious"—thus it was pronounced "Mansir," not "Mankur." Though he held a Harvard Ph.D. and a fancy title at the University of Maryland, even in his later years he could still repair a tractor, and he retained a midwestern matter-of-factness that made his writing, like his speech, vigorous and to the point. Yet an intellectual fire burned in him. He had a jumpy, delighted, almost pixieish excitability when he talked about ideas. He would ask visitors to let him pace while he spoke, and then he prowled the way some people gesticulate, as though the movement helped him form words. The effect was pleasantly gnomish.

Olson was a man who cared passionately about finding out why economies work and don't work, and also about making them work better, especially in the hardest cases. In 1990, he established a center devoted to helping post-Communist and developing economies find their feet. When he died, in 1998, he was on the campus of the University of Maryland, a few miles from where I was working, but word of his death reached me by way of an e-mail from Armenia. Earlier in his career, however, he made his name as a theorist. The larger world first heard from him in 1965 with the publication of a short, tightly reasoned book titled *The Logic of Collective Action*, in which he turned conventional wisdom on its head.

The standard theory was that human beings in general, and Americans in particular (as Tocqueville, among others, had said), were natural joiners, combining readily into groups large and small. The result was interest-group democracy, in which business interests competed with consumer or labor interests, animal-rights interests competed with hunting interests, sludge-making interests competed with environmental interests, and out of the whole raucous bazaar came a more or less balanced policy.

Wrong on all counts, said Olson. First of all, forming groups is not easy, it is hard, and it does not happen naturally. Very small groups, true, are fairly easy to form, but forming middle-sized groups is much harder, and very large groups, representing millions of people, literally cannot be formed without using coercion or offering special rewards for joiners. The reason is this: The larger the group, the greater everyone's temptation to let others do the hard work of joining and organizing.

Suppose that three people in a rural neighborhood share a private road or driveway. They might easily form a group to repave their road; each one will pay something, but all will benefit. If all three chip in, the road is fixed at minimal cost to each. But now suppose there are a hundred people sharing the road. Then the temptation becomes strong for each person not to chip in. Each one thinks, "Someone else can worry about filling potholes. I'll let other people fix the road, and then I'll be able to use it for free." If enough people think that way, the road never gets repaved.

The problem here is an ancient one, namely, that people try to ride for free if they think they can get away with it. It involves what economists call public goods: goods (or services) that everyone can enjoy even if only one person takes the trouble to pay for them. Roads are one classic example; national defense is another. The classic solution is for a majority to require everyone to contribute to road building and national defense, through taxes. Otherwise, too few roads would be built, and too few soldiers recruited, because too many people would wait for someone else to do the building and recruiting.

In *The Logic of Collective Action*, Olson showed that the free-rider problem applies to private collective projects no less than to government. The bigger the class of people who benefit from collective action, the weaker the incentive for any particular beneficiary to join or organize, and thus the less likely that a group will coalesce. "In short," wrote Olson, "the larger the group, the less it will further its common interests."

If that is true, the implications are unsettling. "Since relatively small groups will frequently be able voluntarily to organize and act in support of their common interests," Olson went on, "and since large groups normally will not be able to do so, the outcome of the political struggle among the various groups in society will not be symmetrical." In other words, small, narrow groups have a permanent and inherent advantage, and "often triumph over the numerically superior forces because the former are generally organized and active while the latter are normally unorganized and inactive."

Experience confirms the prediction. A dozen companies making left-handed screwdrivers may organize to get themselves a tax break. If they win a loophole worth $12 million, each earns a cool million, and the investment pays off handsomely. Their tax break comes out of the pockets of everyone else—but the cost is spread out among millions of Americans. And so it would be pointless for someone to try to organize 270 million Americans to win back a fraction of a cent each.

People have tried organizing groups to represent very broad interests, without notable success. The National Taxpayers Union, which lobbies for reductions in what it regards as wasteful government spending, has managed to enlist only about 300,000 members. Out of a total pool of about 120 million Americans filing tax returns, that is a participation rate (about one in four hundred) that borders on insignificance. Out of 100 million or so American voters, not one in three hundred is a member of Common Cause, a group that advocates political reforms to reduce the influence of moneyed special interests.

26

By contrast, the American Federation of State, County, and Municipal Employees—a group representing a narrower interest—boasts 1.3 million members, or one of about every six full-time state and local government workers (not counting teachers, who are organized by other unions). Still, the class of state and local government workers is a big group, which is a reason why five of six workers don't join. A very narrow interest—say, the three major American auto companies—can produce much higher rates of participation.

Olson's argument became a staple of college political science courses and a pillar of a rising economic literature on what's called "public choice." But Olson wasn't finished. If he was right, what would his theory mean for a large country like America? He began to think about the ways in which the interest-group dynamic might affect an economy over time. The result was his 1982 book *The Rise and Decline of Nations.*

On a Tilt

As Olson pointed out in *The Logic of Collective Action*, organizing a group to seek collective benefits is difficult. The effort costs money, takes time, and risks failure, and organizers face an uphill battle against skepticism and apathy. However, one at a time, little by little, over a long period, groups do manage to overcome the obstacles.

Modern trade unions, for instance, didn't appear until almost a century after the Industrial Revolution. Though farmers have plowed the American soil for hundreds of years, farmers' groups didn't appear on a national scale until around World War I, and only since World War II have they really proliferated. Social Security dates to 1935, but the recipients' main interest group, the American Association of Retired Persons, didn't coalesce until more than twenty years later.

"Organization for collective action takes a good deal of time to emerge," wrote Olson. Having introduced the element of time, he then added another element, that of directionality. Once groups form, they rarely disappear. Rather, "they usually survive until there is a social upheaval or some other form of violence or instability." The two elements combine in a conclusion that Olson italicized: "*Stable societies with unchanged boundaries tend to accumulate more collusions and organizations for collective action over time.*"

In effect, Olson posited a social field of force. Just as the earth's gravitational field makes it harder to walk uphill than to walk downhill, Olson's directional force points to the emergence of more and more pressure groups in any stable society. Figuratively speaking, society is not on a flat surface, where groups come and go depending only on the politics of the moment; it is on a tilt, so that groups gradually but steadily pile up. This is true even in small societies such as universities, where ethnic and single-issue groups tend to establish themselves and then colonize bits of the curriculum or the campus. Moreover, if the groups are swept away for some reason, over time they will tend to reemerge. When Newt Gingrich and his Republicans took over the House of Representatives in 1994, they acted on their pledge to eliminate funding for the Babel of House caucuses that had accumulated over the years of Democratic control. By 1998, as David Grann noted in *The New Republic*, dozens of new caucuses had sprouted, including the Missing and Exploited Children Caucus and the Pro-Family Caucus (all competing, noted Grann, to achieve their narrow interests).

What would be the effect of the piling up of interest groups? To see the answer, you have to look at the economics of what the groups are likely to be doing.

Economic thinkers have recognized for generations that every person has two ways to become wealthier. One is to produce more. The other is to capture more of what others produce. The former is productive activity. The latter is redistributive activity—transfer-seeking, an investment of time or energy in transferring wealth from other people to oneself.

Olson pointed out that no group has much incentive to organize with the goal of increasing productivity for the society as a whole. In metaphorical terms, it pays much better for a group to try to enlarge its share of the pie than to try to make the whole pie bigger. To see why, imagine that you live in a country of a million people. Then imagine a group of a hundred people called the Coalition to Make Ourselves Rich (C-MOR). C-MOR's members make up only one ten-thousandth of the society. If they lobby for a universal job-training program that makes the whole society better off by $1 million, then C-MOR's members will pay the whole cost of their lobbying effort, but they must share their $1 million reward with a million people. Each of C-MOR's members winds up only a dollar better off for his effort — hardly worth the trouble, especially given that agitating for social change is expensive. Now suppose instead that the group organizes for a $1 million tax break focused exclusively on C-MOR itself. This time C-MOR members split the booty a hundred ways, not a million. That translates into $10,000 per member, which is fine boodle. For interest groups, then, the bigger payoff is in redistributing the pie, not enlarging it.

Suppose people in a group wanted to focus more social resources on themselves. How might they do it? If they were competitors in a market, they might organize a cartel to exclude newcomers and then jack up prices. And, indeed, businesses notoriously do attempt that. However, cartel formation is outside the scope of this book, and in any case it has turned out not to be as serious a problem as Americans used to think, partly because the economy has changed. Early in this century, heavy industry called for economies of size, summoning forth corporate giants. Today, flexibility and economies of speed matter more, so that gigantism is often the path to downfall rather than domination.

Even in a closed market, maintaining a cartel is difficult; bickering and opportunism tend to crack and then destroy cartels in not much time. In today's relatively open world market, which reaches across national boundaries, maintaining a cartel is more difficult still. If cartels organize the domestic market, as some people believed the Big Three automakers were informally doing through the 1970s, their fat profits lure in imports that bust the trust, as Detroit discovered the hard way. In the early 1970s, populists and consumerists regarded General Motors as a domineering titan, a sovereign economic state impervious both to market forces and to the public interest. "If they wanted to wipe out everybody by 1980," one American Motors executive said in 1976, "the only one who could stop them is the government." If so, someone forgot to tell the customers and the Japanese. By the 1990s, a gasping GM was shutting dozens of plants and laying off workers by the tens of thousands.

There is a second way to organize for redistribution, though. That way is political and substitutes public policy and the strong force of law for private cartels and the weak force of corporate solidarity.

Getting Organized

Consider two real-life bicycle couriers in Washington, D.C. Couriers in the District of Columbia are basically independent contractors working for thirty or so little companies—enough competition so it's safe to assume that the couriers' wages are at about the level that the market will bear. That level isn't very high, partly because fax machines are driving messenger services out of business. One courier, who calls himself Suicide, has a plan: Organize Washington's messengers and strike for better wages. "If we could have a work stoppage," he told W. Hampton Sides in a *New Republic* article describing couriers' peculiar subculture, "you'd hear it around the world! This city would grind to a halt, man, just completely shut down! They would never fuck with us again." In effect, Suicide's idea is to form a union, or a labor cartel. The collective strike threat would win him and his companions better pay or benefits. On the other hand, courier service would become more expensive, and some customers would switch to fax machines or Federal Express. The end result is likely to be that couriers with jobs will earn higher wages, but fewer new couriers will be hired. Money would be redistributed to the ins at the expense of the outs, with some loss of efficiency along the way. Newcomers lose, Suicide wins.

Unfortunately for him, organizing hundreds or thousands of independent couriers is very difficult, as Mancur Olson showed. Another courier, Scrooge, has a different approach: to raise the prices of the competition and so raise the wages that couriers can command. One way to raise the competition's price, of course, is to get rid of the competition, which is what Scrooge turns out to have in mind. "I'm going to create a [computer] virus that will ruin all the fax machines," he says. "I'm gonna send it out over the phone lines like an epidemic. Then watch out. All bike couriers of the world will unite! And we're going to take this country by storm!"

Scrooge's problem is that the mass murder of other people's fax machines is illegal. He will soon figure this out, at which point he may forget about the whole idea. On the other hand, he may not. Rather, he may organize a group, hire a lobbyist, and start a political action committee. If he can't destroy the fax machines, he can achieve a similar result with a law banning them, or at least restricting their use to long-distance calls, or taxing them heavily, or whatever. Or he can seek a subsidy or tax credit for people who use courier services, diverting business away from fax machines and his other competitors. Or, if he prefers, he can seek a direct subsidy for bicycle couriers, capturing a monopoly claim on a chunk of tax money. All of those tactics are safe, effective, legal, and as American as apple pie.

In practice, that kind of anticompetitive group action goes on all the time, and has for years. Beginning in 1874, with the introduction of margarine into the United States, the American dairymen found themselves facing a new kind of competition, just as Scrooge has. The dairymen did exactly what Scrooge wants to do. For years, the National Milk Producers Federation made war on margarine, declaring in 1935 that "the oleomargarine problem" was its top priority. The dairymen successfully pressed for taxes on margarine and duties on imported food oils and for restrictions on the way margarine could be advertised and sold ("Retail packages of oleomargarine must not be over one pound, must bear the words 'oleomargarine' or 'margarine' in type at least as large as any other lettering on the package," and so forth). But that was long ago, you say? In 1991, the dairymen, complaining that milk prices were too low, fought hard but unsuccessfully for a federally enforced, farmer-directed milk cartel. Had they won, a board of dairymen would have been legally empowered to restrict milk supplies and block entry into the dairy business, thus raising milk prices (and hurting consumers, especially poorer ones). Not long afterward, in 1996, a coalition of northeastern dairy farmers managed to sneak a sort of regional dairy cartel into the law. The legislation empowered a group of northeastern states to raise milk prices throughout the region.

The bicycle couriers or dairymen or whoever may fail at first, but eventually some of them succeed in forming groups and capturing subsidies or anticompetitive rules or other benefits for themselves at the expense of others. True, some groups may seek arrangements that they think benefit society as a whole as well as themselves. Bicycle couriers might argue for road improvements and safety rules. Dairymen might argue for purity standards for milk. But Olson found that as groups accumulate, they will tend to make society as a whole poorer than it would have been. Remember, the payoff is always higher for a narrow, focused benefit than for a broad, publicly available one. "The great majority of special-interest organizations redistribute income rather than create it, and in ways that reduce social efficiency and output," said Olson. Groups rarely propose "social benefits" that don't also handsomely benefit themselves.

I remember fondly how a public-spirited car-alarm manufacturer, deeply concerned about public safety, proposed that alarms be made mandatory in New York City. In 1999, the Associated Press reported delectably on a group called the Alliance for Safe and Responsible Lead Abatement. "Its target audience is Americans concerned about the environment. And its stated goal is to protect drinking water from being poisoned by lead paint removed from older homes and apartment buildings." Behind the alliance was none other than the lobby for the lead-abatement industry, which was trying to protect its $50 million a year in business from an Environmental Protection Agency proposal that would let contractors dispose of lead-painted debris in landfills, instead of having it expensively removed by—guess who? You don't need to have X-ray vision to spot the pattern. A lobby demanding that railroads be required to install expensive new safety measures claims to be representing the nation's children and turns out to be backed by the trucking industry. A lobby demanding lower limits on trucks' size and weight claims to be representing the nation's highway users and turns out to be backed by the railroad industry.

Never mind, for now, whether any particular group's motives are high or low. As a society becomes increasingly dense with networks of interest groups, as the benefits secured by groups accumulate, the economy rigidifies, Olson argued. By locking out competition and locking in subsidies, interest groups capture resources that could be put to better use elsewhere. Entrenched interests tend to slow the adoption of new technology and ideas by clinging to the status quo, as, for instance, the dairymen did when they fought the advent of margarine. The groups can even slow the pace of innovation: If fax machines are restricted to long-distance service, fax producers will enjoy smaller profits, and their incentives to invest and innovate decline.

Further, as interest groups and their deals pile up, so do laws and regulations and the like, and so, therefore, do the number of people who work the laws and regulations. "When these specialists become significant enough," wrote Olson, "there is even the possibility that the specialists with a vested interest in the complex regulations will collude or lobby against simplification or elimination of the regulation." At last society itself begins to change. "The incentive to produce is diminished; the incentive to seek a larger share of what is produced increases." The very direction of society's evolution may be deflected away from productive activity and toward distributive struggle.

Olson noted one other effect, but only in passing. The accretion of interest groups and the rise of bickering over scarce resources could generate resentment and political turmoil. "The divisiveness of distributional issues," he wrote, "can even make societies ungovernable." Alas, Olson, the economist, left this lead unpursued. It remained a tantalizing hint that government, too, could be a casualty of the process he had described.

Down, Down, Down

Even without venturing into politics, Olson produced a theory that was more than broad enough. Here, if he was right, was a mechanism explaining why economies, even whole societies, tend to lose their bloom and then wilt. Instead of relying on ad hoc explanations or clichés, Olson identified a systematic and systemic process that, left unattended, would cause gradual economic sclerosis.

And how far might the process go? Recall C-MOR, which represents a ten-thousandth of the population. Now suppose the evidence mounts that C-MOR's small but hard-won tax break makes the society as a whole just a bit poorer. You might suppose that C-MOR would see that its actions were impoverishing the larger society and would mend its ways. But it won't, at least not if it can do simple division. The reason is that the small group collects all the benefit from its loophole, but it bears only a fraction of the social cost. In fact, if you work out the arithmetic, you discover that it pays for C-MOR to keep seeking perks until the social costs of its goody-hunting are ten thousand times larger than the benefits to the narrow group. The bigger the society, the worse this problem becomes. In a society—like America's—of 270 million people, a group of twenty-five widget makers (a ten-millionth of the population) can continue to earn a profit from new subsidies and benefits until those subsidies and benefits cost society *ten million times* as much as the widget-making group stands to gain.

The arithmetic dictates that groups can hope to reap large gains from their pie-reslicing activity even as that very activity dramatically shrinks the size of the pie. In fact, if a society begins to grow poorer, interest groups may struggle all the more fiercely to expand their own share. The calculus of distributive warfare implies that interest-group activity can, in principle, drive a society to complete destitution and then keep right on going. At some point, some countervailing force might kick in, but whether that would happen is not at all clear. The Olsonian forces may, in fact, effectively face no natural limit—no point, that is, where interest groups stop being drawn into the benefits-chasing game by visions of profit. Quite possibly, *there is no bottom.*

However, Olson's forces can exert themselves only on one condition: Because group-forming is difficult and takes time, the society must be stable enough so that pressure groups have time to form and affix themselves to the body politic. Also, groups need maneuvering room to organize and lobby.

Democracies, of course, guarantee the people's right to form associations and lobby their government. Moreover, democracies tend to be relatively stable. "The logic of the argument," Olson wrote, "implies that countries that have had democratic freedom of organization without upheaval or invasion the longest will suffer the most from growth-repressing organizations and combinations." And so stable democracies are a natural preserve of what Olson pungently called interest-group depredations.

However, democracies are not the only societies that are vulnerable to the Olsonian forces. Stable authoritarian societies also provide happy hunting for pressure groups. In many countries, such the Philippines under Marcos and Zaire under Mobutu, interest groups collaborated with the regime to rob the country blind; in the former Soviet Union, the entrenched industrial barons and state apparatchiks made the economy into a desert. For that matter, a large private company can turn sclerotic if operating units or management cliques become vested interests—at which point the company either reforms or goes broke and is replaced by a more flexible company. The tendency toward interest-group sclerosis isn't unique to democracy. But, if Olson is right, it is inherent in it.

At last we arrive back at the question that posed itself to Olson during his student days in Europe. Why did Germany thrive economically while Britain wound down? True, Britain was hurt by World War II, but Germany was hurt even more severely. True, a devastated country like Germany should enjoy a spurt of catch-up growth. But that would not explain why the "economic miracle" continued there long after the Germans were fully caught up to their prewar level. Moreover, it seemed unlikely that Germany's boom was a peculiar case, because the same thing had happened a hemisphere away, in Japan.

Perhaps, then, the explanation is this: Occasionally some cataclysmic event—foreign occupation, for example, or revolution—might shake a society, sweep away an existing government, and shatter the society's network of interest groups. The old order would be scuttled, and the barnacles would sink with the ship. In the aftermath, the restored economy would be freed from its accumulated burden of protective perks and anticompetitive deals.

Now the theory's darkest implications come into view. "If the argument so far is correct," Olson wrote, "it follows that countries whose distributional coalitions have been emasculated or abolished by totalitarian government or foreign occupation should grow relatively quickly after a free and stable legal order is established." And that is just what happened in Japan and West Germany after the war. In the case of Japan, decades' worth—even centuries' worth—of cozy deals and insider cartels were upset by General Douglas MacArthur and his occupation forces. As resources were freed from groups that had captured and monopolized them, an "economic miracle" followed. By contrast, Olson noted, Great Britain is "the major nation with the longest immunity from dictatorship, invasion, and revolution." It has also, in the twentieth century, "had a lower rate of growth than other large, developed democracies."

Sometimes a slashing fire can rejuvenate a forest by clearing away clots of undergrowth and deadwood. Olson was suggesting that something analogous had happened to Germany and Japan. The fires of cataclysm had cleared away the detritus of stability.

His hypothesis suggested a social cycle. A country emerges from a period of political repression or upheaval into a period of stability and freedom. The country is, at first, relatively unencumbered by interest groups and their anticompetitive deals. If other conditions are favorable, rapid growth ensues. South Korea and Taiwan, both emerging from dictatorship and both growing rapidly, would be in that stage today; China, which grew spectacularly as economic controls were lifted, looks to be next. Gradually, however, interest groups form and attach themselves to the body politic. Each group secures some sort of subsidy or anticompetitive rule. Those benefits accumulate, each jealously defended, and all distorting the economy. Over time, growth slows—as it has done in Japan and Germany in recent years—and anemia sets in.

The idea is difficult to test. Olson and a colleague tried a statistical test comparing forty-eight American states. They looked at the length of time each state had been settled and at each state's rate of economic growth. They found a negative relationship: "The longer a state has been settled and the longer a time it has had to accumulate special-interest groups, the slower its rate of growth." The states of the former Confederacy, which suffered governmental upheaval in the Civil War, enjoyed faster-than-average economic expansion; so did the states of the West, which were comparatively recently settled. The pattern seemed to hold also *within* each region; it seemed to hold even when other differences between states, even differences in their climates, were taken into account. Among municipalities, the pattern also held: The most economically troubled cities tend to be the older ones, which often suffer most from fractious interest-group politics, bloated bureaucracies, and aging political machines. Think of Washington, Philadelphia, Detroit.

Still, such tests are hardly conclusive. Scholars have found more than a few bones to pick with Olson: too broad, too glib, too fatalistic, too this or too that. Like all grand unified theories, his seems to explain rather too much—though, to his credit, Olson never said that his ideas explain everything that goes on all the time, but only some of what goes on most of the time.

Yet the evidence in his favor—evidence that he was on to something important—is becoming harder to wave aside. In the 1970s, an intelligent observer of politics could have dismissed Olson's ideas, but in today's Washington a person would need to be a tree frog not to notice hints, traces, even outright demonstrations of Olsonian forces at work. Even more troubling is the evidence of American society itself. Olson's theory coincides eerily well with the most important change in the structure of the American body politic in the twentieth century, namely the breathtaking growth of groupism.

3

Hyperpluralism

THERE IS nothing even slightly new about groups that form to lobby. In America, the word "lobbyist" dates to at least the late 1820s. In 1852, the future president James Buchanan wrote that "the host of contractors, speculators, stockjobbers, and lobby members which haunt the halls of Congress . . . are sufficient to alarm every friend of this country." No modern critic of lobbying could do much better than Senator (and, later, Supreme Court Justice) Hugo L. Black, who declared in 1935: "Contrary to tradition, against the public morals, and hostile to good government, the lobby has reached such a position of power that it threatens government itself. Its size, its power, its capacity for evil, its greed, trickery, deception and fraud condemn it to the death it deserves."

Something has changed since Black's day, though. In the old days, if you conjured up an image of a powerful moneyed interest, chances are you would imagine not a group but a man, with a first and last name (the 1850s' most powerful lobbyist was named—really—Thurlow Weed), rather than a five-letter acronym beginning with N and A, for "National Association of." You might imagine a robber-baron industrialist like Cornelius

Vanderbilt, who in the mid-1800s led the steamship companies in their fight against the railroads. You might imagine a political kingpin like Tammany Hall's Boss Tweed, whose portly figure is still familiar from Thomas Nast's cartoons. A special interest, back then, was really someone special, someone with great personal power or extraordinary personal connections or an unusual personal following. "Quite simply," the journalist Jeffrey H. Birnbaum has written, "lobbying power resided with people who had personal connections to government."

By the middle of the twentieth century, the complexion of lobbying was clearly different, and the implications of the shift are only now being sorted out. In 1950, Representative Frank M. Buchanan of Pennsylvania, who headed a congressional investigation of lobbying, said: "In the 1870s and 1880s, lobbying meant direct, individual solicitation of legislators, with a strong presumption of corruption attached." By contrast, "Modern pressure on legislative bodies is rarely corrupt. . . . It is increasingly indirect, and *largely the product of group rather than individual effort* [italics added]. . . . The printed word is much more extensively used by organizations as a means of pursuing legislative aims than personal contact with legislators by individual lobbyists." The group was displacing the individual, the professional was displacing the amateur, and the groups and professionals were multiplying.

People have noted, and many have bemoaned, the rise of ethnic groupism in America, in which blacks and Hispanics and Asians and women and others separate into groups by gender or skin color or parentage and then demand things. What too many people have missed is that ethnic groupism is merely one part of a much larger pattern. The blacks and Hispanics and Asians and women merely have been doing what everyone else has been doing—namely, organizing into interest groups and making demands. Groupism has exploded, not only along ethnic lines but along all lines.

When people look at the political system and say it works less well than in the past, they naturally assume the reason is that somehow the process has changed. It has. But to focus on process is to troll for the Loch Ness monster with a bamboo rod and a ball of twine. People need to think bigger and deeper. The much more important change is not in the political process but in the body politic. No society can reorganize itself into benefits-seeking groups and expect to function as it did before. The proliferation of interest groups and lobbies since the 1960s—the advocacy explosion, as the political scientist Jeffrey Berry has called it—represents a deep and fundamental change in America's social structure, a change at least rivaling and perhaps surpassing the civil rights revolution in scope and import. Just look at the scale and speed of what happened.

Out of One, Many

One small milestone was passed in 1920 with the founding of the American Society of Association Executives (motto: "Associations Advance America"). That year, sixty-three associations turned up at the first annual meeting of the new group representing group representatives. By the late 1920s, a congressional investigation found about four hundred lobbies in the Washington phone book; in 1950, Frank Buchanan's congressional commission counted more than two thousand. In 1958 came the founding of what later became the largest lobby in America, the American Association of Retired Persons. In the 1960s, the growth moved into a higher gear, and a mere three decades later a moment arrived when arguably *everyone* had an association in Washington. A sign of the times was the opening of the Baha'i religion's Washington lobbying office in July 1987, complete with a staff of four and a budget of $400,000—a telling moment, because the Baha'i faith requires its members to abstain from politics. When I peeked through the Baha'is' window one day, the only remarkable feature of

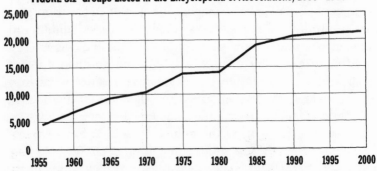

FIGURE 3.1 Groups Listed in the *Encyclopedia of Associations, 1956–1999*

NOTE: Figures prior to 1975 are estimates by the American Society of Association Executives.

SOURCE: Gale Research, Inc.; American Society of Association Executives.

their Washington office was that it looked exactly like every other Washington office.

Counting groups with any precision is difficult, because definitive numbers don't exist, but the numbers of listings in Gale Research Inc.'s *Encyclopedia of Associations* make a good starting point. Those numbers are given in Figure 3.1. In 1956, fewer than five thousand associations were listed. The number had doubled by 1970 and then doubled again by 1990. Over the period 1970 to 1990, an average of about ten new groups were formed every week.

The data suggest a general pattern, though not a universal one. Groups still tended to be relatively sparse until about the time of World War II. Then they started proliferating, and in the 1960s the pace picked up exponentially and finally seemed to moderate in the 1990s. As a result, a disproportionate number of interest groups arrived on the scene quite recently. For example, a study by Kay Schlozman and John Tierney found that 40 percent of the groups listed in a lobbying directory were founded after 1960, and 25 percent after 1970. Those results are typical.

Looking at particular groups serves to confirm the pattern: Within particular sectors and interest areas, the big movement toward organizing into groups began after World War II and sped up dramatically in the thirty years or so beginning around 1960. One impressive example, because of the sheer number of people involved, is the explosion of membership of the American Association of Retired Persons (AARP). Figure 3.2 shows AARP's membership, along with the total number of Social Security recipients—AARP's core (though not its sole) constituency. As recently as 1965, the group still had fewer than a million members, which meant that only one in thirty Social Security beneficiaries had actually joined. That was predictable; banding together takes time. But once the ball starts rolling, momentum builds. In the 1970s, the elderly began joining with a vengeance; between 1980 and 1990 alone, the group tripled its membership. By the 1990s, when the number stabilized, AARP's membership accounted for the vast majority of Social Security recipients. The organization's headquarters in Washington had grown so large as

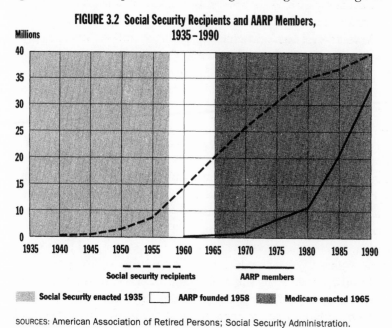

FIGURE 3.2 Social Security Recipients and AARP Members, 1935–1990

Millions

Social security recipients

AARP members

Social Security enacted 1935   AARP founded 1958   Medicare enacted 1965

SOURCES: American Association of Retired Persons; Social Security Administration.

FIGURE 3.3 Membership of the American Federation of State, County, and Municipal Employees, 1936–1998

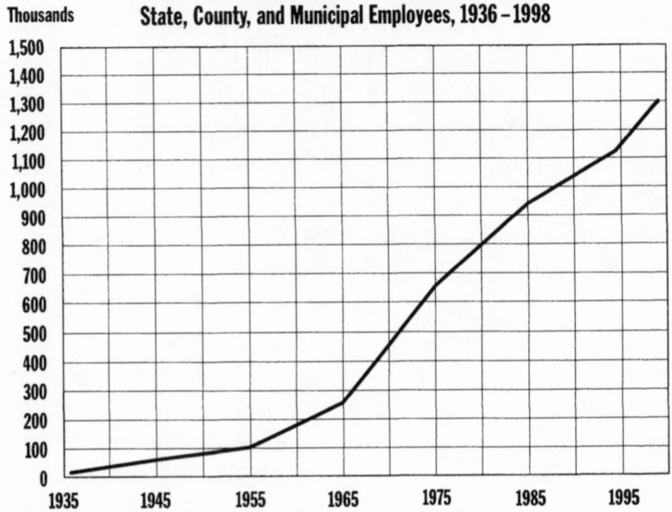

SOURCE: American Federation of State, County, and Municipal Employees.

to have a legislative and policy staff of 125 people, sixteen registered lobbyists, and even its own ZIP code.

AARP's story is not special; it is typical. The American Federation of State, County, and Municipal Employees was founded in 1936, growing out of the Wisconsin State Employees Association. Its membership, charted in Figure 3.3, shows the familiar pattern, though the major growth spurt began earlier than for some other groups. In 1955, the group had organized only about one in twenty-five of its potential members; by 1975, it had organized more than one in eight.

A business group? Same pattern. Figure 3.4 shows the membership of the National Association of Home Builders. The group was born in 1942, grew steadily for twenty years, and then more than tripled its membership from 1967 to 1987.

Another example is the aforementioned American Society of Association Executives, the association of people who run associations. Its membership roster lists individuals rather than

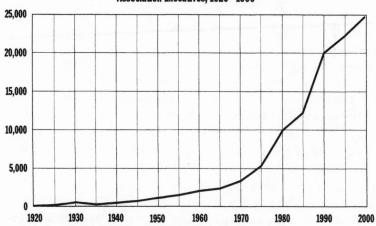

FIGURE 3.4 Membership of the National Association
of Home Builders, 1942-1997

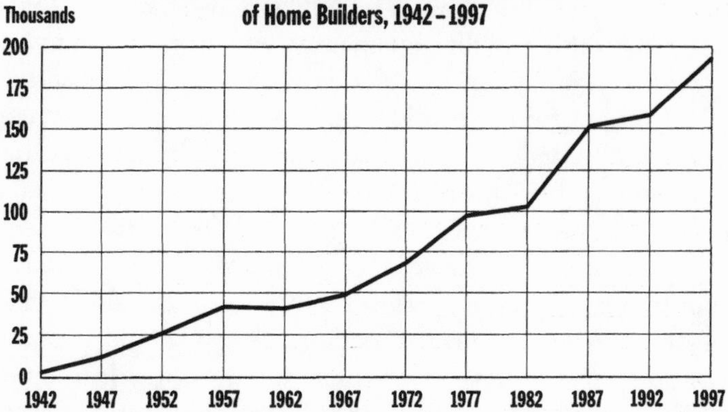

SOURCE: National Association of Home Builders.

groups, and so the numbers don't reveal how many groups there are. But when you look at Figure 3.5, you won't be surprised by the pattern. Founded in 1920, the group grew steadily through the 1960s, and then membership soared, increasing sixfold from 1970 to 1990.

FIGURE 3.5 Membership of the American Society of
Association Executives, 1920-1999

SOURCES: American Society of Association Executives (ASAE); Sam Shapiro, *A Coming of Age: A History of the Profession of Association Management* (ASAE, 1987).

As groups became bigger and more numerous, they also, not surprisingly, started taking up a larger share of economic space. They became million-dollar businesses. According to membership surveys conducted in selected years by the American Society of Association Executives, in 1946 fewer than 25 percent of groups had budgets of more than $500,000 (in constant 1985 dollars); by 1985, two-thirds of them did.

These groups represent every conceivable collective interest. Among them are the Association of Old Crows (for veterans of the counterintelligence community); the National Paint Varnish and Lacquer Association; the Possum Growers and Breeders Association; the American Association of Sex Educators, Counselors, and Therapists; the Bow Tie Manufacturers Association; the Association of Metropolitan Sewerage Agencies; the Frozen Pizza Institute; the association of this and the association of that. In 1998, when Washington was preoccupied with a presidential sex scandal, it seemed fitting that the National Association of Adult Businesses, representing strip joints and adult book and video stores, registered to lobby.

The groups engage in every conceivable kind of activity, including, but not limited to, educating, licensing, confabbing, holding contests, setting standards, certifying tournaments, collecting for charities, selling goods and services, wearing silly hats, giving themselves awards. When they start out, they may or may not intend to get involved in politics. Sooner or later, however, someone in a group usually figures out that it would be worthwhile to seek what Mancur Olson called a collective good: some benefit that the members can obtain from nonmembers by lobbying and agitating as a group.

Agricultural groups began as distributors of information and technology to farmers and ended up as lobbyists for subsidies. Civil rights groups began by seeking equal justice under the law and ended up defending affirmative-action benefits for their constituents. In 1967, a hobbyist named Ray Scott founded the Bass Anglers Sportsman Society (yes, "BASS"); by 1990, the membership was approaching a million. The group sold boat owner's insurance, published a magazine, offered fishing tips, and sanctioned fishing tournaments. And, sure enough, the lure of lobbying proved irresistible. In 1989, Scott personally (and, apparently, successfully) lobbied President George Bush about money for various fisheries management projects; BASS also lobbied on water-quality issues and filed class-action lawsuits against polluters.

For the benefit of offended group members, I'll happily agree that groups do many good things. But that's the subject of some other book. For this book, the main point is that sooner or later every group becomes a pressure group, at least on some issues and some of the time. After all, if you have a rifle, why not hunt? And if you have a membership list and a staff and a budget, why not lobby?

Whose Interest Is Special?

As industries and trades and companies organized, reformers and activists and miscellaneous aggrieved citizens inevitably followed suit. What is astonishing is not that public-interest organizations and grassroots pressure groups formed but that they formed so quickly. With the help of tax breaks and of the general perception that these were good people trying to make society better, public-interest groups have proliferated with startling rapidity since the 1960s. A typical study in 1985 found that fully two-thirds of 250 major public-interest groups had been organized since 1968. By the early 1990s, environmental groups alone numbered an estimated seven thousand. Meanwhile, the older public-interest groups grew. For example, from the early 1970s to 1990, the Natural Resources Defense Council's membership tripled; the Environmental Defense Fund's more than quintupled; the Sierra Club's septupled; the National Audubon Society's almost octupled—and so on.

On the surface, public-interest groups may seem to break

Olson's paradigm of collective action, in which groups pursue benefits for themselves while paying scant attention to the costs imposed on society as a whole. After all, the whole raison d'être of environmental groups and peace groups and consumer groups and antigovernment groups is to change society as a whole, supposedly for the benefit of all. Ostensibly, public-interest groups are outward-looking, seeking to reform the whole country or even the whole world, rather than inward-looking, seeking only to reap benefits for themselves.

In fact, though, public-interest groups don't break the paradigm; they merely enrich it. For one thing, they do rather well for themselves and have a strong interest in staying in business, just as other groups do. "Many of the so-called Big Ten environmental groups are multimillion-dollar corporations," reported *National Journal.* The National Wildlife Federation boasted more than 4 million members and $80 million in revenues in 1997, and its president occupied plush headquarters and earned more than $300,000 in pay and benefits. The people who staff these groups may work for less than they might earn at Fortune 500 companies, but they aren't necessarily selfless servants of the public good. They run business enterprises in the interest-group sector.

More fundamentally, these groups are just as dedicated to transferring resources as any other group is. When they lobby, they want society to divert more resources to some activity they like and away from some activity they don't like. They are out to get something they value, and what they want will cost someone else time or money, or they wouldn't need a law to get it. AIDS activists believe that AIDS research is more important than defense spending or low corporate taxes; they, no less than defense contractors and tax lobbyists, seek to redistribute social resources so as to get more of what they value. Environmental groups that advocate preserving spotted owls or old-growth forests value endangered species and ancient trees more than inexpensive timber, a preference that some home buyers and logging towns might not share. In Tucson not long ago, an advocacy group called the Arizona Center for Law in the Public Interest announced the following antismog agenda: "We're going to take the position that the EPA cut off all funding to any capacity-enhancing roadway project." In its members' minds, this group was a crusader for the public good. But to people who didn't share the rather idiosyncratic belief that tying up traffic was a good way to fight smog, the center was a pressure group pursuing its agenda at considerable expense to the general public.

It is completely legitimate for groups to say, and believe, that they serve a broader public interest. The reason we have a political system is to determine whose claim is in the public interest and whose isn't. The point is not that self-styled public-interest groups are necessarily more self-serving than, say, the National Association of Manufacturers or the National Association of Truck Stop Operators—just that they are not necessarily any less so. It all depends on where you sit.

Moreover, the coin flips: The corporate lobbies that pursue profits and the narrow groups that chase subsidies neither admit nor, usually, believe that they're crassly hunting money. Automakers that lobby against environmentalists see themselves as saving jobs threatened by unreasonable demands. Textile companies that seek import barriers see themselves as protecting low-wage workers and strengthening a vital American industry. Pharmaceutical companies lobby to "make us healthier," real-estate interests lobby to "make housing more affordable," agribusiness lobbies to "preserve America's food-production base," and on and on.

Even in principle, the line between public-spiritedness and pursuit of private gain is subjective. One person's public-spirited crusader for environmental sanity or entrepreneurial freedom is another person's job-destroying Luddite or selfish tycoon. Garment workers' unions long defended federal regulations forbidding people from doing commercial sewing at home. You could say they were fighting to prevent a resurgence of exploitive sweatshops, or that they were trying to throw their nonunion competition out of work. Take your pick.

The fact is that all groups, without exception, claim to be serving some larger good, and almost all believe it. And all groups, without exception, are lobbying for more of whatever it is that their members want, generally at some expense to nonmembers, and also often to the profit of the activists and staff who do the lobbying and raise the money. By the same token, every law, regulation, subsidy, and program creates losers as well as winners, and whether you think justice is served depends on who pays when the bill arrives.

Because the point of this book is to look at the game as a whole and not to cheer for any particular player, I'm going to make an intellectual move that may make some people uncomfortable. Instead of taking any particular viewpoint about justice or fairness, I'm going to treat all interest groups as morally interchangeable players in a giant game. From that point of view, AIDS-research lobbies fit within the same conceptual framework as pharmaceutical lobbies, and gun lobbies are very like environmental lobbies. I like some lobbies, you like others, but never mind. They are all playing by the same rules in the same game. None is really special.

Groups "R" Us

That lack of uniqueness is one reason I renounce calling the groups "special interests." Another is that the "special interest" label is more than three decades out of date. Groups are interested, yes; often narrow, certainly. But the fact is that seven out of ten Americans belong to at least one association (according to a 1990 survey conducted for the American Society of Association Executives), and one in four Americans belongs to four or more. Further, many of these group members have no illusions about what their own and other people's organizations are doing: In the 1990 survey, half of the respondents said that the main function of most associations is to influence the government. And so we're kidding ourselves if we pretend there is anything special about either interest groups or their members. Almost every American who reads these words is a member of a lobby.

Our groups have overrun Washington, covering it and inhabiting every cranny of it. You can see the result by walking into any office building in the city and reading the directory. I tried this myself, using the highly scientific random-sampling procedure of going into the first building I saw when I walked out the front door of my Washington office. The directory of this modest-sized building boasted these groups:

> Advertising Council
> Affiliated Hotels and Resorts
> Agudath Israel of America
> American Arbitration Association
> American Federation of Clinical Research
> Americans for Economic Renewal
> Center for the Advancement of Health
> Congress of Russian Americans
> Consortium for the Study of Intelligence

And that was just through the Cs; I kept reading and came to such delectables as the Institute of Chemical Waste Management, the Hispanic Association on Corporate Responsibility, the National Coalition to Prevent Impaired Driving, and the U.S. Cane Sugar Refiners' Association.

"It's to the point where there are so many causes organized in this way that there's very little space left," Senator Richard Lugar, a Republican of Indiana, told me. Day after day, groups stream in and out of his office, all asking to be seen, more and more of them every year. Lugar, scrambling to see them all, compared himself to an overbooked dentist jumping from chair to chair.

"We have developed enormous skills in this country of organizing for the status quo," Lugar said in a 1992 speech. "Anyone who doubts this need only take a look at the people coming into my office on a normal Tuesday and Wednesday. Almost every organization in our society has a national conference. The typical way of handling this is to come in on a Monday, rev up the troops, give them the bill number, and send them up to the Hill on Tuesday. If they can't get in on Tuesday, strike again on Wednesday.

"I have regularly on Tuesday as many as fifteen constituent groups from Indiana, all of whom have been revved up by some skillful person, employed for that purpose in Washington, to cite bills that they don't understand, have never heard of prior to that time, but with a scoresheet to report back to headquarters, whether I am for or against. It is so routine, it is so fierce, it goes on every week every year, that, you know, at some point you [can't be] immune to it. You try to be responsive. These people don't realize what they're doing, how they're being used, or even what the implications are of what they want."

The old era of lobbying by "special interests" is as dead as slavery and Prohibition. Where influence peddling was once the province of the privileged, it is now everyone's game. Americans have achieved the full democratization of the special-interest deal: influence peddling for the masses.

Why so much organizing, so quickly? Cultural theorists could spin out a dozen plausible theories, and some of those would be at least partially right. Some analysts point to the increasing size and complexity of American society. The country's population has more than doubled since FDR's first year in office, and perhaps people form groups in order to carve out communities amid growing diversity. Also, new technology breeds new activities and new puzzles, and people band together in response. Genetic-engineering associations didn't exist in 1970, and the reason is obvious.

There are many more explanations of that kind. Yet it's a mistake, when dealing with human beings, to overlook crass, material explanations. Like the bank robber Willie Sutton, Americans look for cash where the money is. If the costs of a certain kind of activity fall over time, and if the potential benefits grow, then more people will engage in that activity. And that is what has happened with group-forming.

You Can Afford One

First, the costs. Mancur Olson's work shows that anyone who wants to organize a group not only is likely to be met with apathy from many potential beneficiaries, but also can count on investing a good deal of his own time and money. That is why a group doesn't automatically appear wherever someone thinks it should. However, the costs of organizing have fallen. In 1920, if you wanted to round up ten thousand people, you had your work cut out for you. You would have needed to print and mail thousands of letters, make hundreds of phone calls at expensive rates, travel hither and yon by car on dirt roads, and gather followers one at a time. Today, if you want to round up ten thousand people, you can do a lot of the work from your living room, with a fax machine, a phone, a copier, and a modem. You can travel by air, exchange money in seconds, and join any number of Internet groups, all within a modest budget.

More important still, in 1920 you were more or less on your own, making up a strategy as you went along. You had few examples to emulate and few neighbors who could advise you. Today you can instantly tap into a whole infrastructure of group-forming know-how. You can hire consultants to run a direct-mail campaign, you can buy mailing lists, you can consult by phone with any of thousands of associations already in the business, you can hire any of thousands of experienced professionals who float from one interest group to another. Liberal public-interest groups can visit the Advocacy Institute, which "provides training in advocacy skills, such as long-range strategy planning, coalition-building, media advocacy, and advocacy uses of new communications technologies to a variety of citizen groups at the local, state, and national levels from around the world." Environmentalists can check in with the Whetstone Project, whose business is "to provide technical assistance to grass-roots organizations and to develop new methods of holding corporations accountable." What should be your group's tax status? How should it advertise? How much should it spend? Should it incorporate? Should it lobby directly? What about direct mail? Is there a market for its cause? What exactly should the cause be? Lawyers, lobbyists, accountants, consultants, market researchers, public-relations people, and many more all stand ready to tell you anything you need to know.

The techniques of lobbying have been codified, boiled down, and made handy for ready reference. You can buy *The Lobbying Handbook*, by John L. Zorack. ("The best way to learn the legislative process is to get a job in the United States Congress." "Helping to raise money for Members of Congress is part of the 'softening-up' process that paves the way for successful lobbying." Yours for only $125.) You can buy a copy of Stanley J. Marcuss's *Effective Washington Representation*. If you're a scientist, you can get *Working with Congress: A Practical Guide for Scientists and Engineers*, by William G. Wells, Jr., from the American Association for the Advancement of Science. ("Keep your message simple, focused, and short." "Remember that telephone calls based on 'outrage' and 'demands' don't go over well.") You can buy a thousand other books, magazines, newsletters, and software programs, and there are more all the time.

Finally, your job will be a lot easier than it used to be because you usually won't have to start from scratch. Rather, you can stand on the shoulders of existing groups. Compared with organizing individuals into an interest group, organizing groups into an interest group is fairly easy. A 1992 *Wall Street Journal* article told a typical tale. In 1987, a forty-year-old Minnesota farm activist named Mark Ritchie became fascinated with the global trade talks. Ritchie was an experienced activist who had organized food co-ops and a corporate boycott, and so he began arguing his case in meetings with environmentalists and foundations. In 1990, he procured a $50,000 grant from a Unitarian Church environmental charity. With that money, he hired a veteran environmental organizer, and their Citizen Trade Campaign was launched. Labor groups signed on, followed by populist farm groups, environmental groups, religious groups, and animal-rights groups. Just a few months later, the coalition came within thirty-nine votes of defeating President Bush's request for authority to negotiate a trade pact with Mexico and Canada in 1991. An activist like Mark Ritchie could hardly have hoped to form a group of thousands of individuals so quickly on his own. Instead, he linked existing interest groups. Other things being equal, then, groups breed more groups.

As information moves more quickly and cheaply, as ever more of it is prepackaged by professionals, as new groups form to serve as networkers and facilitators, the cost of group-forming falls. In some ways, that's good: The bigger America becomes, the more important it is for people to stay in touch with each other and find friends in distant places. But in other ways the change is problematic. "A single person with access to the right mailing lists," the journalist Robert Wright notes, "can send solicitation letters to tens of thousands of Americans and, with the money thus reaped, mold this inchoate group into a force to be reckoned with." An entrepreneur, a mailing list, a computer, a bit of cash—another interest group is up and lobbying.

Today, grassroots organizing is as sophisticated as any business going. The National Association of Home Builders has assembled a political manual explaining how to run a telephone bank and a house-to-house canvassing campaign, how to organize "victory caravans" to transport political volunteers, and so on. When Congress considered raising milk-price supports, it heard from thousands of worried managers of fast-food restaurants who were quickly mobilized by their trade association's "action alert" newsletter. With the help of computers, mobilization is now practically instantaneous. In 1993, for instance, the

U.S. Chamber of Commerce set up a computer system that could patch through calls and faxes to members of Congress from a ready pool of about fifty thousand volunteers. ("People on the Hill are getting tired of hearing from old Washington insiders like us," said one chamber official.) Computer-assisted groups can, and do, inundate congressional offices with carefully targeted mail; since the early 1970s, the volume of mail received by the U.S. House of Representatives has roughly quintupled.

In Washington, cynics have come to call this sort of computer-synthesized grassroots activity "astroturf" lobbying. It energizes voters, yes, but not in the old-fashioned way. Steven E. Schier, a political scientist at Carleton College, draws a distinction between the mass mobilization of voters and what he calls the "strategic activation" of voters. In old-fashioned mobilizations, political parties would frame broad, thematic appeals to the general public, "seeking to arouse all possible voters to vote in response to a direct partisan message." Strategic activation, conversely, is more like "narrowcasting." Interest-group executives and polling companies and political consultants craft messages and push buttons so as to arouse a response from a carefully targeted audience of constituents and activists: that is, from "small segments of citizens most likely to 'get their message' and vote or lobby government," observes Schier. Why bother to mobilize masses, which is expensive, when you can activate activists, which is cheap? But the people so activated, Schier notes, are often a highly unrepresentative lot: "Partisan mobilization encouraged heavy turnouts of eligible voters. . . . Activation has no such representative function. It works to further the purposes of particular political elites during elections and when they lobby government, regardless of what most citizens think or desire." In 1999, Hugh Heclo, a political scientist at George Mason University, wrote that it has become routine to send out personalized mailings to "computer-generated lists of potential supporters, profiled by demographic, consumer, and political characteristics." The result is perverse: "This sort of political mobilization appears to be the most effective way to harvest funds, drive up poll numbers, and get supporters to vote—to do everything, in short, except mobilize *the public*, which includes too many ordinary folk who are not true believers and so, as one leading consultant put it, 'are not profitable to work.'"

This is not to say that ordinary people are not involved. In fact, in a peculiar way they are more involved than ever—but their involvement has little in common with the flesh-pressing, ward-heeling politicking of yore. Back when lobbying was a game for tycoons and giant companies, you needed to have deep pockets to buy politicians' attention, or else you needed to have a lot of time to donate to personal activism. Now, with the electorate sliced, diced, and presorted by ZIP code, it's easy to find an interest group, if one doesn't find you first. Much as mutual funds have offered ordinary people access to almost every kind of productive investment, so too have interest groups offered ordinary people access to almost every kind of redistributive investment. Want to invest in rare-metals futures? It's as easy as finding a mutual fund and writing a check. Want to invest in lobbying for government benefits? It's as easy as finding an interest group and writing a check.

What Olson said is still true: You need to put up time and money if you want to organize an interest group or invest in one. But the investment becomes less daunting every year.

Too Sweet to Resist

To the reduced costs that make interest-group activity more accessible, now add the higher benefits that make it more attractive. Never before has organizing groups to lobby for benefits been as potentially lucrative as it is today; never have the sums available been as large or the paths to them as plentiful.

In 1929, the U.S. government's entire budget accounted for a mere 3 percent of the nation's economy. Even through the 1930s, when the economy was shrinking and the New Deal was in full

flower, government's share of the economy was still only around
10 percent, on average. This 10 percent was a notable slice of the
pie, but you could still ignore it and occupy yourself with the
other 90 percent without too much risk. Republicans often charge
Franklin Roosevelt with turning government into a swollen monster, but only after FDR was dead did the stakes in Washington
become so large that no sensible person could ignore the game.

Many objective measures—the numbers and length of laws,
of regulations, of court decisions—suggest that the big jump in
the level of federal activism came in the Johnson and Nixon
years, around the same time as the rate of group formation took
off. Starting in the mid-1960s, government was seeking to do
more things for more people and groups than ever before. Robert
C. Clark, of Harvard Law School, has tracked the increase: "In
the Progressive Era early in this century, there were five new federal statutes enacted in the area of health and consumer safety;
in the New Deal period, there were eleven; during the period
from 1964 to 1979 (the 'third wave,' as it might be called), there
were sixty-two." He notes that the same pattern holds in other
areas of federal activity, such as energy and the environment.

Turn back to Figure 1.1 (Chapter 1) and you'll notice that
before the early 1970s, the number of pages of new laws enacted
by each Congress averaged a bit more than two thousand. Then
it jumped to an average of more than five thousand pages. (And
Ronald Reagan's antigovernment presidency didn't change that a
bit.) The annual page count of the *Federal Register*, where new
regulations are printed, drifted gradually upward from Truman's
day until about 1970. Then, in the space of only about five years,
it tripled, remaining in the higher range ever since, as Figure 3.6
shows. Between 1960 and 1985, the page count of new federal
court decisions in the West Publishing Company's case reports
more than quadrupled. And so forth.

By the late 1970s, the federal government's budget was running to a sum equivalent to a fifth or more of the entire American
economy. To the direct spending must be added thousands of

FIGURE 3.6 *Federal Register* Pages, 1948–1998

SOURCE: U.S. Office of Management and Budget.

laws and regulations that redirect private money, time, and energy. Regulations now cost Americans, economists estimate, several hundred billion dollars a year, or several thousand dollars per American household per year.

Whether you think those amounts are too much or too little depends on how much of the bill you pay and whether you feel you get your money's worth. But what is not seriously in question is that the sums being moved around in Washington— through the budget plus regulations—are now much too large to ignore. They are more than large enough to ensure that everyone has a major stake in at least breaking even when the chips are divided in Washington. Everyone needs a vigilant agent in the capital, and anyone can hope to profit by lobbying well. As one lobbyist told Jeffrey Birnbaum, "The modern government is huge, pervasive, intrusive into everybody's life. If you just let things take their course and don't get in the game, you get trampled on. You ignore it at your peril."

The point is not that government's heightened activism is a bad thing, as such. Government has been doing more because people have called on it to solve their problems, and politicians are eager to help. The point, rather, is that the more actively and ambitiously government moves resources around, the more can be gained by forming a group and lobbying for a bigger share, and so the stronger the incentive to do it. There is no way out of that dilemma; the bad comes with the good. Indeed, a built-in side effect of new government programs is their tendency to summon into being new constituencies—which, in turn, often lobby for yet other new programs, keeping the whole cycle going.

Fifty years ago, the elderly were a demographic category. Today they are a lobby. Why the transformation? Before 1935, the government wasn't giving much to the aged, nor was it taking much from them, so why lobby? But after Social Security and Medicare were in full swing, the elderly had so much at stake in Washington that they would have been crazy not to have organized, both to protect "their" programs and to agitate for new benefits (long-term care, for instance).

In 1920, four farm groups ran offices in Washington: the National Farmers Council, the National Board of Farm Organizations, the National Grange of Patrons of Husbandry, and the American Farm Bureau Federation. On May 12, 1933, President Roosevelt opened the era of modern farm politics by signing the Agricultural Adjustment Act, which was soon followed by the Agricultural Adjustment Act Amendments of 1935, the Soil Conservation and Domestic Allotment Act of 1936, and the Agricultural Adjustment Act of 1938. Farmers now had programs to defend. By the late 1950s, groups had sprung up to represent growers of each subsidized crop—the National Cotton Council in 1938, the National Peanut Council in 1941, the National Association of Wheat Growers in 1950, the National Corn Growers Association in 1957, and so forth. Today American agriculture fundamentally *is* a collection of groups, organized around federal programs. By extension, if American society is increasingly organized as a collection of groups, that must be at least partly because American government is organized as a collection of constituency-based programs.

Too Much of a Good Thing

The point of this discussion about groups and programs isn't to argue for or against Medicare or dairy subsidies or whatever. Rather, it's to look at the interest-group sector as one might any other industry. If the potential rewards of group-forming increase, and if the average costs of group-forming decrease, you don't have to be an economist to see that the likely result will be more and bigger groups.

No wonder, then, that the groups have grown and multiplied. The interest-group industry pays rising returns on investment and enjoys falling costs; its potential base of investors includes nearly the whole adult population, creating a practically unlimited pool of capital; its technological base grows ever more sophisticated; it is supported and staffed by an expanding infrastructure of professionals who know the business. From an economic point of view, the American interest-group sector is a classic growth industry, rather like the American automobile industry of half a century ago.

Well, so what? Maybe more groups are better. At a party in Washington a few years back, I ran into a journalist who works for a prominent liberal magazine. We got to talking about the way federal programs tend to be taken over by the people who can hire the slickest lobbyists with the shiniest Gucci shoes. He agreed with me that it's a problem. But when I suggested it's a fundamental problem, he demurred. On the contrary, the way to deal with the plague of corporate lobbyists is to organize more citizens' groups and public-interest groups to fight them, on the model of Ralph Nader's far-flung organization. I suppressed the urge to roll my eyes. "After twenty years of that," I said, "haven't we learned anything? All you get is an escalating spiral where groups breed more groups, and the system gradually chokes."

He saw the postwar explosion of groups as a flowering of citizen activism that helps to perfect democracy. I saw it as a burgeoning of pressure-group entrepreneurship that seeks to exploit democracy. He thought I was a defeatist, or maybe a corporate stooge. I thought he had his head in the sand. In any case, our argument represented a clash between two views of how America is working. He was talking about pluralism. I was talking about hyperpluralism.

In the political science theories of the 1950s and 1960s, pluralism dominated. The idea was that in a democracy it's only natural for people to form groups, which will compete and negotiate in order to create a reasonably good approximation of what's good for the whole society. If some group becomes disproportionately powerful or begins to abuse its power, an opposing group will form, and the system will be tugged back toward balance. More groups will involve more citizens and interests, thus counteracting the influence of narrow groups and powerful insiders. The more groups, the better.

In the 1970s, the pluralist model began to fall apart. For one thing, it was empirically wrong: Often, countervailing groups did not spring up against narrow interests because, as Olson showed, narrow interests enjoyed stronger incentives to organize and an easier time getting together. There would be no point trying to form a national organization merely to get rid of subsidies for beekeepers.

Moreover, it turns out that not everyone is equally inclined to join groups. The educated are much likelier to be joiners than the illiterate; the rich are likelier to join than the poor. A 1990 survey for the American Society of Association Executives found that people with college educations are more than twice as likely as the less-educated to join four or more associations, and the less-educated are twice as likely as the college-educated to join no groups at all. Groups, apparently, are skewed toward privilege. Environmental groups' members, for example, tend to have above-average incomes. "Readers of *Sierra*, the magazine of the Sierra Club, have household incomes twice that of the average American," noted Terry L. Anderson in *The New York Times*. "Environmental magazines are more likely to feature Rolex and BMW than Timex and Volkswagen advertisements." When such groups lobby for emissions controls or pesticide rules that raise the prices of cars and groceries, they may be reflecting the preferences of people who buy Volvos and Brie more than the preferences of people who buy used Chevies and hamburger. Moreover, the people at the very bottom—the downtrodden and the excluded—tend to be the hardest of all to organize; people foraging for food in dumpsters don't write $20 checks to associations in Washington. It wasn't at all clear, then, that group bargaining would produce fair or even representative outcomes.

Most important, there was growing concern about the side effects of groupism itself. Consider an economic analogy: In economics, inflation is a gradual increase in the level of prices. It's usually a more or less stable rate of increase, so people can plan around it. But if the inflation rate starts to speed up, people start expecting more inflation. They hoard goods and dump cash, driving the inflation still faster. Eventually an invisible threshold is crossed: The inflation now feeds on its own growth and undermines the stability of the whole system. That is hyperinflation, the most dangerous and destabilizing of all economic pathologies. When hyperinflation sets in, the economic system begins to defeat the very purpose for which it exists—namely, to provide a stable market where people can trade and invest dependably. The economy enters crisis, confidence in it plummets, capital flees, and government itself may collapse.

Suppose something similar happens with groups. More groups demand more benefits; more benefits spawn more groups. As the group-forming process picks up speed, an invisible threshold might be crossed. At some point, there might be so many groups, and so many more groups forming every year, that they would begin to choke the system that bred them, to undermine confidence in politics, even to erode political stability. The system might begin to defeat the purpose for which it exists—namely, to make reasonable social decisions reasonably quickly. That would be what James A. Thurber, a political scientist at American University, calls hyperpluralism. In his view, America is now there: "I think we have reached a threshold of so much competition among the groups for scarce resources that we've reached a level of deadlock and crisis."

No Retreat

From today's vantage point, the age of the smoke-filled room, when lobbying was a game for the well-heeled and well-connected, turns out to have had its strong points. In those days, the transfer-seeking game was exclusive, which meant that many people and interests were effectively shut out. But the very fact of its exclusivity meant that it was relatively small; by today's standards, it involved few people and modest sums of money. That game was shady, but at least it was fairly inexpensive. It was controlled by old boys in patent-leather shoes and silk hats, but at least it was under control.

However, there is no point hankering for political bosses and robber barons and smoke-filled rooms. A politics that excludes all but the privileged and the connected is repugnant, and a shady game, however small, is still shady. Say what you like about the corporate lobbies or public-interest groups whose work you find distasteful, they operate more or less in the sunshine according to fairly regular rules, and their combination of openness and inclusiveness (practically everyone is spoken for by somebody) has made American politics among the world's cleanest. Despite some housecleaning after World War II, Japan has basically held to the smoke-filled-room model straight through the postwar period, with the result that a parade of corruption scandals has brought down one government after another. In any case, there is no repealing the group proliferation and the enriched stakes that have turned redistributive politics into a popular, rather than an elite, sport. Having changed, American society will not change back.

The trouble is that the shift from the smoke-filled room to the mass-membership lobby has created a set of problems that Americans have not even begun to learn how to manage. By the standards of a country more than two centuries old, hyperpluralism is brand-new. Experts in universities, to say nothing of the general public, have only recently begun to take a hard look at what's going on. In Franklin Roosevelt's day or even Lyndon Johnson's, social reformers took the structure of American society more or less as a given and built groups and programs upon it. Hardly anyone foresaw that the democratization of interest-group politicking might work to transform society itself into a collection of interest groups—and do so in only about three decades, far too quickly for either the voters or the institutions of government to make a smooth adjustment. Few Americans have reckoned the extent of the change, much less revamped their thinking to accommodate it.

In fact, the standard kind of political thinking makes matters worse, not better. Liberals and conservatives still think they can bring the interest-group spiral under control if they can just beat the groups on the other side. Liberals, like the journalist I met at the party, want to beat corporate lobbyists and the religious right; conservatives want to beat environmental activists and unions. What few on either side have figured out is that they are all trapped together in a self-defeating mind-set. Their mind-set might have made sense fifty or a hundred years ago, when the smoke-filled room was small enough so that you could hope to push your enemies out and slam the door, but it is useless today, when there is no smoke-filled room and there is no door. The more you try to beat the other guy, the more the game expands.

And it does expand. Growing seems to be what it does best. I mentioned that the benefits-hunting industry—the transfer-seeking sector—resembles the auto industry of decades ago. So it does, but with a difference. The automotive industry grows until additional cars become superfluous, at which point profits vanish and investment shifts to other sectors. The transfer-seeking industry appears to be able to generate profits simply by growing. The auto industry grows like bone or muscle. The transfer-seeking industry appears to grow more like cancer. To understand why, it's necessary to look at the curious dynamic of the parasite economy.

4

The Parasite Economy

LIKE MOST of the lawyers in Washington, Mike LaPlaca lobbies. Like a few of them, he wishes he didn't. In 1972, he was a businessman, working in the productive economy. By 1992, when I met him, he was a lobbyist, working in the parasite economy. It had sucked him in, just as it has sucked in thousands of other people. His career was, in that respect, a microcosmic version of America's recent experience.

In 1972, LaPlaca was national sales manager for the Hertz car-rental company. After the constant traveling gave him health problems, he decided to leave business. Having picked up a law degree along the way, he moved back home—to Washington, D.C.—and opened a law practice, emphasizing, naturally enough, franchise law and car-rental companies. He went on about his business until 1989. Then a Republican member of Congress, Lynn Martin (later a secretary of labor), introduced an obscure piece of legislation involving collision-damage waivers. It changed Mike LaPlaca's life.

A collision-damage waiver, as many car renters know, lets you off the hook for damage to your rental car. The waivers are a profit maker for rental companies and are often convenient for renters, who no longer need to worry about being stuck with a big bill if the car crashes. The trouble was that some car-rental companies were pushing collision-damage waivers at customers who, for one reason or another, didn't really need them. Consumer groups, using the sledgehammer logic of political activism, declared that if collision-damage waivers were sometimes being sold misleadingly, then they ought to be banned altogether.

Who, then, would pay for damage to rental cars? That's easy, said the activists: the car-rental company. The consumer rents the car, the business pays for any damage to the car. No customer liability, no problem. The upshot was a bill that said: "No rental company shall . . . hold any authorized driver liable for any damage," except in a few specially defined cases, like drunken driving. Did you drive your rented car into a tree? Did you leave the keys in it so that it got stolen? Not to worry: The car-rental company would have to fix or replace the car. This was a textbook bit of legislative cost-shifting: Car-repair costs would be shifted from consumers to businesses.

One obvious result of such a bill would be to make people less careful about their driving. Renters would damage more cars (who cares? The rental company will pay); costs would go up throughout the whole system. But another result was more subtle and interesting, and explained why the two industry giants, Hertz and Avis, both threw their weight behind the liability bill.

A cost increase doesn't necessarily affect all companies the same way. The costs of fixing and replacing damaged cars are relatively easy for a huge company, like Hertz or Avis, to absorb. But small rental companies don't have a lot of cash. To keep afloat, they rely on their cars' coming back safely and then going back out the door. If you're a small operator with only a handful of cars, you're in trouble when you have to write a few checks to replace $16,000 cars.

Suddenly Mike LaPlaca's legal clients were looking at a law that they believed would drive up their relative costs. "What the bill does if it becomes law," LaPlaca said, "is to put enormous pressure on smaller companies to raise their prices." In New York State, where a similar law had passed, dozens of little car-rental companies, with names like Ugly Duckling and No Problem Rent-a-Car, went bust. "Only large companies with thousand-car fleets can absorb such loss expenses," wrote the owner of a Budget Rent-a-Car franchise in California. "We could go out of business with just a few major losses." The fact that the two biggest companies, Hertz and Avis, were strongly supporting the bill only confirmed the smaller companies' belief that they were under attack. A classic distributional struggle—consumer activists and big companies on one side, small and midsize companies on the other—was now under way.

When people believe their interests are under attack, they band together to form an interest group. In 1989, shortly after the liability bill was first introduced, Mike LaPlaca organized a coalition of car-rental companies to fight the liability bill.

Until 1989, small and midsize car-rental businesses had never maintained much of a presence in Washington, because Washington had never paid the industry much attention. The car-rental business was one of the least regulated transportation industries, and for many decades it functioned well. But by the time I met LaPlaca, things had changed. The Car-Rental Coalition and its member companies had spent roughly $1 million retaining five lobbyists or lobbying firms—a figure that did not count time donated by hundreds of executives and workers in the car-rental business (or, of course, the money spent by their opponents).

Moreover, if an interest group expects to gain clout with politicians, it needs to give them a reason to pay attention. The Car-Rental Coalition created such a reason in 1992 by forming a political action committee, or PAC. Like all PACs, the coalition's PAC invested in friendly politicians rather than in new jobs or factories. "We were making contributions literally minutes before the election," LaPlaca said.

Feeding a Washington lobby is now a regular cost of doing business in the car-rental industry, even for tiny companies that got along without representation in the past. Car-rental customers pay the price. Only one class unequivocally wins: The lawyering, lobbying, and politicking class of Washington's K Street is several million dollars richer.

No doubt because he was new to the world of lobbying and power-politicking, LaPlaca spoke of his experience with a note of outrage. "I'm an innocent at this, and I can say I was shocked," he said. "I lived fifty-two years without ever having to petition the Congress on behalf of myself or a client. And in many ways I wish I could go back to the fifty-second year."

Shed no tears for Mike LaPlaca. He earns several multiples of the average family income and works in pleasant offices on H Street in Washington. But do wonder, as he himself outspokenly does, whether there isn't something peculiar and insidious about the forces that bent his career. Although we normally think of wealth as money, the real source and meaning of wealth is the career product of a human being's talent and energy. The diversion of a career from the business sector to the lobbying sector affects wealth in the most fundamental sense.

Note, then, the lessons of LaPlaca's story:

One, everyone involved was doing what made sense for him—looking out for his interests. Consumers were looking out for their interests (as they saw them); so were the little companies; so were the big companies; so were the politicians. And the lawyers and lobbyists were looking out for their clients' interests.

Two, though some of the players may in fact have been acting out of cynicism and opportunism, their actions could also be squared with reasonable viewpoints and decent motives. Take your pick; we'll never know. But it doesn't matter anyway, because either way—

Three, the end result was a new interest group, a new political action committee, and several new lobbying jobs, at a cost in the millions. That is how the parasite economy grows, despite, or because of, the best intentions of all concerned.

Making and Taking

As a thought experiment, imagine you're the president of Acme Big Flange Company, and you have an additional—"marginal," in econospeak—$1 million to invest. Obviously, you want the highest return possible. You are locked in a stiff competition with, say, mini-flange mills. The question you face is how best to invest your $1 million so as to get the jump on the competition. What are your options?

First, you could buy a new high-speed flange-milling machine or a better inventory-control system. Either of those would improve your company's productivity. However, in a developed economy, where most competitors are technologically up-to-date, such investments are unlikely to improve your company's productivity dramatically. Rather, the improvement will be incremental. (Remember, this is a *marginal* $1 million; you already would have made the most lucrative investments.) Over a decade, you might earn an annual return of something like 10 or 15 percent on your investment—maybe $100,000 or $150,000 a year.

Not bad. But there is a second option to consider. For $1 million you could hire one of the best lobbyists in Washington. This fellow is a former staff member of the House Valve and Flange Subcommittee: He knows the legislators, he knows the issues, and he is persuasive and ingenious. With his help, you could invest some of your $1 million in campaign contributions to members of the Valve and Flange Subcommittee. Though you can't count on buying anyone's vote, your money would buy you access, which your competitor might not enjoy. Your lobbyist and your PAC might win you a tax break, a subsidy, or, best of all (because least visible to the public), a law or regulation hobbling mini-flange mills. Any such tax break, subsidy, or regulation could easily be worth, say, $10 million a year.

So here is your equation. New machines earn a return of $100,000 or $150,000 a year; a successful lobbyist earns potentially fifty or a hundred times that amount. Which is the better investment?

The example is hypothetical but hardly far-fetched. This is from *The New York Times* of October 22, 1992:

> It was an obscure provision buried deep in the arcane language of a 1,000-page trade bill, but Senator Alfonse M. D'Amato was on the case. A handful of sugar refiners, including one with a plant in Brooklyn, stood to gain $365 million in tariff rebates and Mr. D'Amato was all for it.
>
> With his help, the provision squeaked through the Senate in the summer of 1987. That fall, five years before his next race, Mr. D'Amato received $8,500 in campaign contributions from the sugar refiners.

Assuming that the sugar refiners spent about $8,500 for a tariff rebate worth $365 million, this was no ordinary investment. Never mind 15 percent or 150 percent; the rate of return was better than four *million* percent. You can't earn that kind of money by opening a car wash. And, frankly, if you met an investment opportunity that paid $42,941.17 for every dollar you put in, you would be a fool to pass it up.

No wonder, then, that people invest. "If I throw in a million here or a million there, I might get a hundred million back," said one Washington lobbyist (and, yes, former House of Representatives staff member). "And there are probably enough cases like that so they keep throwing money in."

Actually, in any economy, rich or poor, there are always lots of cases like that. You just have to hunt for them. When one person starts hunting, others follow, not wanting to be left behind. When I spoke to Gordon Tullock, an economist whose pioneering work in the late 1960s opened up the academic study of this kind of behavior, he said, "I think it may be that the thing feeds on itself. Every time you have a successful lobbying effort, that advertises the value of lobbying."

economic argu-
ment

This game of trying to capture a larger share of existing wealth is transfer-seeking. Unlike productive investment, it poses a social problem. From any particular individual's point of view, productive investment and transfer-seeking are more or less equivalent. Both are ways of investing your time and energy to make yourself better off. But from a social point of view, the two are very different. Whereas productive investment makes society wealthier, transfer-seeking investment makes society poorer, in two ways.

First, the process of transferring resources from one pocket to another is never perfectly efficient; something is lost along the way. Agents take fees; negotiations take time. Conflict further adds to the cost: If I don't want you to get what I have, I'll do everything possible to make the transfer expensive and difficult.

Second, and what's more profound, the game destroys wealth relative to the proper baseline for comparison, which is the wealth that *would* have been created if people weren't busy trying to grab pieces of each other. Every bit of energy people spend fighting over existing wealth is that much less energy spent producing more wealth. The negative sums of transfer-seeking, then, are the sums that would have been produced but are not: the inventions not developed, the crops not planted, the equipment not bought, the employees not hired, and, in all other forms, the investments forgone.

And how large might the negative sums be? Consider a second thought experiment.

Suppose you have $100. Suppose I want $100. In principle, how much might I be willing to spend to get your $100? The answer is, up to $99, because if I invested that much and captured your $100, I would come out a dollar ahead. And, again in principle, how much might you be willing to spend to keep your $100, once you realize I'm after it? Answer—$99 again.

If you add the numbers, you quickly see a startling result. In principle, the two of us can rationally consume almost $200 fighting over an existing $100. Yet no wealth would have been produced.

Of course, in practice it would be rare for two people to spend $19,999 fighting over a $10,000 car. If, for instance, the chances that any particular car will be stolen are only one in ten, you might spend only about $1,000 guarding your car. However, the broad point holds: An investment in capturing wealth from someone else is likely to summon forth a roughly equal and opposite defensive investment, and the sums involved can grow very large.

But doesn't transfer-seeking create jobs? After all, if I hire a lobbyist to win a tax break, that money doesn't disappear into a black hole. Rather, it hires secretaries, rents office space, buys a copy machine, and so on.

True, but from an economic point of view, paying people to capture more of other people's money is like hiring people to steal cars. If I hire workers to build cars, the result is new jobs and new cars. But if I hire someone to steal existing cars, I have merely moved a job out of the productive sector and into the car-theft sector. My employees will buy screwdrivers and crowbars and wire cutters, thus creating business for hardware stores—but meanwhile a car owner (or insurance company) will be several thousand dollars poorer and will have that much less to spend or invest. Similarly, I can create jobs in the roof-repair industry—and also in the roof-guarding industry—by going around punching holes in people's roofs. But no one would think those jobs were making society as a whole better off. They create activity, but they destroy wealth.

Actually, the example of someone who drills holes in roofs is not as whimsical as it may sound. It brings us within eyeshot of the central peculiarity of transfer-seeking—the peculiarity that earns it the distinctive adjective "parasitic."

Pay Them or Else

If someone climbs on your roof with a hatchet, he puts you in a difficult position. You're going to have to respond, or else you're going to be out the price of a new roof. He may protest that he is doing the morally right thing, helping humanity, taking what is rightfully his, or whatever. You don't much care. If you let him alone, your roof is a goner. Assuming you can't get rid of him violently, you may decide it's cheaper to pay him to go away than to fix your roof.

In the economy, as in nature, a parasite is set apart from a mere freeloader by its ability to force its target to fend it off. This is the sense in which transfer-seekers are, not so loosely speaking, parasitic: Not only are they unproductive themselves, but *they also force other people to be unproductive.*

Is that really so unusual? What about corporate takeover artists? Wall Street financiers and brokers who just move money around? Freeloaders who ask for handouts? Aren't they parasites, in some sense?

In some sense, maybe. But not in the particular sense at issue here. None of those people really fits the bill, because none has the power to make you engage in a distributional struggle.

A corporate takeover artist certainly does command the attention of entrenched company managers, who resent the intrusion. But takeover artists merely offer money for a company; it's up to the stockholders to take the deal or not. Managers may feel obliged to fight the takeover in order to save their jobs. They are in the position of a caretaker who doesn't want the house sold: He'll try to block the sale or keep his job, maybe by promising to fix up the property. (Corporate takeover threats are often productive: They can make managers perform better, so that the stockholders are less willing to sell.) But the would-be buyer of the house isn't a parasite; he's a purchaser.

By the same token, financiers and brokers and other such middlemen are also not really parasites. You hire them because they know, or are supposed to know, how to move money around and where to put it. Using old resources more productively creates new wealth. That's why bankers, who borrow money and lend it out again, are not only productive but also essential. Similarly, a Wall Street trader who sees an underpriced stock may buy low, sell higher, and make a killing—but in the process he is moving capital away from an overpriced company and toward an investment that is more productive. That kind of middleman is like a professional librarian who offers, for a price, to catalog a big book collection. You hire the person to make your assets more productive.

And what about the guy with his hand out on the street, or the guy selling pet rocks, or the inept stockbroker? Are these people parasites? Again, they flunk the basic test: They are not forcing anyone else to fend them off. You can brush off the beggar, you can leave the store without the pet rock, and you can fire the stockbroker and go it alone. A bad stockbroker or a pesky real-estate agent can take your money if you do hire him, but only a transfer-seeker can take your money if you *don't* hire him.

In America, only a few classes of people have the power to take your money if you don't fend them off. One is the criminal class. People who break into your car or rob your house (or punch holes in your roof) are members of the parasite economy in the classic sense: They take your wealth if you don't actively fight them off. Such people are costly to society, not only for what they take but also for the high cost of fending them off. They make us buy locks, alarms, iron gates, security guards, policemen, insurance, and on and on. David N. Laband and John P. Sophocleus, economists who have studied transfer-seeking, once estimated that, in 1985 alone, American criminals invested at least $324 billion in "illegal wealth transfers." Recall how two people can spend $200 fighting over an existing $100, and you won't be surprised to learn that, according to Laband and Sophocleus, American individuals and companies spent about $340 billion that same year trying to fend off thieves (we spent almost $10 billion just for locks).

Criminals, however, aren't the only ones who play the distributive game. Legal, noncriminal transfer-seeking is perfectly possible—on one condition. You need the law's help. That is, you need to persuade politicians or courts to intervene on your behalf.

Consider Scrooge, the bicycle messenger from Chapter 2. If

he spreads a computer virus that shuts down fax machines, he's a criminal. But if he wins a law that taxes fax machines or that subsidizes couriers, he's a Republican. Or a Democrat. In 1999, the American Society of Anesthesiologists went to battle against the American Association of Nurse Anesthetists over a proposed regulation allowing nurses to administer anesthesia to Medicaid and Medicare patients without a doctor's supervision. No doubt for the best of reasons, the anesthesiologists were not keen on losing market share to inexpensive nurses. Similarly, and also no doubt for the best of reasons, businesses seek tariffs, unions seek minimum-wage laws and laws against hiring permanent replacements for strikers, farmers seek subsidies, consumers seek lemon laws, environmentalists seek regulations on industry, plaintiffs seek damages, postal workers seek bans on competition, car-rental companies seek liability legislation that hobbles their competition, and so on, and on, and on.

These groups all think they are doing society a favor, and no doubt some of them are. Many redistributive laws and regulations are worth having, though many also are not. For now, however, focus not on the value of particular laws or benefits but on the dynamics of the game as a whole. As each group seeks transfers, other groups respond. And that is the magical talent of the parasite economy. To fend off a politician, lobbyist, or lawyer, you need to hire another politician, lobbyist, or lawyer, whether you want to or not. If your business competitor starts to move legislation that costs you money, you would be stupid not to hire a lobbyist of your own to block it. If your competitor opens a political action committee to donate to a key politician, you could lose your shirt if you don't do the same. Similarly, when you get sued, you don't have the option of ignoring the lawsuit; for months or even years, you are going to spend a lot of time and money on lawyers.

Fending off transfer-seekers isn't cheap, as anyone knows who has ever been sued. In 1993, a Texas jury needed less than four hours to exonerate American Airlines in a predatory-pricing suit brought by American's competitors, but American was stuck with a $20 million legal bill nonetheless. Lawyers can cost $200 an hour, lobbyists $10,000 a month, and politicians whatever the market will bear. And the energy and money you spend on them will be diverted from investments that would have been more productive for you.

What is peculiar about the parasite economy, then, is its ability to siphon off resources that people would rather invest elsewhere. Activism on one side draws counteractivism on another; motion begets more motion. "For example," write the political scientists Allan J. Cigler and Burdett A. Loomis, "the National Association of Manufacturers . . . originally was created to further the expansion of business opportunities in foreign trade, but it became a more powerful organization largely in response to the rise of organized labor. Mobilization of business interests since the 1960s often has resulted from threats posed by consumer advocates and environmentalists." Mike LaPlaca was drawn into the parasite economy because it was attacking his clients. That is how the parasite economy grows, even if society as a whole would be better off if it shrank.

Paved with Good Intentions

Who are these evil parasitic people, and why don't they just mend their wicked ways?

Meet Milt Brown. He is gentle and genial, a retired consultant who lives in Phoenix. His wife, Catherine, is a woman whose graciousness and sincerity serve her well in a business—real estate agentry—that could do with more of both qualities.

They don't like being taken advantage of, though. Mail from a group in Washington told the Browns that Milt was a "notch baby," one of a group of Social Security recipients who believe (wrongly, but that's another story) that they are entitled to more in benefits than they receive. Milt got angry and began paying the group $10 a year to get his fair share. He kept investing for four years, until he realized that the benefits increase he might receive would be only about $10 a month instead of the $50 he had first supposed—not worth the trouble, he figured.

"When someone tells me, 'Gee, you should get another fifty dollars a month,'" he later said, "I'm going to do what I can to get it." Remind Milt Brown that any additional Social Security money he received would have come out of someone else's pocket, and he would remind you that he was not seeking anything he wasn't entitled to. He just wanted his fair share.

So is Milt Brown a seeker after justice? Or is he a vulture-eyed predator?

Inevitably, the first reaction when I talk about the parasite economy is, Who, me? People point their fingers at lawyers and lobbyists and politicians—*they* are the problem, yes? Yes—and no. They are the professional *agents* of legal transfer-seeking. They don't go fishing for goodies without the enthusiastic support of the people who hire them. Those clients are transfer-seeking *investors*, because they invest their money or their votes, or both, to obtain and keep benefits and subsidies. Put together investor and agent, and the parasite economy is in business. Of course, the two sides can get together more easily if someone takes the initiative to form an interest group, round up members, and hire lobbyists or file lawsuits. People who do that are transfer-seeking *entrepreneurs*. Often, the agents act as entrepreneurs, imagining new benefits or legal claims and then rounding up clients to seek them.

"Well, surely you don't mean *me*—I'm one of the good guys." After they're finished blaming lawyers and lobbyists—as though lawyers didn't have clients and lobbyists didn't serve interest groups—that's what people always say. Public-interest advocates are especially indignant if you suggest that they, too, are playing the transfer-seeking game. When I talked about transfer-seeking with a liberal environmental activist I know, he said: "I don't hear you making distinctions between different kinds of parasites. I would suggest there's a distinction between people who do what they do because they believe it's in the public interest [i.e., himself] and people who do it purely for financial gain [i.e., his corporate enemies]." Then when I talked with an antitax activist who works for a conservative public-interest group, he said of lobbying and lawyering: "It's an evil thing that happens on the left—and it's a necessity on the right. As long as there are criminals [i.e., his liberal enemies], you need to have policemen [i.e., himself]." He loathes the environmentalist. The environmentalist loathes him. Each is valiantly protecting the country from the depredations of the other. Each is, therefore, the selfless public servant.

In Washington you soon discover that everybody is a selfless public servant. Not only does everybody say so, but almost everybody believes it as well. One of the transfer-seeking game's most wickedly ingenious defenses is that it allows every individual player to think that he is serving the greater good while everyone else is evil. The conceptual breakthrough comes when you realize that the parasite economy doesn't care whether the people feeding it are vicious opportunists or high-thinking moralists; it thrives just as well either way. In the transfer-seeking game, *motive doesn't matter.* That is another peculiarity of the parasite economy. Whether the people engaging each other in distributive struggles are idealistic or cynical, the economic outcome is the same: People devote scarce reserves of time, energy, and money fighting back and forth over existing wealth, and the transfer-seeking professionals always make out well.

Indeed, idealistic activists can be much more expensive than cynical opportunists. A man who wants to take your car just for the money can often be warded off by an alarm, which may make the effort not worth the trouble. But the man who believes he is entitled to your car can be much more persistent. "Dammit," he thinks, "that's *my* car, and no bastard is going to keep it from me." The merely greedy give up when they stop seeing dollar signs, but the outraged don't stop lobbying or suing until they get their rights. In fact, someone who is morally outraged is easily capable of spending *more* than $10,000 to get your $10,000 car: Even if he suffers a financial loss, he makes his point and makes you miserable. He might even destroy the car if he fails to get it; better to ruin the car than allow you to enjoy it.

A tapeworm doesn't hate you and isn't out to get you. It is just trying to get what it thinks is its fair share. Similarly, the investors in the transfer-seeking economy aren't out to wreck the economy. They are just trying to get what they think is their fair share.

Or, rather, *we* are just trying to get *our* fair share. If you seek or receive any sort of benefit from Washington (or the state capitals), you are in on the game. It is safe to say, indeed, that every American is implicated in transfer-seeking. If you think otherwise, consider Table 4.1, which shows, by income class, who receives direct entitlement subsidies from the federal government. Benefits flow to all income groups, roughly in proportion to their share of the population. Rich, poor, and middle—all are enjoying benefits and feeling entitled. America is the land of the free and the home of the subsidized.

Chessboards and Slot Machines

You may be wondering why I keep referring to transfer-seeking as a game. It certainly isn't a game in the sense of being childish or inconsequential. In the sense I mean, a game is a social system with a set of rules and players and an inner dynamic of its

TABLE 4.1 Distribution of Federal Direct Entitlement Spending, by Income Group

Taxable Income	Percent Share of Population	Percent Share of All Benefits
Below $10,000	21.9	23.4
$10,000 – $20,000	20.4	22.3
$20,000 – $30,000	16.3	16.3
$30,000 – $40,000	12.1	11.4
$40,000 – $50,000	9.0	8.0
$50,000 – $75,000	12.2	10.5
$75,000 – $100,000	4.2	3.6
$100,000 – $200,000	2.8	3.1
Over $200,000	1.1	1.5

SOURCE: Progressive Policy Institute.

own, such that no individual player can predict who will win. To find out who wins, you have to play.

Some games are closed and self-limiting—chess, for instance, where someone wins (or the game stalemates) and that's that. Other games are open-ended and can become all-consuming—playing the slot machines, for instance; the insidious dynamic ("My next coin might win, and I've invested so much already") can trap you until you've lost all your money.

Transfer-seeking appears to be a classic open-ended game. If you look at its implicit logic, you see a potential spiral:

1. Someone can always make a bundle investing in legal transfer-seeking, so someone will always do it. But whatever one person wins, someone else must lose.
2. Therefore, when someone enters the game or expands his position, he effectively forces someone else also to enter the game or expand *his* position. Every new player drags in other new players.
3. The more people and groups play, the more money there is to be made or lost in the game. As the stakes rise, you risk more if you ignore the game, and you gain more if you play it well. Therefore, more is invested. Return to Step 1 and repeat.

On paper, this logic looks like an ideal engine for an open-ended, self-perpetuating game, the sort of game that can keep going and even expanding until it bumps into some outside constraint. In reality, is that happening? To find out, you have to get a handle on the size of the parasite economy.

A Parasite Census

Unfortunately, the Commerce Department's national accounts don't include a line for transfer-seeking, and the Labor Department's employment figures don't have a "wealth-sucking parasites" category. Even in principle, it is impossible to know just how much transfer-seeking goes on, because economists, true to form, disagree on what exactly counts as transfer-seeking.

Still, there are things you can count. If you don't know the amount of construction activity in your city, but if you do know that the number of contractors and architects has doubled over the years while the population stayed the same, you can make some reasonable, albeit imperfect, inferences. Similarly, if you don't know how much transfer-seeking goes on in America, but if you do know that the number of transfer-seeking professionals has increased relative to the economy and the population, you can infer that Americans are probably investing more in transfer-seeking. Since most transfer-seeking professionals are lawyers or lobbyists, you have a clue where to begin.

Since 1955, the number of law degrees granted annually in the United States has more than quadrupled, even though the population grew by only about 50 percent over the same period. In effect, a larger and larger share of American talent has been going into the legal business. The result appears in Figure 4.1, which shows the number of lawyers per million of U.S. popula-

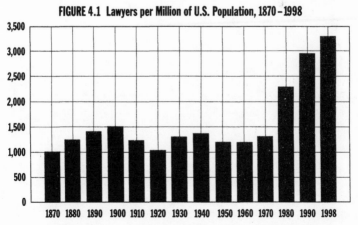

FIGURE 4.1 Lawyers per Million of U.S. Population, 1870–1998

SOURCE: Ronald H. Sander and B. Douglass Williams, *Law and Social Inquiry,* Summer 1989; U.S. Department of Labor; U.S. Census Bureau.

tion since 1870. For a hundred years, the proportion of lawyers stayed about the same; then, between 1970 and 1990, it more than doubled, as Figure 4.1 shows. The number of lawyers in Washington, D.C., grew even faster than the national number, quadrupling just between 1972 and 1987.

Not surprisingly, you find a parallel pattern if you count lawsuits, as Figure 4.2 shows. The number of filings in the federal courts drifted mildly upward from 1950 to the mid-1960s; but then it took off, nearly quadrupling by the mid-1980s. "Comparable figures for the state courts are not available," according to the legal scholar Marc Galanter, "but a sense of the growth of state judicial activity can be gathered from the increase in lawyers employed by state courts, from 7,581 in 1960 to 18,674 in 1985." When I asked Brian J. Ostrom, of the National Center

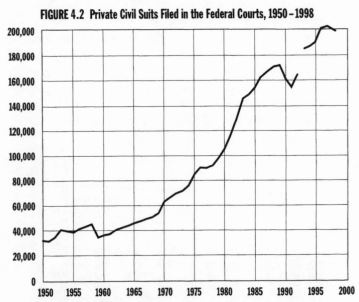

FIGURE 4.2 Private Civil Suits Filed in the Federal Courts, 1950–1998

NOTE: Series is discontinuous between 1992 and 1993 because of change from years starting in June to years starting in September.

SOURCE: Administrative Office of the U.S. Courts.

for State Courts, about state lawsuits, he said, "The amount of litigation in state courts grows every year. It's always increasing—by an amount in excess of population growth. The process of people making mutually acceptable bargains among themselves seems to be breaking down."

The increase in lawyers and litigation probably has several causes. One might be, as Ostrom noted, an increase in people's contentiousness. Another cause might be lawyers themselves. To some extent, they can act as transfer-seeking entrepreneurs. Long before science had any real idea whether electromagnetic fields from power lines caused cancer, lawyers were lining up clients and preparing to sue power companies. One enterprising lawyer, reported *The Wall Street Journal*, carved out a niche as "the leader of a nationwide group of law firms eager to turn EMF [electromagnetic fields] into a legal battleground." Another lawyer said, "All it's going to take is one or two good hits [i.e., big judgments against power companies] and the sharks will start circling." The spectacular fees, sometimes in the billions of dollars, awarded to lawyers and firms who bankrolled the lawsuits against the tobacco companies in the 1990s made luridly clear that litigation had become one of the most lucrative businesses in America. Lawyers' constant scouring of the law for new claims and claimants, and then for new defenses against those new claims and claimants, can and most likely does feed litigation and distributional struggle.

Almost certainly, however, the biggest cause of more lawyers and more litigation is more laws. To take just one example, in 1990 Congress passed, and the president signed, the Americans with Disabilities Act. The act was billed as a civil rights measure, but it was also a broad new economic entitlement, transferring resources from society generally to the disabled. As such, it was a good example of how transfer-seeking can be driven equally well by idealism (advocates for the disabled wanted their rights) and by pecuniary interests (activists for the disabled wanted more social spending)—indeed, the two are hard, or even downright impossible, to tell apart. The idea was to widen handicapped people's access to all kinds of jobs and to buildings, transit systems, and so on. In an attempt to fit the law to a complex world, Congress wrote the disabilities act vaguely, requiring, for instance, "readily achievable" measures and "reasonable accommodations." But what did that mean? Thrashing out what the law required kept a legion of lawyers busy. Responding to those lawyers' lawsuits and petitions kept another legion of lawyers busy.

From one point of view, the disabilities act was a civil rights measure seeking to expand justice for the handicapped. But from another point of view, it was a public-works jobs program for lawyers, and a new battleground for distributional warfare in general. Which view was right? Both. As the number of laws and claims escalates, as issues become more complex, as the law struggles with ever finer distinctions, more lawyers become necessary. For better and for worse, legal entitlements and lawyers come together as a package deal.

Lawyers do a lot of things besides litigate back and forth over existing wealth, and to blame the lawyers is in many instances to confuse the symptom with the illness. Lobbyists, by contrast, are wholly creatures of the transfer-seeking economy. That makes them an even better thing to count than lawyers or lawsuits.

There are, alas, only estimates, because there is no licensing requirement for lobbying, and many people lobby who aren't full-time lobbyists. One measure is the number of people who register with the Senate as lobbying on Capitol Hill, though that is only a small fraction of all lobbyists. As Figure 4.3 shows, the number tripled in the decade after 1976 (the year when the records begin). Because of a change in the Senate's method of counting, the data aren't continuous, but the series starting in 1988 shows the same upward trend.

Various other counts confirm the pattern. *Congressional Quarterly* reports that the number of people lobbying in Washington at least doubled and may have quadrupled between the mid-1970s and mid-1980s. (State capitals, by the way, also

FIGURE 4.3 Lobbyists Registered with the Senate, 1976–1995

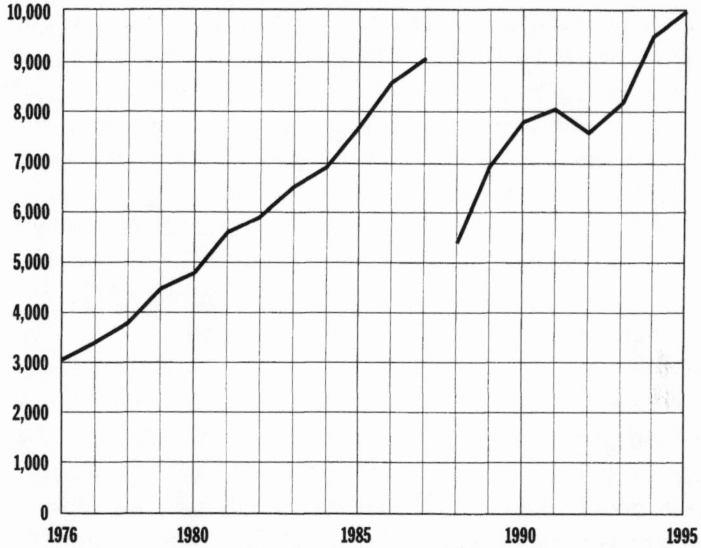

NOTE: Pre-1988 data include some inactive lobbyists excluded from later counts; comparable data unavailable for years after 1995.

SOURCE: Secretary of the Senate.

show healthy increases.) Between 1961 and 1982, the number of corporations with Washington offices increased tenfold. "The chief beneficiaries of this trend," write the political scientists Cigler and Loomis, "are Washington-based lawyers, lobbyists, and public-relations firms." Meanwhile, many companies that already maintained lobbying and public-affairs offices expanded them; one study found that almost two-thirds of the companies it surveyed had increased their public-affairs staffs between 1975 and 1980. The Washington office of General Motors employed three people in 1968 and twenty-eight in 1978, though no cars were built in the District of Columbia. By 1992, roughly 92,000 people worked in Washington for groups and firms seeking to influence policy, according to a count by the political scientist James A. Thurber.

Another indication of whether the transfer-seeking economy is growing is political spending. If the amount that people are investing in, say, the computer business triples over some period, you can assume that the sector is growing and that it has earned favorable returns over the period. The same inference holds for politics: If the investment in political campaigns grows over thirty years, you can assume that more people and groups are spotting politics—ergo, transfer-seeking—as a sound investment.

And, indeed, political spending has grown dramatically, far outstripping inflation (and also increasing, though less dramatically, relative to the size of the economy). Figure 4.4 is based on data compiled by Herbert E. Alexander of the University of Southern California. It shows, in constant 1996 dollars, the estimated total spending on political campaigns—federal, state, and local—in each major election cycle since 1952. The data fit the usual pattern: upward creep until the mid-1960s, and then an upward zoom. Like any other rewarding investment, politics was attracting venture capital.

Perhaps you could wave aside an increase in the number of lawyers *or* of lobbyists *or* of political contributions *or* of interest

FIGURE 4.4 Real U.S. Expenditure on Political Campaigns, 1952–1996
(millions of 1996 dollars)

SOURCE: Herbert E. Alexander, University of Southern California.

groups. But, as far as I can see, there is only one way to read the fact that *all* of those numbers rose sharply beginning in the 1960s and early 1970s and continued to rise through the Reagan-Bush 1980s. America was a society increasingly structured for, and thus dedicated to, transfer-seeking.

Perpetual Motion

In time, a curious thing happens. As the parasite economy thrives, transfer-seeking agents become wealthy and numerous. They become a powerful interest group in their own right. On the one side, they develop and pursue claims on the behalf of their clients. On the other side, they act as an interest group to keep the game going. When there are enough of them, they may begin using their access to government to draw more resources into lobbying. At that stage, the parasite economy may take on the peculiar ability to grow entrepreneurially. In effect, it goes into business for itself.

Most Americans are aware of the power of business interests to influence politics with money. Few are aware, however, of the extent to which the influence business now *is* a business interest. By 1990, reports the Center for Responsive Politics, a watchdog group that monitors money in politics, fully 10 percent of all business-sector contributions to congressional campaigns came from lawyers and lobbyists. For the 1997–1998 political cycle, the center examined various interests' contributions to candidates and political parties, with the grand total running into the hundreds of millions of dollars. The real estate industry gave more than $22 million, the securities and investment industries gave more than $23 million, and retirees and their groups gave more than $26 million. But at the top of the list, with almost $40 million in political contributions, were none other than lawyers; and not too far down the list were lobbyists, who gave almost $6 million—an amount that put them only a nose behind the tobacco industry.

When the parasite economy reaches this peculiar self-referential stage, one can no longer be certain whether association professionals and lobbyists work for their group members or the members are worked by the association professionals and lobbyists—or whether there is even a difference. Lobbyists conceive tax breaks and build coalitions of businesses that become clients who pay the lobbyists to seek the tax breaks from politicians who seek contributions from the lobbyists who deliver subsidies to clients who make contributions to politicians. The agents excite the clients, and the clients excite the agents, and the agents excite each other and thereby excite the clients. The transfer-seeking economy begins to look like a swarm of bees exciting itself into a state of perpetual frenzy.

Government itself becomes a marketable resource and a profit center for an expanding group of career-minded professionals, many of whom use government jobs as stepping-stones to lucrative careers lobbying government. According to data compiled by *CongressDaily/A.M.*(a daily report on Congress), a third or more of the House of Representatives members who left office in the 1990s went to work as lobbyists and consultants. Though no one can prove that politicians and Capitol Hill staff members initiate laws and programs and regulations to create jobs for themselves with interest groups and lobbying firms, everyone suspects it happens, a fact that is itself corrosive of democracy.

These resource-shuffling professionals have a weird incentive: Any kind of distributional struggle benefits them. The more transfer-seeking battles they manage to spark, the better off they will be. Every new legislative fight, every new lawsuit, every new regulatory struggle means new fees for politicians and lawyers and lobbyists, at least in the short and medium term. They win, as a class, no matter who else loses.

Most of what happens in Washington is driven by ideological passion, the desire to do good, or the fear of being harmed. Lobbyists and politicians are typically not cynical people. They are doing their job. But that is the problem: The job of transfer-seekers is to seek transfers. A lobbyist is paid to stay alert to new opportunities or, when possible, to create them. His job is to call a potential client and say, "If you hire me, I think we can get the subcommittee chairman to insert a provision letting us depreciate Luxembourg." A politician's job is to keep himself in office by giving things to people who want things. Everyone wants to keep the gaming tables busy. One House member, on hearing that the Car-Rental Coalition wanted to stop a bill, told Mike LaPlaca to substitute a bill of his own. When LaPlaca replied that no bill was necessary, the member retorted, "Don't you know why we're here? We're here to pass laws."

In the public's mind, the standard model of lobbying in Washington involves special interests buying influence, in a sort of legalized bribery. In fact, the process more often involves politicians shaking down special interests, especially lately, as politicians have become surprisingly brazen about putting the touch on lobbies. When the Republicans took over both houses of Congress in the 1994 elections, they immediately made clear that the money flowing from business lobbies, which had mildly favored the powerful Democrats, had now better begin to favor the powerful Republicans. The money obliged, being neither inclined nor well-positioned to argue. Democrats, of course, play the same game. Back in the early 1990s, when the Democrats controlled Congress, Edward J. Markey, a Democrat from Massachusetts, was a master of the art of collecting corporate contributions. Markey had begun his political career as an anticorporate liberal, but by the time he assumed the chairmanship of an influential Energy and Commerce subcommittee, he had learned the value of business money, and business money had learned the value of Markey. At one of his fund-raisers, 125 lobbyists paid $500 each to hobnob with him. Why? Not because this was their favorite social activity. "Everybody's here," a telecommunications consultant told *National Journal*. "Bullshit walks and money talks. You gotta be here."

Indeed you do. In 1995 only three Internet-related bills were introduced in Congress; by 1998, the comparable number was 175. This was largely due to the vast expansion of the Internet itself: In 1995, the World Wide Web contained only about 10,000 pages, whereas it contained 320 million by the end of 1998. The Web was kicking up all sorts of issues, ranging from smut to encryption to taxation, and no doubt the vast majority of those 175 bills were designed as good-faith attempts to solve what their sponsors perceived as real problems. But, of course, in the parasite economy, motive doesn't matter. "Congress has found a new field to plow," a high-tech lobbyist told *National Journal*'s Louis Jacobson. "Companies have realized they have no choice. . . . Congress is going to regulate, so therefore they have to get involved." And so Cisco Systems' lobbying budget went from nothing in the first half of 1997 to $420,000 a year later. Microsoft's lobbying budget doubled over a similar period (to $2.4 million). AOL's tripled (to $1.3 million). High-tech companies, which only recently had been ignorant of Washington, were hiring pin-striped lobbyists by the dozen—not because they wanted to but because they felt they had to. "Techno-geeks have made their fortunes," wrote Jacobson, putting a sharp point on the matter. "Now K Street's influence peddlers are demanding—and getting—their share of the loot."

Plainly, these professionals in the interest-group business have their own reasons to stir the pot. These are not underpaid people. In 1995, according to a *National Journal* survey, the average salary of trade and professional associations' top officers was well over a quarter of a million dollars (not counting benefits and perks). For the people heading up finance, insurance, and real-estate lobbies, the *average* salary was $372,000. The top people at unions earned $189,000; at public-interest groups, $124,000. Like anyone else in business, these people want to build their organizations and earn rising paychecks, which means generating new demands that bring home more benefits for the membership. "Washington has become a major marketing center," writes Jeffrey Birnbaum, "in which issues are created by interest groups and then sold like toothpaste to voters from Portland, Maine, to Portland, Oregon."

The combination of ideological agendas, group demands, and agents' appetite for fees is more than potent enough to ensure that the transfer-seeking game keeps itself constantly energized.

The more motion, the better. Bill Clinton rode to Washington on a promise to take America back from the special interests by breaking "gridlock"—that is, by trying to pass lots of laws. Actually, plenty of laws had been passing already, but now the lobbyists and interest-group professionals were ecstatic. "The one thing everyone agrees on," Tom Watson, a lawyer with the firm of Crowell and Moring in Washington, told *Legal Times* shortly after the election, "is that the government will now be more interested in regulating business. We are all expecting about a 33 percent increase in fees." Lawyer-lobby shops went straight to work loading up on former government officials and Capitol Hill staff members. At firms with good Democratic connections, reported *Legal Times*, "the jubilation was palpable." But Republicans would make out just fine, too. "This Congress and the promises that Clinton made," said Tom Korologos, a high-powered Washington lobbyist, "means an almost automatic defensiveness from the corporate community on most issues it faces." Translation: money for lobbying. Parasite heaven.

The mere possibility of government action pulls resources into the whirlpool. Figure 4.5 shows the number of health-care groups

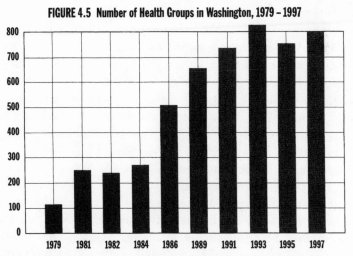

FIGURE 4.5 Number of Health Groups in Washington, 1979 – 1997

SOURCE: National Health Council, *Health Groups in Washington*, various editions.

in Washington from 1979 to 1997. In less than two decades, the number increased nearly eightfold. Why? From 1960 to 1990, the proportion of health care paid for by the government doubled, to two-fifths. Add the talk of health-care reform, and you had Washington staging a show that no one could afford to miss. In July 1991, the American Hospital Association moved its top offi-cers to Washington, believing that they "should be closer to the action." In March 1992, the American Nurses Association moved its headquarters—and a half million pounds of office furniture and equipment—to Washington, after twenty years in Kansas City. "We have nursing's agenda for health-care reform," they said. And so it goes. In 1971, 19 percent of trade and professional asso-ciations were headquartered in Washington; by 1990, 32 percent, and counting. That is Mike LaPlaca's story, writ large.

In their ability to attract resources merely by being active, politicians and, to a lesser extent, lobbyists and lawyers resem-ble a man standing in the center of a trampoline, who can draw objects on the edge toward him just by bouncing up and down. One House staff member, who has worked on the Hill for two decades, said, "The power of a member to call a hearing or get his chairman to call a hearing, and therefore shake the tree, is very, very real, and it bothers me a lot. And members can play it even if they're not playing it." That last observation was interest-ing. When I asked what it meant, he replied that well-meaning activity stirs the pot no less than cynical activity. Never mind the motives; if a politician holds a hearing or submits a bill, all the affected industries juice up their troops and make campaign contributions. Even if there's only a one-in-ten chance that a bill will actually pass, no one can take the risk of failing to drop a few dollars into the machine.

Significant bills revising the tax code passed in 1981, 1982, 1983, 1984, 1986, 1988, 1989, 1990, 1993, 1996, and 1997—"more frequent and detailed changes in taxes than ever before in American history," wrote David E. Rosenbaum in *The New York Times* in 1992 (before the more recent tax changes). Investment and saving incentives were expanded and then withdrawn; a

Medicare surtax on the elderly was adopted and then repealed; real estate loopholes came and then went and then came again; corporate taxes went down and then up; excise taxes fell while payroll taxes rose. In the 1960s, the tax code and related rules filled two volumes, whereas in the 1990s they filled eight; just in the five years after the 1986 tax reform passed, Congress made about 5,400 changes to the tax law through twenty-seven differ-ent pieces of legislation. Constant rewriting of the rules acted as a subsidy for tax lawyers and accountants, but it made life mis-erable for people trying to invest and plan. "Changes in the law," noted Rosenbaum, "forced people to alter the way they saved and spent and invested their money." Hank Barnette, the chair-man of Bethlehem Steel, told *The Wall Street Journal*, "It makes long-term financial planning very difficult." Yet—wasn't this odd?—the overall tax burden did not change much over the whole period. And—wasn't this also odd?—politicians never seemed to grow any more satisfied with the tax code. Chances are they're fiddling with it some more as you read these words.

Wherefore all the activity? Why, during the period of putative gridlock, was a new record set for tax-law churning, leaving people apparently as unhappy as ever? There were many reasons. One was that as a million groups clamored for a million tax breaks every year, they were bound to pull the tax code hither and yon in a random walk. Imagine many people pulling on a circular fire net, each trying to drag it his own way, and you see why the tax code wanders all over the place. Another possible reason is hinted at by the fact that in 1985, as the Reagan administration's tax-reform effort got under way, contributions to the House tax-writ-ing committee doubled from the level of 1983, the previous nonelection year. As the House moved to pass the reform bill in December 1985, reported *Congressional Quarterly*, "One Democrat was overheard suggesting to another that the party pre-vent a final vote so the bill would remain in limbo for a few more months. 'Why kill the goose that laid the golden egg?' he asked."

In 1992, after rioters and looters sacked much of south-central Los Angeles, what began as an urban-relief bill turned into—surprise!—a tax bill. There would be new tax breaks for small savers, college bowl games, insurance agents, bingo players, yacht owners, tuxedo renters, users of reloaded shotgun shells, and so on. There would be higher taxes for securities dealers, people who move, people who join clubs for business reasons, and so on. What fun. Fun, at least, if you were a politician counting the receipts, or a lobbyist counting the fees, as affected interest groups circled past the tollbooth.

The real champions of the game were the temporary tax credits. Some of those credits mattered, especially the credit for research and development. Because temporary credits need to be renewed every year or six months, the result is frenetic activity for politicians and lobbyists, and business for both. "It's a degrading process," said one lobbyist. "Law firms and lobbyists are always the gainers."

As citizens, the lobbyists and lawyers and politicians and interest-group professionals want to solve many problems while minimizing fuss; as transfer-seeking professionals, however, they soon learn that their paychecks and campaign coffers reward them for solving few problems while maximizing fuss. As citizens, they wish society had less need of people like themselves; yet, as professionals, they are adept at creating jobs for one another by prospecting for transfer-seeking opportunities. They believe that they serve the public or at least provide a necessary service. Yet the public despises them.

To the public, Washington looks increasingly like a public-works jobs program for lawyers and lobbyists, a profit center for professionals who are in business for themselves. From the public's point of view, the lobbying business is self-serving, elitist, and corrupt. But the public is only half right.

The Trap, Again

That the parasite economy is self-serving is true. But the transfer-seeking industry is no more self-serving than any other business. Lobbyists and group organizers and transfer-seeking entrepreneurs are working stiffs and capitalists, like anybody else. They see opportunities and they take them. It's just that they work in a sector that tends to destroy wealth.

If the parasite economy were the product of a few evil elites and corrupt Washington insiders, it would be comparatively easy to control. The problem is that it isn't the product of a few bad people.

That lobbies are elitist is true only in the limited sense that they are disproportionately run by elites. Plenty of people with high-class law degrees work in interest groups, lobbying firms, and government itself. In fact, of the eighteen jobs in the Clinton administration's first cabinet, fourteen were occupied by lawyers—an ironic achievement for an administration that prided itself on its diversity.

Despite the often-stated contention that Washington is run by corporate moneybags, however, in no sense do lobbies represent only an elite (though elites certainly enjoy disproportionate representation). They represent groups, which include practically everybody. Ultimately, the lobbying sector keeps producing jobs because Americans keep organizing to lobby. The parasite economy thrives because America's countless and diverse groups are, if anything, represented too well.

That lobbies are corrupt is hardly true at all. Corruption implies secrecy and money under the table. The parasite economy, by contrast, is like a New York Stock Exchange on which government benefits are sought and traded openly and (for the most part) honestly. Everyone can join a group and invest in lobbying government—and everyone does. It's worth remembering, too, that virtually all of those investors, far from being "corrupt," conceive of themselves as doing worthy or useful things: aiding cutting-edge industries, giving veterans their fair share, supporting small businesses, helping the elderly afford health care, and the like.

In the first chapter, I mentioned that politics seemed caught in a kind of trap. Government tried to do more, yet people were less satisfied; politicians railed against special interests, yet special interests proliferated. Now the nature of that trap emerges. From the individual's point of view, it always makes sense to hire a lobbyist, or vote for a politician, who can bring you a subsidy or use public resources to solve what you believe are pressing problems. But if everybody follows this seemingly sensible logic, everybody spends more and more time chasing everybody else's money and protecting his own. That logic, ultimately, is why the game is not self-limiting. The lobbying and political classes can stir the pot, and they do, but the fire beneath it is the deceptive logic of transfer-seeking.

In 1936, Senator Richard B. Russell, finding himself in a difficult primary race, made his case plain. "The farmers are awake to the fact that my opponent is promising them nothing except to cut off their checks," he declared, mincing no words, "while I stand for larger benefit checks." He buried his opponent. Today the amounts changing hands are much bigger, and the brokers are far more numerous and sophisticated, but the same logic applies. When Senator Arlen Specter, a Republican from Pennsylvania, had some trouble in the 1992 election, he responded by touting his seniority, which he dedicated "to using every bit of influence I can." "On the campaign trail," reported *The Economist*, "Mr. Specter has something for everyone. He fights as hard as the best Democrat for import quotas on steel. Roads? He has brought back $1.28 for every tax dollar sent to Washington." That was the logic of transfer-seeking. Senator Alfonse D'Amato, the New York Republican, "makes the clearest, rawest pitch in politics," reported *The Washington Post* in 1992: "Look what I done for you lately." D'Amato said, "If you put the pie out, don't blame me for wanting a slice of the pie for my people—who've gotta eat also." That, too, was the logic of transfer-seeking. In 1997, a conservative Republican senator named Sam Brownback, of Kansas, opposed the nomination of a secretary of commerce who, said Brownback, had failed to identify enough "corporate welfare" to be excised from the department. "But," reported *The Washington Post*, "the senator quickly noted that one program that should not be considered corporate welfare was the government's subsidy of ethanol as a motor fuel, a program dear to the heart of farmers who grow corn in Kansas."

I'll not declaim here about public greed and the decline of civic virtue. As I hope the preceding pages make clear, people invest in transfer-seeking because it seems to make good economic sense or because they believe it's good for society, not because they want to rob each other blind. I'll also not launch a diatribe against "corruption" or "elite lobbies" in Washington that are out of touch with "the people." That whole way of talking misses the point. I'll argue that the main reason to worry about the growth of the transfer-seeking economy, and about trying to control it, is simply this: It is expensive.

It's expensive in two fashions. The political cost is the toll on government, which I discuss in Chapter 6. Before getting to that issue, though, I want to consider also the economic cost, which is payable in cash and paid in a thousand almost invisible ways.

5

Hidden Costs

I'VE MENTIONED that this book is about side effects. Before talking about the costs of devoting more and more resources to lobbying and other forms of transfer-seeking, I want to emphasize that point again.

To say that medicines have side effects is not to say that medicines are worthless and should be abolished. It is to say that you need to be careful and selective. Taking higher and higher doses of more and more medicines, in hopes of curing more and more diseases, will cripple or kill you. The same is true of government benefits. Every program does some good for somebody, or else it wouldn't exist. Many programs—unemployment insurance, say, and space exploration and veterans' benefits—deliver real benefits to society. But if you neglect to be selective or forget to keep track of the costs, many individual programs that seem worthwhile on their own merits may add up, collectively, to a wildly incoherent and expensive jumble that nourishes thousands of ravenous lobbies and breeds more of them every month.

With medicines, it's fairly easy to be careful. If you take too much or too many, you get sick. But federal programs are different from medicines in this respect: The benefits flow to the recipient, but the side effects are borne by society as a whole. If medicines made their users feel better while making nonusers sick, you would expect a lot of people to be using too many medicines. Something like that seems to have happened in the universe of federal transfer programs.

The very first bill that President Bill Clinton signed into law required businesses to grant workers time off for family needs. "Only Scrooge, it seems, could oppose the Family and Medical Leave Act of 1993," wrote James V. DeLong in *The New Republic*. Yet the fact is that this new middle-class entitlement, like countless others that it was piled on top of, wasn't free. Any business manager can tell you that holding a job open for up to twelve weeks per year per employee is a headache. Businesses would have to maintain workers' health coverage during leaves; a three-month leave might cost the employer well over $1,000. Workers might not return after the leave, DeLong noted, "so any worker who leaves a job within a year of the birth of a child, or for any health-related reason, can get three extra months of health insurance coverage quite easily."

The benefits of mandated family leave were obvious — so obvious that only sourpuss economists and annoyed business groups objected. But the costs were obscure. To pay for family leave, consumers would pay slightly higher prices and employees would be paid slightly lower wages. Some employers would try to avoid hiring young women or others who seem likely to use family leave. Other employers would substitute part-timers, who weren't covered by the act. There would be new lawsuits, new paperwork, new rules, new kinks in the labor market.

Was the family-leave act worth the cost? Maybe, maybe not. The problem, however, was that few voters were willing to believe that there was any cost at all. They believed they had received a free gift from their politicians, when in fact they had merely cadged from each other. Later they might pout and rage at the price, cursing government and demanding still more benefits to salve their pain.

Here is a key to the transfer-seeking economy's ability to grow even when society would be better off if it shrank. Benefits from lobbying—subsidy checks, tax breaks, favorable regulations, court awards, and so on—are highly visible; but the costs—the waste, the inefficiency, the rigidities, the complexities, the policy incoherence as subsidies and deals redistribute money in every direction at once—are diffuse and often invisible. Maritime interests are only too well aware of the large subsidies they receive ($112,000 per job, at costs to consumers running into the billions each year): In 1997 and 1998, according to the Center for Responsive Politics, they spent more than $10 million on lobbying, and their political action committees donated more than $1 million to federal candidates. But are you aware of the higher shipping costs you pay? Of the investment forgone because of the tidy lump of money that the maritime lobby has captured? And even if you were, would you care enough to antagonize this determined and well-funded lobby, for the sake of the productivity of the economy as a whole?

As I've repeatedly noted, I'm not out to attempt to assess the worth of particular government programs. Instead I'll operate on the assumption that you will decide for yourself whether arts subsidies or farm subsidies are worthwhile. The point is to look at *systemic* costs: costs arising from the accumulation and interaction of programs as lobbies weave a dense web of programs and benefits and subsidies and anticompetitive rules. Rather than try to cover all the bases, I will focus on costs of three orders: (1) the cost of direct investment in the transfer-seeking economy; (2) the cost of defensive maneuvering against potential transfer-seekers; (3) the cost of the subsidies and rules that transfer-seekers put in place.

First-Order Cost: Parasite Food

How much do we feed the parasite economy and its professionals? It's hard to know, but some of the components give a sense of the magnitude.

We have a rough idea what we feed lawyers, though lawyers do a lot besides transfer-seeking. "A conservative estimate is that legal services now account for 2 percent of the economy's output," the economics columnist Robert J. Samuelson writes in *The Washington Post*. "In 1991, law firms collected an estimated $100 billion in revenues, up from $10.9 billion in 1972. That's double the growth rate of the total economy." Between 1967 and 1996, the revenues of for-profit law firms quadrupled in constant dollars and doubled as a share of the economy. By no means did all of the increase disappear into a black hole. Some of it was productive. But some of it came because legal costs escalated as more litigants fought over existing wealth.

When combatants drag each other back and forth, the frictional costs are bound to be high. A RAND study looked at nationwide tort litigation in 1985 and found that the costs of the litigation process itself—mostly lawyers' fees—"consumed about half of the $29 billion to $36 billion that were spent on litigation," leaving only the other half for actual compensation and damages. A dollar in legal costs for every dollar paid to a wronged plaintiff is a lot of friction. This is probably not a very productive way to spend $15 billion or more every year.

Agents' fees also include payments to lobbyists and politicians. How much lobbyists earn in aggregate isn't known. The economists David N. Laband and John P. Sophocleus have estimated that about $4.6 billion was spent on state and federal lobbying in 1985. Today, of course, the sum would be more. In a 1999 report called *Influence, Inc.*, the Center for Responsive Politics, using more direct methods than Laband and Sophocleus (the center tallied lobbying expenditures reported to the Senate), concluded that in 1998 lobbies spent about $1.4 billion to influence Congress and the executive branch. "There were more than 38 registered lobbyists and $2.7 million in lobbying expenditures for every member of Congress," said the center. (The center counted only money that groups listed as spent specifically on lobbying. Associated expenses—for instance, the cost of running a Washington office—weren't included. The center's Larry Makinson guessed that the $1.4 billion figure "is conservative, to put it mildly.")

As for politicians, in 1996 the direct investment in them ran to about $4 billion, according to Herbert E. Alexander of the University of Southern California. Harder to count are indirect investments in politics, which tend not to be reported. Executives travel back and forth to Washington to lobby for tax credits; insurance companies treat politicians to junkets in Barbados. "Regulated Industries Were Eager to Bankroll Presidential Galas," headlined *The Washington Post* in the wake of the first Clinton inaugural. You could call that sleazy, and it was, but no regulated business can afford to be on Washington's bad side. If you're a company or group with a stake in public policy, then baseball tickets and honoraria for politicians are investments you had best not neglect.

Still harder to count are the amounts spent as Americans struggle to stay up to speed on the transfer-seeking game. If you're a lobbyist or group organizer, you'll need magazines, books, electronic-information services, databases, seminars, who's-who directories, consultants, and more. Those materials don't come cheap—a fact that is itself further evidence of the high return on transfer-seeking investment. A subscription to *National Journal*, a weekly on government and politics that is required reading for parasites (and a publication with which I'm affiliated), costs more than $1,000 a year.

If you lobby and know what's good for you, you had better buy this stuff, as the publishers and seminar organizers will be happy to remind you. "Keep track of the political influences that affect your bottom line—before it's too late," a promotional mailing for *State Legislatures* magazine warns ominously. In the transfer-seeking game, what goes into one person's pocket comes out of someone else's, so don't be the slowpoke who gets taken to the cleaners. Why buy the National Conference of State Legislatures' books on annual state tax and spending actions?

Because, says a mailing, "Whatever your business, you have a serious stake in state taxes and spending. . . . *Isn't a $70 investment worth the potential impact on your bottom line?*" Italics in the original, and well deserved. Wouldn't it be a shame if you were slammed with a $7 million tax surcharge, all because you neglected to feed $70 to the parasite economy?

Add up the costs of paying for transfer-seeking professionals and paraphernalia, and you have a sum somewhere in the tens of billions. A surprising aspect of that sum is how small it is—in the range of 1 percent of the gross national product. Remember, however, that much of this money is siphoned from the pool of investment capital, which runs to less than $300 billion (on a net basis). Diverting precious capital from productive investment is not a very good idea.

In the early 1990s, when a slow economy was squeezing their profits, American steel companies filed six dozen lawsuits alleging unfair competition from foreign producers. "A financial windfall for Washington's trade bar," was the way *National Journal* described the legal action. The initial filing involved more than 2 million pages of allegations in 650 boxes; several major law firms each reported assigning the equivalent of a dozen full-time lawyers to the cases; each foreign defendant company hired its own battalion of lawyers, as did each country named in a suit; and all parties concerned acknowledged that the legal fees would run into the tens of millions of dollars. One lawyer joked, "It's an enormous contribution to the services balance of trade." Ha, ha. The American steel industry suffered for decades from chronic underinvestment, and swaths of it remain technologically laggard. Do we really want to see heavy industry investing its scarce capital in lawsuits? And remember how the game grows: Foreign companies must defend themselves, diverting still more capital from steelmaking to lawyering. "In anticipation of the U.S. filings, two Mexican companies filed antidumping suits against seven U.S. flat-rolled producers," the Commerce Department reported. "Canadian producers indicated that they

too were preparing antidumping suits against U.S. steelmakers."
To pay the lawyers, steel prices must go up, making refrigerators
and cars more expensive. Yet, when the returns on investing in
lawsuits become higher than the returns on investing in machin-
ery, what do you expect?

Second-Order Cost: Defensive Maneuvering

If you stopped at first-order cost, you could safely conclude that
the parasite economy isn't all that expensive to support.
However, the direct costs of paying transfer agents are only the
tip of the proverbial iceberg. To bring more above the surface,
move to another hidden cost, one that is even harder to trace
with any precision but that is probably an order of magnitude
more expensive.

This second-order cost is the cost of defensiveness and uncertainty generated by the very existence of the transfer-seeking
economy. On a block where burglaries are common, people
spend heavily on alarms and guards and outdoor lights, even if
they never wind up being burglarized. Something a bit like that
happens in a society where transfer-seeking is common.

Although defensive maneuvering is an important factor in lobbying (everyone needs a lobbyist because everyone else has one),
its effects probably show up most clearly in the area of litigation. If you want to give someone benefits or help him solve his
problems, one way is with a direct subsidy or a regulation requiring others to help him. Another way, however, is to give him a
legal claim against someone else. Once he enjoys the right to
sue, he can go to court seeking compensation or damages. As
always, important social goals are served this way. Again, though,
there are side effects, which become more noticeable as new
laws create more grounds for lawsuits.

David Meglathery is the principal of a public elementary
school in Connecticut. He has worked in education since 1968
and has seen many changes, including one he doesn't much like.

These days, it is not uncommon for parents to threaten a lawsuit when they're unhappy. When Meglathery caught a child stealing pencils from the dispensary, he suspended him for one morning, and the father threatened to sue. "It has become a part of the frustrated parent's repertoire," Meglathery says. Plus, Meglathery has been named as a defendant in an employment suit. Plus, "there's no such thing as an accident any longer," and so the playground seesaw is gone, as is the merry-go-round, as is the jungle gym. "Basically," he says, "playgrounds have been stripped of their equipment." Playgrounds are probably safer, but that isn't an unalloyed blessing. "It has eliminated a few risks that were there, but it has also eliminated a lot of opportunities for kids to cooperate and do some imaginative and creative things." And today's safer playground equipment is so expensive that "most school budgets"—including his own—"do not contain the money for them."

School principals are in the trouble business. "You're dealing with people and you're constantly being bombarded by crisis situations," Meglathery says. Nowadays, he is always second-guessing himself. "It just isn't worth getting involved in a lawsuit, even though you know you're right. It restricts my ability to be as effective as I could be, because of caution, because of anxiety. You live with it day and night. You wonder, am I going to find a letter in my mailbox that's going to summon me to a situation where I'll have to testify?"

Until a few years ago, when he decided it was time for a change, Steve Lichtman owned a small plumbing-supply company in Michigan City, Indiana. His family had been in the business since the 1930s, and he prided himself on knowing his customers and his business. He also learned the joy of being sued. His wife got into a low-speed fender-bender, and he was sued for a sum in the low six figures. The other driver reported being fine at the scene but showed up at the deposition in a wheelchair. "The lawyers told us that if it went before a jury it could go into boxcar numbers," he said. "So we just settled."

At work, his liability-insurance costs kept rising smartly. That meant less money, he told me, for new workers. To jockey for advantage, customers sent lawyer-letters and dropped hints about suing. He never knew when a lawsuit might strike from out of the blue. "It always seems like you've got to look over your shoulder," Lichtman said.

Welcome to the high-claims world, where there are multiple laws allowing people with complaints to attach themselves to other people who have money or insurance. Because those claims bring some benefits, you cannot assume the high-claims system is terrible and should be junked. But neither can you assume that more claims equal more justice, more efficiency, or anything else. Claims against schools may mean that fewer kids break bones on playgrounds, but they may also deprive many kids of jungle gyms and merry-go-rounds. Is that fair? Is it progress? It's not obvious.

Rather, the high-claims system constitutes a more or less blind gamble. Lawsuits undoubtedly deter some bad behavior, enforce some contracts, spread some existing risks, and punish some wrongdoers. But they also undoubtedly discourage some beneficial enterprises, open loopholes in some contracts, create some new risks, and terrorize some innocents. And we have no way of knowing whether the balance sheet comes up positive or negative.

To see why, imagine that you decide to reduce fire injuries by holding firefighters liable for fire damage. "Now," you think, "they'll be darn sure to put out every fire." Maybe, but maybe not. Chances are that litigation will drive up the cost of firefighting. The city may cut back on the fire department or cut child nutrition or education. Both actions are plausible given that, for instance, in the space of a single decade (1976 to 1986), Washington State's legal costs rose ninefold as it faced ever more lawsuits; and that by 1985 there were more than 54,000 claims pending against the federal government, demanding more than $140 billion. New Jersey, plagued by claims against its transit systems, staged a bogus bus accident in 1993. "Video cameras inside the bus and outside filmed seventeen people scrambling onto the bus before the police arrived," reported *The New York Times*. "All later claimed to be injured in the accident. Another two who were never even on the bus also filed claims." In 1998, New York City spent nearly $400 million fighting lawsuits and satisfying jury verdicts and settlements — money diverted from other city needs. The number of settlements and judgments against the city grew by more than 40 percent just between 1993 and 1997. "New York City," observed Saul B. Shapiro, a lawyer, "is subject to trial by jury virtually every time someone trips on a crack in the sidewalk, slips on ice, or drives into a pothole."

Moreover, once the inevitable horror story gets around about a firefighter who was taken to court and stripped of all his worldly possessions, people may start fleeing or avoiding the business. In New York State, where a third of all obstetricians have been sued four or more times, one out of every six had stopped delivering babies by the early 1990s. In 1986, according to Peter Huber of the Manhattan Institute, a new claim was being filed against the makers of whooping-cough vaccine every week; "one former manufacturer faced one hundred suits demanding more than $2 billion in compensation, or two hundred times the total annual sale revenues of the vaccine." Manufacturers retreated from the business, and by 1986 only two major companies were investing heavily in vaccine research. "In America," noted *The Economist*, "fear of litigation and of political fallout has encouraged some companies to abandon contraceptive development. This restricts the contraceptive options open to American women — IUDs are virtually unobtainable, and all the compounds used in chemical contraceptives in the United States today were available in the 1960s." From 1977 to 1985, the manufacturers of small airplanes saw their liability-claim payments rise ninefold. The result, as they retreated from the business, was to keep older, less safe planes on the market, even though, as Huber obvserved, "the new models kept off the market were notably safer than the old ones people went on using instead." One study of small manufacturers of farm equipment in California found that 22 percent had dropped product lines out of fear of liability litigation. And so on.

In the same way, litigation against firefighters may result in more fire damage rather than less. Now, the key word here is "may." The point isn't that litigation necessarily makes matters worse on net, but that there is no a priori reason to suppose it makes matters better. We don't know.

And what about the victims of fire? At least they will be compensated for their losses, because there will be someone to seek compensation from—yes? Alas, that isn't clear, either. Because litigation is expensive and often traumatic, very few people who suffer personal injuries ever sue—about 2 percent, according to RAND research. Those who do sue may receive awards out of all proportion to the losses they suffered, or they may receive nothing. And the process will take months.

The litigation system does, of course, compensate some people, albeit almost arbitrarily. But its very arbitrariness creates negative elements on the other side of the equation: defensiveness and fear. You might at any moment be sued, but you might not. One consequence is business uncertainty, which can cloud the investment climate, complicate decision-making, and introduce ever more lawyers and paperwork into deal-making. Everyone hires more lawyers and buys more liability insurance, even though most people won't actually have to pay a claim (just as everyone buys locks, even if most people aren't actually robbed). Insurance, of course, is expensive. For instance, in the 1980s, doctors' liability premiums rose by about 15 percent a year; much of that cost was passed on to patients.

Moreover, many people become more careful than they need to be, and that's harmful too. In 1989 alone, according to the Council of Economic Advisers, defensive medicine—medical procedures protecting doctors from lawsuits, rather than patients from disease—cost at least $20 billion, or more than a sixth of total physician expenditures. In fact, one reason for the rush to health-maintenance organizations in the 1990s was because they were harder to sue.

And there is that other consequence, anxiety. You never know when a transfer-seeker will come to get you. Maybe he has a good case or maybe not, but either way, you'll pay the lawyers — just as you'll pay the lobbyists if your competitor goes after you on Capitol Hill. This problem can become worse as transfer agents — lawyers, in this case — learn how to churn the system to get the most out of it. The legal scholar Dan Dobbs described the process this way:

> Some kinds of claim offer potential recoveries so great that many people may be induced to assert them, even though the win-rate is very low. But if one out of every ten plaintiffs is able to win such a claim, that means nine out of ten defendants must pay attorney fees and other expenses of suit even though they are entirely innocent. The innocent nine are hostages for the liability of the tenth. The costs to them in money and in life disruption may far exceed the gains to the one plaintiff. I count this a very high cost indeed.

I think the only fair conclusion today is that we have no idea whether the high-claims legal system is making us better off or worse off on net. Indeed, about the litigation system there is little that we do know. Among those nuggets of uncontested knowledge is that the system handsomely benefits the professionals who work it. When Arista Records became the target of an enterprising class-action suit, on the grounds that the company's pop duo Milli Vanilli didn't do their own singing, Arista settled. Eighty thousand or so alert fans could send in for $1 refunds on singles, $2 on cassettes, and $3 on compact discs. That might have made the fans feel a little better. But the lawyers felt a lot better, because they walked away with considerably more than $3 each.

Figure 5.1 gives a clearer idea of this second-order cost. The data were compiled by the Tillinghast–Towers Perrin consulting

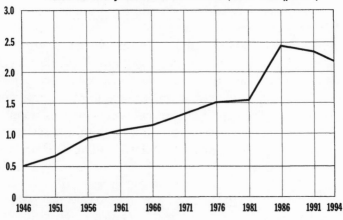

FIGURE 5.1 Tort System Cost as a Share of GDP, 1946–1994 (percent)

SOURCE: Tillinghast – Towers Perrin.

company from insurance-company data and show the annual costs of the tort system (which is only one part of the civil-litigation system) as a share of the gross domestic product (GDP) since 1946 (the most recent data being for 1994). The curve rises smartly over the period and follows the same sort of post-1960s leap that became so familiar in Chapter 3. By 1991, when the trend had leveled off, insurance companies were paying more than $132 billion in damages, claims, legal expenses, and administrative costs. That accounted for more than 2 percent of the national economic output—almost twice the level of 1966. A remarkable thing was how much money did *not* go to injured parties. "If viewed as a mechanism for compensating victims for their economic losses," reported Tillinghast, "the tort system is extremely inefficient, returning less than 25 cents on the dollar for that purpose." If compensation for pain and suffering is added, the injured still received less than half. Lawyers and administrators, especially the former, wound up with the remainder. The example was yet another confirmation of the iron law of the parasite economy: No matter who else loses, lawyers and lobbyists always win.

In the context of transfer-seeking, litigation is a cousin of lobbying. In both kinds of activity, the system is supposed to provide fair compensation or serve society's larger interests, but it necessarily also creates opportunities for redistributive entrepreneurism and profit-hunting; in both, the parties on all sides wind up feeding middlemen and hiring expensive professional agents; and in both, the very existence of the transfer-seeking activity leads to defensive maneuvering—companies maintain huge legal staffs, for instance, or they open more Washington offices—that may itself feed the cycle. There are, of course, some important differences between the cousins. For one, relatively few Americans actually litigate, whereas most Americans lobby, if not personally then through their interest groups. More important, a lawsuit seeks a direct transfer from a particular person or company, whereas lobbying usually seeks transfers from the economy at large—from taxpayers or consumers as a class. This type of transfer brings me to the next kind of cost.

Third-Order Cost: Subsidy Madness

This cost is the steepest of all. It is the cost of the goodies themselves: damage done as industrious transfer-seekers weave distortions and inefficiencies into the economy.

If you could maintain a limited portfolio of carefully selected subsidy programs, chosen to work together, this cost wouldn't be a serious problem. Markets are not perfect, and every society needs laws and programs to soften life's sharpest edges. By picking a group of core programs and then holding the line, you might be able to meet the most important social needs. The problem arises because subsidies, once enacted, are fiercely defended and rarely go away. As they pile up, they begin to affect the economy somewhat in the way that a hundred drugs used simultaneously might affect a patient.

To see why, go back to Scrooge the bicycle messenger.

Suppose he succeeds in his campaign to restrict fax machines to long-distance use. He now captures local business communications that otherwise would have traveled by fax. But the reason people were using fax machines instead of bicycle messengers was that faxing was cheaper. Forced to use a more expensive option, people find that communications costs have increased. What used to cost two or three dollars now costs five or six. Less is left over to be spent on other things. That is what economists call a "deadweight loss". People pay more, but they don't get more. Wealth is destroyed. Meanwhile, the fax-machine business becomes less profitable, and so fax-machine makers invest less in research and development. At the same time, the coddled messenger business becomes less competitive, and so couriers invest less in making themselves faster and cheaper. Communications technology improves more slowly than it would have. Again, a deadweight loss.

If the story ended there, you could say, "Well, protecting Scrooge's job costs some money, but it's worth it." Unfortunately, the story doesn't end there—far from it: Subsidies and protective rules breed other subsidies and protective rules, in a chain reaction that never really ends.

Thanks to Scrooge, fax makers are outraged and financially pinched. They want redress. Since they couldn't stop Scrooge's fax ban from passing, their lobbyist advises them to ask the government for a tax break. Suppose that they get it: The tax code is now artificially encouraging faxing, but the regulatory code is artificially discouraging faxing. The policy has become incoherent, doing two opposite things at once. More inefficiency.

Meanwhile, suppose, not implausibly, that the government pays for its tax break for faxers by raising the tax on telephones. Now phone calls are more expensive, and resources are diverted from *that* sector. People begin using e-mail when a phone call would otherwise have been cheaper and more efficient. Again, they are paying more to do effectively the same thing: another deadweight loss.

The phone company, in turn, covers its losses by lobbying regulators to raise prices on mobile-phone service. But—oops—Scrooge depends on his mobile phone to find out where his next delivery is. So the same system that subsidizes him is also raising his costs. He is collecting in one pocket but paying from another. More incoherence.

The chain goes on and on, around and around. Pretty soon the plumbing system of tax breaks and subsidies and regulatory favors is a tangled mass moving resources in every direction at once. It is incoherent and at war with itself. You install pipes to divert water from my sink to your bathtub; someone else diverts this same water from your bathtub to his toilet; and I divert this same water yet again back to my sink. Before long, everyone is rerouting everyone's water and pipes are running in and out of every door and window, all in a mad jumble, and with a lot of leakage along the way. The result is the net impoverishment of all classes but one—namely, the class of plumbers and pipefitters, of whom there are more every year, getting rich laying ever more convoluted networks of pipe.

Eventually, as everyone seeks subsidies and everyone pays for everyone else's subsidies, the economic distortions become too numerous to count. Money flies in every direction simultaneously. Increasingly, people make their investment decisions so as to maximize subsidies rather than productivity. For investment advice, they buy books like *Tax Guide for Residential Real Estate*. ("Home ownership and real estate renting are among the best tax shelters—*if* you know how to put the tax breaks to work for you," advises the book's publicity kit.) The economy loses efficiency. It either grows less quickly than it would have, as is the case in today's America, or it goes into subsidy shock and stagnates or even shrinks, as happened in many Third World and socialist economies. The one consistent exception is the sector that makes its living by buying and selling subsidies. That sector grows.

The chain I've just described is unrealistic only in that it makes the mess seem less messy than it really is. Here is how American farm policy works.

Though fewer than 2 percent of Americans now live on farms, agricultural interests make up a powerful political bloc, well represented in every state and well organized in Washington. They are expert at farming the tax code and cultivating Capitol Hill. So they demand and receive massive subsidies—enough, as the writer James Bovard has pointed out, to buy each full-time American farmer a new Mercedes-Benz every year. Those subsidies to farmers pump capital into farming and drain capital from other sectors. The inevitable result is that farmers are encouraged to produce more food than the market will buy. To stop them from overproducing, the government, having paid them to grow crops, used to pay them also *not* to grow crops. That began to seem so ridiculous that, more recently, the government instead began encouraging farmers to export their surpluses, or, in some cases, it put limits on imports. Sometimes, as with peanuts, Washington limited outright how much farmers could sell. (Follow?) The policy is incoherent, just as if you were stepping on the gas pedal and the brake at the same time. Accordingly, the waste is large.

But it is not self-limiting. If one country tries to cope with its subsidy-induced food surpluses by driving up exports or shutting down imports, other countries will soon do the same. After all, this is a game that everybody can play. In the developed nations, all of which run expensive agricultural programs working at cross-purposes with themselves and each other, farm subsidies cost consumers and taxpayers the staggering sum of about $300 billion *a year*, according to estimates by the Organization for Economic Cooperation and Development, or about $275 per citizen per year. Some of that money makes its way to farmers, but much of it evaporates in the form of higher farmland prices, and much is simply wasted because of the economic distortions and counterdistortions it causes. A 1988 Purdue University study found that for every farm job saved by subsidies, the American economy paid $107,000 in lost nonfarm output, $80,000 in federal spending, and $14,000 in higher food prices. (Imagine how many jobs all that money could have created, had farm interests not monopolized it.) When two Australian economists, Kym Anderson and Rod Tyers, studied farm subsidies and protection among developed nations, they found that the cost came to about $1,400 a year for each nonfarm household in 1990. Worse, for every dollar of farm subsidies reaching producers, thirty-seven cents were wasted.

And that occurred just in agriculture, one small corner of the universe of subsidies and countersubsidies and counter-countersubsidies. In America, the tax bill of 1981 handed out giant tax breaks to the politically powerful real-estate industry. The result was to shift resources artificially into office buildings and away from, say, commercial research and factories. That, in turn, contributed to the massive overbuilding that brought down the savings-and-loan industry, at a cost of hundreds of billions.

Or again: One of the main reasons American health-care costs have soared is that health benefits have been exempted from the income tax. If your boss were to give you an extra $1,000 in cash, you would pay a chunk of it in taxes; but if he gave you the same amount in added health benefits, you would pay no additional taxes. Of necessity, such a policy amounted to a big subsidy for health-care consumption. It artificially diverted resources into health care and out of other sectors, feeding health-care inflation and sapping the rest of the economy.

Or again: When the sellers of smaller and cheaper kinds of mobile phones needed radio frequencies, the existing frequency users moved in Congress to prevent the government from granting them. The result of such maneuvering was to delay the introduction of new technology and raise its cost.

One can go on and on in this way. The vast majority of subsidies and anticompetitive deals distort resource flows and slow the economy's ability to adapt. In today's globalized economy, that problem may be even more serious than it was in the 1950s or 1960s. Robert J. Shapiro, an economist associated with the "New Democrat" Progressive Policy Institute in Washington (he went on to join the Clinton administration's Commerce Department), has argued that a global market "puts an enormous premium on flexibility and innovation" because companies need to innovate and mobilize quickly to meet needs of disparate local markets. "In economic life, the only force I know that drives innovation is competition," says Shapiro. "This is the fatal flaw of subsidy policies. They insulate sectors from the full force of competition, and insulate them from the need to be innovative in order to be more productive." As subsidized sectors fall behind, growth slows. Shapiro concludes: "Then the demand for subsidies increases as people try to protect their rate of return. It's a vicious cycle."

The reason the cycle is so hard to break is that the costs of economic distortion and rigidity are so hard to see. They are marbled all through the economy and embedded deeply within it. When you go to the store, the labels don't tell you how much marketing orders or farm subsidies increase the prices of bread and fruit. To make matters worse, lobbies work hard to hide the costs of their benefits. Interest groups, Mancur Olson wrote, "have an incentive to seek [subsidies] that are the least straight-forward or the least conspicuous, not those that have the lowest social cost." Given a choice between a direct cash payment from the Treasury or a rule raising prices, business lobbies almost always choose the latter, because it's harder for irate taxpayers to notice.

Yet, though the costs of economic goody-hunting are hard to see, we know that they exist, that they are large, that they twist economies in ways large and small. The economists David Laband, Frank Mixon, and Robert Ekelund, Jr., illustrated the bending of economies in a particularly amusing way. When they compared state capitals with similar noncapital cities (and con-trolled for extraneous factors), they found that the capital cities boasted a disproportionate number of golf courses and fancy restaurants. They reasoned that this was because golf courses and fancy restaurants are favorite business venues of lobbyists. Moreover, the larger the state government's share of state income, the more fancy restaurants in the capital. The more the swirl of subsidies expands, the better the parasite professionals dine. Like the plumbers we hire to divert each other's water, they win no matter who else loses.

Grand Total

Now suppose you want to add up all these costs.

Scholars who do this kind of work, according to Robert D. Tollison, an economist who specializes in transfer-seeking, come up with a range of cost estimates, all of them necessarily squishy. About the lowest is 3 percent of the gross national product a year. At the other end of the range, David Laband and John Sophocleus figured that Americans—including criminals as well as legal transfer-seekers—invested about $1 trillion in transfer activity in 1985, which would have been about a quarter of the GDP that year.

However, most estimates cluster in the range of 5 percent to 12 percent of GDP every year. In 1998, that would have been $400 billion to $1 trillion. If those estimates are in the ballpark, then by hunting for redistributive goodies Americans make themselves about 5 percent to 12 percent poorer than they otherwise would be. When I asked Tollison whether 5 percent to 12 percent seemed like a lot, he said, "Even the smallest number, 3 percent, is a lot of wealth to be pissing away, if you can help it." For instance, 3 percent of GDP, if it became available for investment, would increase the amount of gross private investment by about a fifth; if it were saved, it could roughly double the American pool of personal savings.

And now I'll try to show why you should care. Figure 5.2 is one of the most basic of all economic charts. It shows, in inflation-adjusted dollars, the amount of output produced per worker

FIGURE 5.2 Domestic Product per Worker, 1947–1998 (1992 dollars)

SOURCE: U.S. Commerce Department; U.S. Labor Department.

in the economy since 1947. It also shows the most important single economic phenomenon of the postwar era: In the late 1960s and early 1970s, the economy's productivity growth rate shifted to a slower track. If real output per worker had continued to rise after 1973 at the same average rate as it did before, by 1998 it would have been about 40 percent higher than it actually was. In other words, Americans would be about 40 percent richer.

Economists don't know all the reasons for the falloff; even when they muster every possible explanation, they still can explain only about half of the productivity slowdown. But the effect is clear: a marked sluggishness in the rise of living standards. After 1973, real compensation per worker rose at only a fifth of the previous rate. More tellingly, the median family income, which doubled from 1947 to 1973, turned almost stagnant—partly because families themselves were changing but also because the engine of wealth, namely productivity, was turning so slowly. Before the early 1970s, rising family income had seemed an American birthright; afterward, it seemed a struggle.

You may have noticed that the productivity curve in Figure 5.2 looks a little bit like the growth curves for groups and lawyers and political contributions and so on—except upside down. The period of hyperpluralism and the period of slow growth roughly coincide. It's also interesting to note that growth picked up somewhat, though not to its pre-1973 level, in the economic expansion of the 1990s, a period when the formation of lobbies seems to have slowed. All this may be, literally, a coincidence. We don't know. Transfer-seeking is certainly not the sole culprit in the post-1973 economic sea change and probably isn't even the main culprit. On the other hand, it is very likely that the substitution of transfer-seeking for productive investment is at least one of the factors behind slow long-term growth. "I don't think we have good measures," remarks the economist Gordon Tullock, "but I'm sure the costs are very large."

If Americans are serious about improving long-term growth and productivity—undoubtedly the most important economic need of our time—then we are going to have to get more serious than we have been about the problem of parasites. We need to think about ways to interrupt, or at least contain, the cycle by which transfer-seeking grows.

Today it is painfully clear that Americans have no handle on the cannibalistic forces unleashed by the revolution of groups and claims and activists and lobbyists and lawyers. In our desire to solve problems, we created a government with vast power to reassign resources, while in our desire to look out for ourselves we created countless new groups. What we did not create, and still don't know how to create, was a way to control the chain reaction set off when activist government and proliferating groups began interacting with each other. Worse, instead of demanding less, we keep demanding more. Groups and activists doggedly, often hysterically, deny that their incessant invention of demands feeds distributive warfare and exacts an economic toll. So they reinforce the public's own denial.

All of that needs to change. Just now, the transfer-seeking game appears to have control of us, rather than we of it.

Not Fatal, But . . .

Despite everything, the parasite economy is not about to bankrupt America. The United States is a rich country with a resilient and resourceful economy. Companies are clever at adapting. Foreign competition helps curtail the worst excesses. I've been careful not to talk about an economic "crisis," because there isn't one. Transfer-seeking activity is a constant drag on the economy but is not a killer—at least not in the foreseeable future. That isn't a reason to stop worrying. In fact, it may be a reason to worry all the more, since the transfer-seeking mentality is so insidious, and its costs so well hidden. Still, the economic costs appear to be bearable, at least so far.

There is, however, that second kind of cost. Granted, lobbies and groups probably can't wreck the economy. But what if they can wreck the government?

6

Demosclerosis

It is April 10, 1992. Four U.S. senators, two Democrats and two Republicans, have marched to the Senate floor with a brave and foolhardy proposal. They are going to take a stab at curtailing federal entitlement spending.

Entitlements are the huge check-writing programs whose benefits are guaranteed ("mandatory") by law: Social Security, Medicare, farm subsidies, veterans' payments, welfare, student aid, many more. Most of these are not little "special-interest" programs benefiting the few at the expense of the broad public. Rather, they are among the most popular programs the government runs, distributing Washington's bounty to millions of Americans and accounting for roughly a sixth of all personal income.

The middle class loves entitlement programs, which is precisely why they are so difficult to control. For the last several decades, they have been eating the federal government alive. Entitlements account for fully three-quarters of all federal domestic spending, and the proportion is steadily rising. By way of discipline, what the gang of four have in mind is an overall limit on the growth of entitlement spending. Bowing to the inevitable, they have exempted Social Security, which is viewed as too popular to touch. Other entitlement programs will collectively grow under their plan, but not as rapidly as in the past. "We do not seek to end entitlements or even to reduce them," Charles Robb, a Democrat from Virginia, tells the Senate. "We do, however, believe that it is necessary to restrain their growth. That is, first and foremost, what this amendment does."

Actually, that's not all it does. It also lights up the civil-defense network of every lobby in Washington. Indeed, well before the proposal reaches the Senate floor, the interest groups are sounding alarms and manning battle stations. Within two hours of the four senators' first detailed discussion of their proposal, their offices are receiving telegrams, says New Mexico Republican Pete Domenici, "from all over the country, saying that this is going to hurt a veterans' group, this is going to hurt people on welfare, this is going to hurt seniors on Medicare." Bill Hoagland, an aide to Domenici, later recalled, "We were inundated. Just about every interest group you can think of was strongly opposed. It was very dramatic, how quickly they all came to the defense."

The American Association of Retired Persons calls the proposal a "direct attack." The National Council of Senior Citizens deems it "outrageous." Children's Defense Fund: "unacceptable." Committee for Educational Funding: "unconscionable." Food Research and Action Center: "devastating." American Federation of Government Employees: "unfair and unconscionable." Veterans of Foreign Wars of the United States: "totally unjust." Disabled American Veterans: "unconscionable." American Legion: "incredible." Paralyzed Veterans of America: "inherently unfair." The National Cotton Council of America, the U.S. Rice Producers' Group, the National Farmers Organization: "unfair." American Postal Workers Union: "irresponsible, simple-minded." And so on.

On the Senate floor, opponents of the spending cap move to exempt disabled veterans. This is a way to kill the cap without actually voting to kill it: Once disabled veterans are exempted, there will be votes to exempt farmers, children, Medicare recipients, nannies with overbites, and everybody else. Each such vote will allow senators to go home and boast about "saving" a program; and each will allow another clutch of interest-group professionals to tell its membership, "See how badly you need us!" Perversely, the end result of this string of votes will be to entrench the very programs that the four senators are trying to restrain.

The veterans' exemption passes overwhelmingly; the game is over. The senators withdraw their proposal. It is dead. In fact, it never had a chance.

Maybe the senators' plan deserved to die, maybe it didn't. Either way, it served a purpose. It provoked a stark demonstration of the forces that are petrifying government.

The key words are "are petrifying"—not "have petrified." "Demosclerosis"—government's progressive loss of the ability to adapt—is a gradual but continuing process. It is not like an acute fever, which attacks in a sudden crisis and galvanizes the immune system to respond with an all-out, decisive counterattack. It is more like hardening of the arteries, which builds up stealthily over many years. Like arteriosclerosis, it can be treated only by a long-term change in behavior: a disciplined regimen of self-reform. Also like arteriosclerosis, demosclerosis gets only worse if it is ignored.

To understand it, you need to begin with the right question. That question is not "Why does nothing get done in Washington?" Things always get done in Washington, today no less than ever. To frame the issue as a matter of whether "things get done" is to set off in the wrong direction and wind up hunting for ways to "speed up the process" and so on, which is almost entirely beside the point. The crucial question, rather, is this: Why is it that what Washington does is less and less effective at solving problems?

Out of Kilter

In the American system, of course, it is supposed to be hard to change things. If the founders had wanted government to move quickly and easily, they wouldn't have bothered with competing power centers and a Bill of Rights. They wanted action to be deliberate, in every sense of the word. And they were right. An institution as powerful and as susceptible to abuse as government ought to move carefully and, where possible, tactfully. Just making change easier (for instance, switching to a parliamentary government, in which a single party controls the whole government) might not solve the problem. In fact, it might make the problem worse, by removing some of the checks and balances that stop interest groups from grabbing goodies at will.

Demosclerosis happens not because change is difficult but because change is easier in one direction than in another. The problem, in other words, is asymmetry—a long-term imbalance of forces. Mancur Olson pointed out one such asymmetry: New interest groups form faster than old ones go away. Now here is another, which the founders could not have foreseen and which few people understand even today: In an interest-group democracy, all kinds of action are difficult, but they are not *equally* difficult.

Imagine a rocket ship headed for Jupiter on three thrusters. Now imagine that the thrusters are slightly out of balance. At first, you might not notice. After a little while, though, the rocket would be a little off course, and then a lot off course, and then it would be hurtling aimlessly into deep space. To prevent this from happening, you would have to spend energy just working to keep the rocket pointed straight. If you let it slip off course, you would have to struggle all the harder to bring it back. Control could become difficult or even, eventually, impossible. You might run out of fuel long before you reached Jupiter. In any case, you could never relax for long. You might need to exert yourself constantly just to keep control.

An interest-group democracy faces a similar problem. To create a new subsidy or anticompetitive deal is hard, but to reduce a subsidy that already exists is much harder. And to completely eliminate a subsidy or an anticompetitive arrangement is hardest of all.

Consider that as few as three or four well-placed congress-men (sometimes even one or two) can create a new subsidy pro-gram, if they are careful not to step on the wrong toes. After all, when you add a new program—assuming you're fairly clever about it—few interest groups or politicians complain, and the beneficiaries stand up and cheer. But once a subsidy program or an anticompetitive deal is in place, three or four congressmen can almost never get rid of it, because the people enjoying the subsidy can always line up ten or twenty members to defend it.

When you try to trim programs, interest groups complain bit-terly and fight hard, as the four kamikaze senators discovered. But woe unto him, above all, who makes bold to grab a subsidy or a special deal by the roots and pull it out entirely. Try doing that, and the affected group flies at you with the fury of the des-perate or the damned. It recruits powerful politicians to block you; it floods your office with mail; it finances your political opponents; it does whatever else it needs to do. Unless you want to be shot, stabbed, and set on fire, the cardinal rule in Washington is: Never challenge someone's sinecure.

Ask Ed Derwinski. He is an affable former congressman who landed in 1989 as the secretary of veterans affairs, overseeing a massive health-care system with more than 170 hospitals, twice that many clinics, and a quarter of a million employees.

Most VA hospitals opened decades ago, when America was a very different place. "What you've got," Derwinski says, "is a structure that, if you invented it today, 50 percent of the facili-ties would be located elsewhere. I felt the system needed shak-ing up. But I had been in government a long time, and I realized you couldn't shake it up." Derwinski knew better than to pro-pose closing any hospitals, even if closures would help improve service in the system as a whole. The veterans' lobbies would scream, the bureaucracy would resist, the mayors would cry foul, the local congressmen would throw a fit, and the White House would panic. He did propose some consolidation—turning duplicative hospitals into, say, specialty clinics or nursing homes—but in the end was able to do very little even of that.

Then he committed the cardinal sin. Ever so gingerly, he threatened a monopoly franchise. Derwinski and the secretary of health and human services proposed letting nonveterans use a VA hospital.

In the poor town of Tuskegee, Alabama, the only private hospital within a thirty-five-mile radius had shut down; meanwhile, the large VA hospital there had plenty of extra space. Local residents were driving miles for medical care, even though there were empty hospital beds in their backyard. And so Derwinski proposed opening the VA hospital to needy local patients, for a three-year trial period. He did not propose to turn away any veterans: Only spare space was to be used, veterans would receive priority over nonveterans, and the VA wouldn't pay an extra cent.

The veterans' groups rose up in fury. Although representing only a minority of all veterans, they were tightly focused, politically astute, well financed, and well connected to sympathetic politicians at every level of government and in every city, county, and state. Derwinski liked to call them "professional veterans." In their opinion, the veterans' health-care system belonged to veterans, and only to veterans. With his rural-health proposal, Derwinski was challenging their franchise.

"This is a ridiculous idea," said the head of the American Legion. "Just the tip of the iceberg," said the head of Veterans of Foreign Wars. The VA health-care system "must meet the needs of those it was designed for—veterans," said the head of the Disabled American Veterans. If there are empty hospital beds, said the veterans' lobbies, then extend medical benefits to more veterans and their families.

The strafing began. "Our members have deluged congressional offices, the White House, and the VA with letters and telephone calls to object to this proposal," said the Legion. The VFW called on its posts to "send a telegraph [sic] to President Bush demanding an end to the Rural Health Care Initiative and also (if you agree) *demanding* that Secretary of Veterans Affairs Ed Derwinski be fired!" In the Senate, Alabama's Richard C. Shelby rose to proclaim that "veterans' hospitals are the exclusive domain of veterans and their qualified dependents." The Senate voted ninety-one to three to kill the test program, whereupon Derwinski retired it, whereupon the veterans' lobby retired him. In the 1992 campaign, President Bush, seeking the support of veterans' groups, gave them Derwinski's head. Bill Clinton, taking the hint, promised in his campaign to "be a good president for the nation's veterans," endorsed a bundle of new benefits for them, and, upon winning, appointed a professional veterans' lobbyist to head the VA. That appointee immediately journeyed to the Tuskegee hospital and "there he made it clear [reported the *Chicago Tribune*] that he still opposed allowing nonveterans in the VA system."

Game, set, and match.

Nothing that happened to Ed Derwinski was unusual. You want to update the sadly archaic banking laws? In 1991, the Bush administration sent Congress a banking-reform package. Under ancient statutes dating back to the early years of the New Deal, banks were barred from a variety of money-making activities. They could not underwrite securities, operate mutual funds, sell insurance, or open branches across state lines. Yet their modern competitors—mutual funds, for instance, which didn't exist when the banking laws were written—could perform many such functions with impunity. And so banks were placed at an artificial disadvantage, which restricted their ability to find profits. Weak banks, in turn, weakened the whole financial system.

What happened? "Bank reform succumbed to a frenzied attack by lobbyists," said *The New York Times*. "Small bankers, fearing competition, tore away interstate banking. Insurance firms, fearing competition, tore away insurance underwriting. Securities firms, fearing competition, tore away the proposal to let banks sell stocks and bonds." In the end, *National Journal* reported, "every administration proposal for permitting banks to widen their business horizons—every single one—was picked off in the carnage." The end result was surely one of the most bizarre policies of our time: As the twenty-first century approached, the country limped along with financial rules written in the age of gramophones and green eyeshades.

By the middle of the 1990s, the banking rules were so obviously antiquated that federal regulators more or less waved financial institutions around them, like road crews diverting traffic around a broken water main. But reform attempts repeatedly came to grief, held up by the refusal of this or that lobby to sign off on this or that reform bill, by opposition from this or that member of Congress, or by bureacratic infighting between federal agencies. Congress, to its credit, kept trying, if only because the 1920s and 1930s regime had become ludicrous and wearisome to everyone affected by it. Yet the country was forced to live under that archaic regime until the regime had in essence collapsed altogether, not because living that way made sense but simply because removing the old rules was so difficult.

You want to reform an agriculture program? You may be able to trim a subsidy a little, if you work very hard, but suppose you want to withdraw someone's monopoly claim completely. Take the sugar program, a classic anticompetitive arrangement that subsidizes growers by artificially pushing up sugar prices and restricting imports. The program costs Americans $1.4 billion a year in higher grocery bills, according to the General Accounting Office. The benefits are highly concentrated; almost half of them flow to 1 percent of the sugar farms. Sugar parasites are voracious.

Senator Richard Lugar of Indiana tried to whack them. "As we tried to reform the farm budget," he said in a speech in 1992, "I made a specific motion to abolish the sugar program. The administration wanted to cut the support price from eighteen cents to sixteen. Well, my motion to abolish got two votes, Slade Gorton of Washington and my own. I'm ranking [Republican] member of the Agriculture Committee, and I could only get two votes. Five votes out of twenty to cut the support price from eighteen to sixteen. No change in the tobacco program, no change in peanuts, no change in wool, no change in honey or mohair or any of the rest of it."

In 1996, with Republicans now in control of the Congress, a band of conservative free-marketers and urban farm-welfare opponents went after sugar again. "It's anti-free-market and it's corporate welfare," said Dan Miller, a Republican House member from Florida. They got as far as a vote on the House floor, one of the most dramatic of 1996. "The sugar vote capped a year-long, multi-million-dollar advertising and lobbying battle that pitted well-heeled sugar cane and beet planters against a powerful coalition of manufacturers, consumer groups and environmentalists," wrote David Hosansky in *Congressional Quarterly*. One representative denounced sugar lobbyists for filling the halls of the Capitol "with pockets full of money"; another thundered that eliminating the sugar subsidy would "bring pleasure to Fidel Castro." Having made some strategic concessions that slightly narrowed the terms of their subsidy, the sugar interests argued that their program had been reformed already; what worried most representatives more than the arguments, though, was the very real possibility that excising the sugar program could leach enough support from that year's massive farm bill to cause its collapse. As the votes were counted, dozens of sugar lobbyists sat silently in the House gallery, only to break into cheers when the results came in: The attack was repelled by a vote of 217-208, with only a few votes to spare. In truth, this was not quite the near-death experience for sugar that it appeared to be, for the Senate would probably have rescued the program anyway. Still, Miller professed disappointment. "We just need to work harder," he told me dejectedly, though it was difficult to see how much harder he and his allies could have worked.

You want to reform the schools? Another classic anticompetitive franchise protects public-school employees, who enjoy a monopoly claim on tax dollars for education. (By contrast, people spend their Medicare money at any hospital and their food stamps at any grocery store. No provider enjoys a monopoly claim.) What happens when you try to nibble at that franchise?

The Bush people timidly tried in 1991. They wanted to finance 535 "break the mold" schools, both public and private, to be chosen competitively in Washington and funded directly from there. They also proposed some mild incentives for localities to try school voucher plans, which let parents spend public money at private schools. In both cases, the idea was to stimulate innovation by circumventing the entrenched establishment of public-school employees and administrators.

Under intense opposition from those groups, the voucher measure was demolished. "Break the mold" schools turned mostly into block grants for state education agencies and local school districts: more money for the entrenched providers. There would be no going around them to finance new competitors. Later on, the Clinton administration, needing support from the public employees' unions, carefully avoided reopening the issue. The Clinton people steered a mile wide of vouchers. They even renounced experiments. Hell no, said Richard W. Riley, Clinton's secretary of education: "I can't see spending public money to see if something is worthwhile when I'm 100 percent sure it's not."

I multiply examples to make a point. Getting rid of some client group's well-tended perquisite is not impossible, but it is very difficult. It requires endurance, willingness to face daunting odds, and an appetite for pain. (Representative Miller, the sugar opponent, told me after his House defeat that various sugar interests had put a $500,000 price on his head, meaning they were spending that much in an effort to defeat him.) Digging out an interest group and its favorable deal is like digging out a splinter embedded deeply in your foot—so painful that you'd usually rather just limp.

Try, Try Again

All right, so it's harder to get rid of subsidies and perks than to create them. So what? How does that asymmetry erode government's ability to adapt? The crucial element—the nub of the argument—is trial and error.

We tend to think of trial and error as a small and sterile idea, a mere commonplace ("If at first you don't succeed . . ."). The method of trial and error certainly seems unglamorous by comparison with, for example, the method of large-scale planning. It is tempting to think that lowly trial and error merely roots out mistakes, whereas planning builds cathedrals. To take such a view, however, is to sadly underestimate the power of trial and error, for trial and error is the key to successful adaptation and problem solving in large, complex systems.

In the large, complex system of biological evolution, species undergo mutations. Mutations themselves aren't evolution. Evolution occurs when a mutant proves better adapted to its environment than its predecessors or its competitors. The critical trick is to find the *useful* mutation, though you never know in advance which mutation will be useful. The vast majority will fail. A few, however, succeed brilliantly. Those high achievers then proliferate by outcompeting their rivals. That is how life adapts to changing environments. And if you replicate the trial-and-error process throughout billions of species over billions of years, you get a biosphere whose nearly infinite complexity and diversity and flexibility put any cathedral—or any other planned and static structure—to shame.

The genius of a capitalist economy is that it uses the same kind of evolutionary strategy. Stalin was able to build state-of-the-art factories in the 1930s and 1940s; what he could not do was keep the factories up-to-date. His economy could not adapt. Capitalism, by contrast, is good at adapting, and the key to its adaptability is that it makes many mistakes but corrects them quickly. Then it makes many more mistakes and corrects those. Hopeful entrepreneurs open businesses, and corporate executives try new marketing strategies; most fail, but every so often someone hits on a brilliant innovation. You never know in advance which innovation will turn out to be brilliant. But the point of the method of trial and error is that you don't need to know. The successful innovations proliferate by outcompeting their rivals.

The process is similar with another complex social system, science. No one knows in advance which idea will turn out to be right. Most new ideas, in fact, are wrong. The key to science's success is that it tries out a million hypotheses every day and abandons most of them. The survivors are our knowledge base. And so the knowledge base adapts through trial and error.

To see the full implications of demosclerosis, it is necessary to apply the same kind of evolutionary thinking to government. In a bafflingly complex world, you can no more know in advance which government programs will work than you can know in advance which mutations will succeed or which new products will be profitable. The only way to find out is to try a program and evaluate the result. Moreover, in a world that changes quickly, today's successful program is tomorrow's anachronistic failure. The only way to stay abreast is to keep trying new programs and let the successful ones outcompete their rivals. In other words, the way for governments to learn what works in a protean world is by trial and error.

However, something has gone badly wrong.

The Living Dead

The Reagan administration believed in killing domestic programs, mostly because its conservative officials disliked government. Ronald Reagan, a popular president who effectively controlled Congress in the critical early portion of his first term, made a point of trying to eliminate federal programs. But during his eight years in office, only four major programs—general revenue sharing, urban-development action grants, the synthetic-fuels program, and the Clinch River breeder reactor—actually were killed.

President Bush had no better luck. For fiscal 1993 alone, the

Bush administration proposed ending 246 federal programs. Unlike Reagan, Bush wasn't trying to spear any big (or controversial) fish; if all 246 had been eliminated, the budgetary savings would have come to only $3.5 billion, or a quarter of 1 percent of federal spending. You might think that clearing the waters of such small fry would be fairly easy. But you would be wrong. Out of 246, a not very grand total of eight programs actually disappeared, including the commission on the Constitution's bicentennial (which had occurred in 1987) and a NASA asteroid flyby. The total savings came to an even less grand total of $58 million. In a budget of $1.5 trillion and thousands of programs, that was all the president could get rid of.

It is scarcely an exaggeration to say that, in Washington, *every program lasts forever.* When you stop to think about it, this is an astonishing fact—indeed, almost incredible. How—why—can it be?

Go back to the world of hyperpluralism described in Chapter 3. Remember that one sure way to get an interest group started is to set up a redistributive program. Soon after the program begins, the people who depend on it—both the program's direct beneficiaries and its administrators and employees—organize to defend it. They become an entrenched lobby. They have money, votes, and passion. They have professional lobbyists and rapid-response "action alert" systems. They are slick and sophisticated. When necessary, they scream and yell. At any given moment, it's always safer to placate them than to defy them.

Suppose, then, that you want to get rid of the Rural Electrification Administration (later renamed the Rural Utilities Service), as the Reagan and Bush administrations wanted to do. The REA started as a New Deal relief program in 1935, when only 10 percent of American farms had electricity. A few decades later, its mission was accomplished. Not only did the vast majority of farms have electricity and telephone service (99 percent had power and 96 percent had phones in 1990), but they were more likely to have such service than the average American household. In fact, the rural electrical subsidies often flowed to the nonpoor and even the nonrural. Many people began wondering whether the country really needed the REA.

Those people faced a formidable obstacle. In 1942, hard on the heels of the rural electrification program, the National Rural Electric Cooperative Association arrived on the scene. Today the association represents a thousand far-flung rural electrical cooperatives; the cooperatives boast ten thousand local directors and six times that many employees; those people are well connected, politically active, and regularly in touch with members of Congress and each other. If anyone makes a move to abolish the rural electric programs, those people, as well as several other lobbying groups, swarm out of the woodwork. "There were so many," recalled one former government official who opposed the program, "they had support everywhere. It was hopeless." To back them up, the association's political action committee donated almost $800,000 to about 360 congressional candidates in the 1995–1996 election cycle alone. And the association, with its imposing building in the suburbs of Washington, wasn't going away. Interest groups almost never go away. Like everyone else, they want to keep their jobs.

These people have more than just the power of a strong grassroots lobbying network. They also have the power of conviction. They believe in the rightness of their cause, and they bolster their belief with two appealing arguments—need and fairness.

Proponents of the need argument say, "We need federal money because, having relied on it for all these years, we can't get along without it." When I asked Bob Bergland, a former secretary of agriculture who later was head of the electric-cooperative association, why his members still needed subsidies, he replied: "There's a level at which some of these marginal [rural electric] systems simply won't be able to pass on the costs." (However, he also conceded that rates would go up "not much" without the subsidies.)

Proponents of the fairness argument say, "Our competitors

self-defeating

are subsidized, so it's only fair to subsidize us." Bergland made this argument, too, accurately pointing out that municipal and private utilities enjoy various kinds of tax breaks and indirect subsidies. It would hardly be fair to punish the rural cooperatives while leaving their competitors untouched.

To understand why programs never die, it's essential to see that both of those arguments—need and fairness—are available to *every lobby in Washington*. Because groups that receive subsidies (or other kinds of benefits) soon rely on them, *every* reduction creates some genuine hardship cases. And because nowadays everyone is subsidized one way or another, *every* reduction hurts some people relative to others. Even in principle, there is no patently "unneeded" program or "fair" reduction. Turn over every stone in Washington, but you will never find one. That is another reason lobbies don't go away: All are defending something that is economically vital and morally urgent for somebody.

but it all is politics

Can't you at least get rid of the programs that fail? In principle, maybe, but not in practice. One problem is that people disagree about which programs have failed, and even about what "failing" means. Evolutionary systems get around this problem simply by forcing all businesses, ideas, and species to compete. "Success" isn't argued about; it's whatever prevails. If the federal government worked on a trial-and-error basis, it could try many rival programs to solve any particular problem, and then abandon all but the one that worked best. It might start with a dozen competing welfare systems and close all but one of them—and then close that system, too, when a better one came along. The trouble, though, is that in today's world each program instantly generates an interest group, and each interest group lobbies to keep its own program open, drumming up campaign contributions and producing stacks of studies "proving" the program's success. In the end, we get stuck with all twelve programs instead of finding the best one, and before long they are working at cross-purposes and shutting out any new rivals.

So why don't all these lobbies cancel each other out? After

all, they compete for the government's money and attention. And, to some extent, that helps curtail excesses. As a rule, though, lobbies work hard to avoid head-on confrontations with other lobbies, for exactly the same reason that politicians work hard to avoid confrontations with lobbies: Challenge someone's sinecure, and you get his fist in your face. If farmers tell the government, "We want you to kill the ranchers' subsidies and give us the money," they can count on a bruising fight with the cattlemen's association. On the other hand, if they say, "The ranchers are receiving land-use subsidies, so please raise our price supports," they avoid antagonizing any powerful group directly. The choice is obvious. There are occasions when a direct conflict is inevitable—for example, the showdown over sugar in 1996—and those are the times when programs are most vulnerable. Precisely because of that vulnerability, however, everyone looks for accommodations that keep everybody happy, which is why you can't rely on competition between lobbies to control lobbying.

Thus, when I asked Bob Bergland whether he would favor cutting his own *and* his competitors' subsidies, he demurred. "We think a good argument can be made for support on all sides," he said. In other words, subsidize our competitors *and* us— which is exactly what usually happens. Other things being equal, lobbies and subsidies tend to reinforce each other rather than to undercut each other. And now we're back where we started: Since everybody is subsidized, to cut any particular group's subsidy is "unfair." The circle closes.

The result is that, with rare exceptions, we are stuck with everything the government ever tries, including some rather bizarre things. Strange to say, late-twentieth-century America was a land where you needed a government license to grow peanuts. This was because commodity markets were turbulent in 1934. "The chaotic agricultural and economic conditions that caused the Congress to establish the peanut program fifty-eight years ago no longer exist," noted the General Accounting Office in 1993. "Most peanuts in the United States today are produced by large agribusinesses rather than by the small family farms that dominated agriculture in the 1930s." Did the peanut program end, once it became a protection for big agribusinesses that employed slick lobbyists to keep newcomers out of the markets? On the contrary: The incentives to defend it only grew. A fifth of the peanut growers controlled more than four-fifths of the peanut licenses, which they could sell or rent for anywhere from $50,000 to $6 million. Of the third to half a billion dollars that the peanut program cost American consumers every year, as much as a fourth was deadweight loss: wealth that was simply destroyed. But that loss was spread very thin. On the other hand, a $6 million peanut license is worth fighting for.

By way of long-lived anachronisms, it would be hard to beat the federal subsidy for wool and mohair. The program was set up in 1954, when wool was a vital strategic commodity for military uniforms. (Mohair growers, who sell the fleece of Angora goats, sneaked into the program and came along for the ride. Don't ask what an Angora goat is; the point is that there were a lot of them in Texas, which was robustly represented on the House and Senate agriculture committees.) In 1955, a year after the program was created, the American Sheep Industry Association was founded. Eventually it boasted 110,000 members and a budget of more than $5 million, some of which it spent on (what else?) lobbying Washington to preserve the subsidies around which it had formed. In any case, the wool and mohair program failed: Wool production went down, not up, because market forces overwhelmed the subsidies. But even if the program had succeeded, its main rationale disappeared soon after it was born. Synthetic fabrics were developed, and the Pentagon struck wool from its strategic-commodities list. That was in 1960. Nevertheless, in 1992, the wool and mohair program spent a tidy $191 million. Why did Bill Clinton inherit Dwight Eisenhower's failed strategic-fabrics policy? It survived because it was ably defended by the small but devoted group of people who benefited from it, in some cases richly (several dozen farmers routinely drew subsidy checks of more than $100,000 a year).

If anyone asked the wool growers or the American Sheep Industry Association why the program was still necessary in the 1990s, they said, predictably, that wool farmers needed the money and that their competitors, especially overseas, also were subsidized. When I asked the same question of a professional lobbyist who used to work for the wool growers, he chuckled and answered more frankly. "There's nothing more permanent in this town," he said, "than a temporary program."

In 1993, a remarkable thing happened. Congress, determined to show that it could get rid of at least *something*, managed to eliminate the wool and mohair subsidy, along with an equally peculiar honey subsidy that dated to 1950. Those two programs were about all Congress was able to get rid of, and accomplishing even that much required a crusade on the part of a few representatives and senators. Nonetheless, effective on December 31, 1995, the National Wool Act was repealed (though duties on wool imports remained).

Well, that didn't seem entirely fair, now, did it? So in April 1996, Congress passed a new farm bill whose Section 759 was titled "National Sheep Industry Improvement Center." This, it turned out, was an entity empowered with up to $50 million of federal funds to "enhance production and marketing of sheep or goat products in the United States" and to "design unique responses to the special needs of the sheep or goat industries on both a regional and national basis." Two western senators, including one very conservative Republican, had dropped this trifle into the farm bill because life was not easy out in wool country, and because, as a wool lobbyist told *Congressional Quarterly*'s Hosansky, "I think it's the kind of thing you look to for an industry that no longer has any support whatsoever as a direct payment." As of 1996, an indirect payment would have to suffice.

Apparently life was not easy in mohair country, either. In 1998, the Texas people and the Mohair Council of America inserted into a giant appropriations bill a provision letting mohair growers take out interest-free federal loans. "There's nothing free about this deal," the head of the mohair council told *The Washington Post*, "except the loans are interest-free the first year." That seemed logical enough: no subsidy except for the subsidy.

O death, where is thy sting? Grave, where is thy victory?

Life in the Frozen Lane

Not only are programs virtually impossible to kill, but once put in place they are also hard to change. Every wrinkle in the law, every grant formula and tax loophole, produces a winner who resists subsequent reform, unless "reform" happens to mean more money or benefits for the lobbies concerned. America's basic welfare program for the poor was designed in the 1930s primarily to meet the needs of widows, who weren't expected to work. As the world changed, the program didn't. By the 1970s, many scholars understood that some aspects of the welfare program actually deepened poverty by encouraging fathers to leave home, yet the old policy persisted almost as though no one knew any better. Between 1935 and 1996, when, in the signal accomplishment of the Gingrich Congress, welfare was overhauled, only one significant reform of the program was made; and that change, the 1988 Family Support Act, was a modest measure affecting only a minority of welfare recipients. If a complicated program takes sixty years to update, it can hardly be expected to adapt to changing real-world problems.

But surely it's possible to change an outmoded funding formula, at least? Don't count on it. In 1989, Pete Perry, an acting head of the federal Economic Development Administration, decided it was time to change the way regional economic-planning districts were funded. There were almost three hundred such districts all over the country, drawing an average of about

$50,000 of federal money every year. Perry had a sensible reason to change the formula: The formula was that there wasn't any formula. Rather, each district received more or less what it had received in earlier years, with an occasional cost-of-living adjustment. By the late 1980s, after two decades when some regions thrived and others decayed, funding bore no relationship to need or anything else. Some of the least needy districts were receiving some of the largest amounts. Moreover, funding wasn't related to districts' performance. And so Perry decided to try a new system. Grants for each district would be based on such factors as local population, income levels, unemployment, geographic area, and the planners' past performance. If a district had grown richer, some of its money would be rerouted to a needier district.

"That," he said, "hit the fan." The people who ran the planning districts enjoyed robust support from local bigwigs. They also maintained a pressure group: the National Association of Development Organizations (NADO), which was founded shortly after the Economic Development Administration was established. When I paid a visit to NADO's executive director, Aliceann Wohlbruck, she agreed that planning-district funding made little sense. "There's no great logic here," she said. "We really agree there are things in the programs that need to be changed. We want to work to improve the program." But her idea of improvement did not include reducing or eliminating funding for any existing district. "I think you've got to have a hold-harmless," she said. "If you've had the same level of funding for twenty-five years, how do you tell people you're going to cut it?"

Not the way Pete Perry told them, apparently. His proposal drew an action memo—URGENT, all capitals, bright pink paper—from Wohlbruck to NADO's constituents. They dropped a blizzard of mail and phone calls on members of Congress, who complained to the secretary of commerce. By the time the dust had settled, Perry's new formula was dead, and Congress had raised the minimum level of funding for all the planning districts. End of reform.

To make government work under such conditions is a task only for the masochistic or the criminally insane. Americans love to complain about government workers and managers. "Waste, fraud, and abuse," they grouse. What Americans overlook, or do not understand, is that their organization into tens of thousands of permanent interest groups is making public servants' jobs impossible.

Imagine that you are appointed to be head of a bankrupt corporation. Your mission is to straighten out the company's finances and bring its equipment and product lines up-to-date. "Okay," you say, "let's get to work." But there's a catch. You're told that you cannot drop a single product, close a single factory, or get rid of any old equipment. Sure, you can develop new products. But you also have to keep the old ones on the market. You can manufacture the latest ergonomic office chair but not drop your line of 1950s-style Naugahyde dinette furniture. You can open a new factory but not close any old ones. At most, if you concentrate your energy on a few intense battles, in any given year you can drop one or two products and streamline one or two plants. But the effort will be exhausting.

"Impossible!" you say. "No one could revitalize a corporation under such conditions!" You quit. And you're right.

Talk to anyone who has managed a federal government agency in the age of hyperpluralism, and you soon find that this imaginary situation isn't so imaginary. Orson Swindle, for instance, ran the Economic Development Administration for a few years during the Reagan administration. He wanted to reform the EDA's University Center program, which gave each of fifty or so universities about $100,000 a year to help plan local development projects. The trouble—as he saw it—was not with the concept itself, which he supported, but that once a center was set up, it kept receiving funds forever. "If the program has merit," Swindle said, "then why don't we wean some of the centers that had been on it for twenty years?" The better centers could stand on their own—selling their services and raising local contributions, for instance. And as money was freed up from existing centers, the EDA would spend it to start new ones. In fact, that was how the program was originally supposed to work when it was set up in the 1960s. "We would never have to ask for any more funds," Swindle said, "and we'd have more and more centers."

Unfortunately, that trick never works. The existing centers and their interest group, NAMTAC (the National Association of Management and Technical Assistance Centers), didn't care for the idea that "their" funding would be diverted to establish new rivals. "Very violently opposed" is how the centers' reaction was described by NAMTAC's Washington representative.

"The people that are in NAMTAC," observed Hugh Farmer, a retired civil servant who had worked at the EDA almost since its doors first opened, "are major universities from across the country, and they have quite a lobbying effort with Congress. They make their living by doing this." They went riding up to Capitol Hill, guns blazing, and without much trouble obtained a law barring any reductions in existing centers' funding. Swindle's attempt to make the program more flexible had instead locked it in place. The program had become a kind of permanent entitlement for a few dozen lucky universities.

So much for innovative management. A disillusioned Orson Swindle wound up as a senior adviser in Ross Perot's 1992 presidential campaign. Hugh Farmer, too, left the EDA with a bitter taste in his mouth. "I was frustrated by the fact that we couldn't change anything, we couldn't try new things," he said. "I think EDA is in a position where it's not being effective because it's too inflexible and it's too set in its ways. It's frozen and inflexible. Or it's semifrozen. It's kind of slushed. You're allowed to move a little to the left or right, but you can't move very far."

In 1991, President Bush appointed Diane Ravitch, a Democrat, to be assistant secretary of education in charge of educational research. She had plans and ideas. She got nowhere. She soon discovered that all but 5 to 10 percent of her department's research budget was preassigned, by law, to entrenched recipients. "There's a little bit of discretion," she told me, "but the vast bulk is frozen solid."

A handful of established regional laboratories virtually monopolized a key chunk of the research budget. They maintained a lobbying group, which was run by a former aide to a key member of the House Appropriations Committee. Another grantee, a center for civics education, was run by a man whose lobbyist had previously worked for the chairman of the House committee overseeing education. (You may sense a pattern. Recall that many politicians, Capitol Hill staff members, and government officials later go to work as lobbyists or interest-group professionals. That is probably another reason programs are hard to eliminate: Policymakers would prefer not to offend their future employers.) I asked Ravitch whether she tried to get rid of the civics program. "There was no point trying to get rid of it; he [the lobbyist] was close to all the guys on the Hill," she replied. "You can't get rid of those things. They don't do it." In the end, she managed to kill one program, called Leadership in Educational Administration. "Amazing," she said. That tiny program spent only $7–8 million at its peak.

She couldn't kill; therefore she couldn't create. She had hoped to develop videos for parents and a computerized information network for educators: "But there was no interest group for that." In the end, she found, there were only two ways to do the job. One way, the popular method, was to shovel money out the door to the established clients. The other way, always contentious, was to reexamine priorities and fight trench warfare against the established clients. The former approach was politically painless but unsatisfying; the latter was politically painful and almost always unsuccessful.

"At first," she said of her days in Washington, "I thought it was about people really solving problems. But what it's really all about is people protecting their districts and the organizations they're close to. If you don't get the interest groups' support, you can't change anything, but if you change anything, you don't get their support. That's the conundrum."

"At the beginning, I thought I could shape the agency. But I couldn't do that. That was already done. My priorities were irrelevant. And that, for me, was a devastating discovery."

How Big Is Too Big?

What would become of a giant, complicated social system if it couldn't discard its failures and overhaul its anachronisms, or couldn't modify them quickly enough? Imagine an economy in which every important business enterprise was kept alive by a politically connected coalition of enterprise managers and government officials. Over time, the world would change, but the universe of businesses wouldn't. Obsolescent companies would gobble up resources, crowding out new companies. They might change, but in ways more suited to pleasing their political patrons than to increasing their efficiency. The economy would cease to adapt.

That is what happened to the Soviet economy. It collapsed.

In principle, the U.S. government's situation is like the Soviet economy's, though the U.S. government doesn't seem likely to collapse. In both cases, the method of trial and error reached the point of critical failure.

In Washington, old programs and policies cannot be excised except at enormous political cost, and yet they continue to consume money and energy. As a result, there is less and less money or energy for new programs and policies. Every time a peanut-subsidy program from the 1930s or an EDA university-center program from the 1960s becomes entrenched, it occupies a spot where an experiment might have been performed or a start-up venture might have been tried. The old crowds out the new.

A second consequence, which is at least as important, is that when every program is permanent the price of failure becomes extravagant. The key to experimenting successfully is knowing that you can correct your mistakes and try again. But what if you have only one chance? What if you are saddled with your mistakes forever, or at least for decades? Then experimentation becomes extremely risky. In fact, an experiment that you can try only once and then are stuck with is not really an experiment at all. In a one-shot environment, the very possibility of experimentation, which by nature is a trial-and-error process, breaks down.

To make this point clearer, let me invoke the physicist Freeman Dyson. In many of his writings, Dyson has argued that size matters. But he doesn't mean size just in the physical sense. Rather, if you want to know whether a machine is worth building or a program is worth undertaking, you have to scale it to make sure it's flexible enough to adapt to a changing world. "Never sacrifice economies of speed to achieve economies of scale," writes Dyson. "And never let ourselves get stuck with facilities which take ten years to turn on or off." Otherwise, projects are out-of-date by the time they open for business. Speed can make all the difference:

> Judging by the experience of the last fifty years, it seems that major changes come roughly once in a decade. In this situation it makes an enormous difference whether we are able to react to change in three years or in twelve. An industry which is able to react in three years will find the game stimulating and enjoyable, and the people who do the work will experience the pleasant sensation of being able to cope. An industry which takes twelve years to react will be perpetually too late, and the people running the industry will experience sensations of paralysis and demoralization.

Detroit's automakers learned the hard way that a car requiring five years to bring to market is a very different product from a car requiring two or three years to bring to market, even though the two might be physically identical. Slow-to-market cars from General Motors were always behind the market.

Quick-to-market cars from Toyota were on top of the market. Quick is beautiful.

Moreover, Dyson argues, not only should a project or institution be quick enough, but it also should avoid one-shot operations, which don't allow you to fail and try again. Among human beings, it is axiomatic that almost nothing goes right the first time. Any reformer who depends on hitting the bull's-eye with his first arrow is doomed. When locked in place, first-try "solutions" soon cause more problems than they solve.

"The right size," according to Dyson, "means the size at which you can afford to take a gamble." If a project is so big that you're stuck with it even if it fails, don't do it. In other words, the right size for any program or institution is no larger than the biggest size that still lets you correct your mistakes in time. Larger, and you either fail to solve problems, or you cause more problems than you solve. By those standards, government today is scaled incorrectly.

all about size, again

Rigor Mortis

The size of government is the great ideological divide in American politics. Liberals want government to do more; conservatives want it to do less. But big versus small is not, in itself, the best place to draw the distinction. The more important question is not how big government is but how flexible. *kh huh.*

Flexibility depends not only on the size of government but also on the society in which government is embedded. In a society with few lobbies, government can be large yet still quite flexible. A few decades ago, when fewer lobbying groups were around to defend everything, the government could be more experimental and so was better able to solve problems. But as Americans increasingly organized themselves into transfer-seeking lobbies, they eroded their government's flexibility and thus, in effect, made themselves harder to govern. Today, the federal government is swimming in molasses instead of water. It can't correct its mistakes in time. Therefore it has great difficulty solving problems. And, of course, more lobbies form every day.

People sometimes look at Franklin Roosevelt's period of governmental experimentation and say, "If we could do it then, we should certainly be able to do it now." But they miss the point, which is that society has changed. In a society dense with professional lobbies, FDR's brand of experimental central government cannot exist. Roosevelt was able to experiment in ways that are inconceivable today, not only because his government was smaller and more manageable but also partly because there were far fewer organized lobbies around to interfere with change. He was able to move programs into place quickly. On the seventeenth day of his administration, he proposed the Civilian Conservation Corps; three weeks later, it was law. On November 2, 1933, he was given a proposal for a Civil Works Administration employing people to repair streets and dig sewers; by November 23, the program employed 800,000 people, and five weeks later, 4.25 million, or fully 8 percent of the American workforce. Just as important, Roosevelt was able to eliminate programs. He ordered the Civil Works Administration shut down at winter's end; its total life span was only a few months. Similarly, the Civilian Conservation Corps was dissolved in 1942, once the war effort made it superfluous. In those days, the government had some capacity to move programs on line quickly, try them out, and then get rid of them when their time had passed. It could declare a problem solved and then move on to the next project, and it could correct its errors, if not perfectly, then far more easily than it can today. But this error-correcting capacity—which is the capacity to solve problems—has steadily diminished.

Today we must expect that anything the government tries this year will still be with us fifty years from now. Even the most promising policies and programs cannot be made to work when you lack the flexibility to fail, adjust, and try again. By eroding the capacity for error elimination, demosclerosis has changed the very parameters of the doable.

A good example is so-called industrial policy, which seeks to use targeted subsidies to support industries deemed to have special strategic or economic value. The only way such a policy could ever work is through constant experimentation and tinkering. First you might subsidize steel, but if that didn't work you could switch to research support for computer chips, and then if that failed or became unnecessary you could tinker with patent rules for biotech. You would constantly move your resources around, hunting for approaches that work. Ira Magaziner, a business consultant and industrial-policy proponent who worked for the Clinton administration (most notably by designing its disastrous health-care plan), has said: "What you could loosely call industrial policies are, by their nature, trial-and-error policies, similarly as they would be in companies." In FDR's day, industrial policy might have been possible. (In fact, something like it was tried and rejected.) But in the age of demosclerosis, each industry runs a sophisticated lobby and can capture and then cling to any resources you throw in its direction. Any industrial policy soon turns into an encrusted mass of subsidies for anachronistic industries with high-priced lobbyists. It blocks, rather than advances, useful change.

Or again, suppose you think a national system of high-technology trains is a good idea. In a nonsclerotic world, the government can help develop such a system and, if it fails, adjust it or go on to the next thing. But in a demosclerotic world, the case is very different. You begin setting up a system of, say, magnetic levitation trains this year. With luck, it's mostly ready ten years hence. Long before then, however, appears the National Association of Maglev Development Authorities (NAMDA), which boasts thousands of influential members around the country and runs a half-million-dollar political action committee. NAMDA's job is to make sure that the existing high-tech train systems (translation: its members' jobs) are funded forever. The result: Twenty years hence, the country is burdened with an obsolete train system that blocks other advances in transportation.

The point is not that defended programs never die; now and then, they do. The point is that purging a program is such a slow, agonizing process that the rate of calcification outstrips the rate of adaptation. If you think again about the example of the rocket with unbalanced engines, you quickly see that such an asymmetry of forces can, as it plays out over time, have enormous consequences. In fact, in a demosclerotic environment, the government may find itself trapped in a cycle in which its attempts to solve problems ultimately diminish its problem-solving capacity. With enormous effort, it may succeed in reforming, say, the welfare or banking laws. But a decade later, a thousand lobbies will have nailed the reforms in place, including the ones that failed. The very process of reform may thus be hijacked by the forces of reaction and turned against itself.

"Medicare is a state-of-the-art 1965 benefits package," Willis D. Gradison, the head of the Health Insurance Association of America, said, by way of illustration. "It's a good program. It just wouldn't be done that way today. And if you look at the changes we've made in Medicare, it's amazing how narrow they are." Indeed, Medicare was a shining reform in its day. But then it calcified. Decentralized private plans evolved new ways to deliver care; by the early 1990s, insurance companies were funneling their customers into health-maintenance organizations, almost half of which the insurers themselves owned. Medicare did no such thing. It failed to evolve.

Eventually, caught in an impossible bind, the whole system may begin to go critical. Driven by the demands of a changing world, the government has no choice but to pass new programs. Yet at the same time, driven by the demands of the organized lobbies, the government struggles desperately to keep doing everything it ever tried for every group it ever aided. And so, lacking any better option, Washington just piles new programs on top of old programs. Laws are passed, policies adopted, programs added or expanded—things "get done"; but, as layer is dropped upon layer, the accumulated mass becomes gradually less rational and less flexible. To form a mental picture, imagine that you were forced to build every new house on top of its predecessor. That could work for a while, but eventually you would have a teetering, dysfunctional mess. Similarly, accumulated programs and policies work to every end at once and often block each other, sometimes creating new problems, which may create the need for still other programs, leading to still more interest groups and entrenchment. Bit by bit, program by program, the government becomes dysfunctional.

As Americans heap ever more tasks on their government, while simultaneously organizing themselves into ever more lobbies, is it any wonder that government fails to meet expectations? And as government disappoints, is it any wonder that Americans despise it? By the 1990s, when polls showed that public confidence in the federal government had fallen to record lows, government and the public had become like the ill-tempered farmer and the arthritic nag. The farmer loads more and more on the nag, the nag becomes weaker and weaker, the angry farmer beats and whips the nag, and the battered nag becomes weaker still.

In the period beginning with the New Deal and peaking with Lyndon Johnson's Great Society, Washington seemed one of America's most adaptive and progressive forces—which, at the time, it probably was. What Roosevelt's and Johnson's visionaries did not foresee was that every program would generate an entrenched lobby that would never go away. The same programs that made government a progressive force from the 1930s through the 1960s also spawned swarms of dependent interest groups, whose collective lobbying had turned government rigid and brittle by the 1990s.

Demosclerosis has thus turned progressivism into its own worst enemy. Yesterday's innovations have become today's prisons. One of the main paradoxes of demosclerosis, and one of its nastiest surprises, is that the rise of government activism has immobilized activist government.

No one setting out to write a fresh policy today would think to banish banks from the mutual-fund business, or make peanut farmers buy licenses, or forbid United Parcel Service to deliver letters, or grant massive tax breaks for borrowing. Countless policies are on the books, not because they make sense today, but merely because they cannot be gotten rid of. They are like dinosaurs that will not die, anachronisms whose refusal to go away prevents newer, better-adapted rivals from thriving. In a Darwinian sense, the collectivity of federal policies is ceasing to evolve.

A Stricken Giant

As the disease of demosclerosis advances, it causes a paradoxical and pathetic symptom: bogus national poverty. In Washington, it became the conventional wisdom in the 1980s and 1990s that programs and ambitions that were once affordable had become "too expensive." For a time, penury seemed a result of the fiscal pressure from chronic budget deficits, but after the deficit melted away the budget remained as tight as ever. The deficit, apparently, was not the sole problem. In the 1940s, America could "afford" the Marshall Plan to set Europe back on its feet; in the 1990s, America could not "afford" any remotely comparable effort to help the former Communist countries find political and economic stability. In the 1960s, America could "afford" a program to send astronauts to the moon; in the 1990s, America struggled mightily to "afford" even a modest orbiting space station. Subjectively, in the world of feelings, the government was poor, or in any case much poorer than in the fat years of Kennedy and Johnson. But objectively, in the world of fact, this was absurd.

The United States is now wealthier than any other country in human history, including its prior self. Per capita disposable income, adjusted for inflation, is more than twice as high as in 1960, when the federal government could "afford" almost anything. Real wealth per capita is at least 75 percent higher than in 1960, and real economic output per capita has more than doubled. To speak of the American economy as though it were "poor" or unable to buy what was once affordable is, by this standard, preposterous.

Likewise, the federal government is not poor, either in absolute terms or relative to its postwar heyday. The government's income, after adjusting for inflation, is more than three times its income in John F. Kennedy's day; government spending, also adjusted for inflation, is more than four times higher than in 1945, the peak of the mighty mobilization for World War II. The notion that taxes have been slashed to unusually low levels is simply wrong: Measured as a share of the economy, the government's receipts in the 1980s and 1990s were well in line with the postwar norm and slightly above the level of the "wealthy" 1950s and 1960s. In objective terms, the federal government is better able today to "afford" initiatives than ever before in history.

So here is another paradox: As the nation grew objectively richer, it felt subjectively poorer. Why? If government is "poor," if it is unable to "afford" things, that is because of its inability to unlock resources from entrenched claimants and reallocate them for new needs. It is not poor; it is paralyzed. It is not malnourished; it is maladaptive. It is trapped in its own past, held there like Gulliver in Lilliput by a thousand ancient commitments and ten thousand committed clients.

Microgovernment

By the middle of Bill Clinton's presidency, a peculiar term had begun to circulate through Washington: "microinitiative." Behind its emergence was a poignant story, revealing of Washington in its throes.

Clinton had come to office with grand ideas. He had staked

his 1992 campaign on an ambitious plan to make the economy more productive. People could disagree with his platform, but it had the "vision thing" in spades. At its heart was the notion, then popular in the Democratic Party, that the country needed a massive government capital-spending program to improve physical and human infrastructure: roads, bridges, job retraining, smart highways, high-speed rail, electric cars, environmental technologies, information highways, and so on. In fact, Clinton's ambitious public-investment program was the main plank of his economic platform in 1992: "In the absence of increasing investment in this country, including public investment, you can't get growth going again," he said.

Clinton came to office believing, as many of his supporters did, that his vigor and his vision and his mandate would let him restore to government something of the creativity of better days. In the opening weeks of his term, he spoke passionately and often of experimentation. In his inaugural address, he declared, "Let us resolve to make our government a place for what Franklin Roosevelt called 'bold, persistent experimentation.'" So important to him were Roosevelt's words that he repeated them in his first national address to the public, a few days before the State of the Union message: "Our every effort will reflect what President Franklin Roosevelt called 'bold, persistent experimentation,' a willingness to stay with things that work and stop things that don't." He sent the same message again in his subsequent economic address: "I have to say that we all know our government has been just great at building programs," he said. "The time has come to show the American people that we can limit them, too, that we can not only start things, but we can actually stop things." The passage was ad-libbed, and it showed a crystalline comprehension of what had gone amiss.

To make room for experimentation, however, Clinton would need to eject some of the countless experiments from yesteryear that were still hanging around. In his 1992 campaign, he had talked about change, but he never built much real support for it.

Instead, he promised more of everything to practically everyone, at no cost except to foreigners and "the rich." He promised a $200 billion "Rebuild America" fund for new infrastructure and human-capital programs. He promised to hire 100,000 new police officers and expand drug treatment. He promised national job-retraining programs, community-service jobs for welfare recipients, more money for AIDS and schools, more Medicare benefits. He promised an investment tax credit, a tax break for start-up companies, an expanded tax credit for the working poor, a children's tax credit, a tax reduction for the middle class. He promised a lot of other things besides. And, in addition to promising more spending and lower taxes, he promised to *reduce* the budget deficit.

Clinton was boxed in by his rhetoric. He had no mandate to do anything unpopular, which meant he was in no position to force Congress or the pressure groups to accept any change that was unpleasant to them. "We decided early on that we weren't doing this as an academic exercise," a Clinton adviser told *Time*. "We wanted a program that could get through Congress." Under the circumstances, his administration had little choice but to produce an economic plan that contained almost no restructuring of the government. Clinton's budget proposal in 1993, when he had his first and, as it turned out, last chance to make a serious change in Washington's entrenched priorities, was a conventional miscellany of standard Washington maneuvers. The budget did not propose the elimination of a single major or even midsize program, and its offering of mostly trivial terminations accounted for less than 5 percent of the total reductions in spending that Clinton proposed—nothing beyond the routine.

In September 1993, the president's own National Performance Review declared that "the federal government seems unable to abandon the obsolete. It knows how to add, but not to subtract." Alas, learning to subtract was not a priority for the Clinton administration. Under the heading "Eliminate Special Interest Privileges," the panel made four suggestions: eliminate highway demonstration projects mandated by Congress (these were often pork), cut unneeded air-service subsidies to small communities, and abolish the honey and the wool and mohair subsidies, which were already under heavy fire in Congress. Other eliminations were few and mainly inconsequential. When someone complained that the task force's four hundred recommendations included only fifteen program eliminations, Clinton's budget director, Leon Panetta, replied, "I would kiss the ground and thank God if we could eliminate fifteen."

Where you cannot demolish, you cannot build. After the inauguration, Clinton was trapped with no option but to scale back his "investment" agenda. Congress, demanding more by way of deficit reduction, scaled it back even more. What finally emerged, according to the Economic Policy Institute, a liberal think tank in Washington, was a fiscal 1994 federal budget that included *less* for government investment—that is, for infrastructure, education and training, and civilian research and development—than President Bush had spent the year before.

Even sadder was the fate of Clinton's national service program. More than any other initiative, national service defined his vision of what he had called "our New Covenant": Young people could work for their country to repay their student loans, learning citizenship and responsibility. "Just think of it," he rhapsodized at the 1992 Democratic convention, "millions of energetic young men and women, serving their country by policing the streets or teaching the children or caring for the sick. . . . That's what this New Covenant is all about." A year later, the end product was miniaturized by "fiscal reality," alias demosclerosis. To fulfill anything like Clinton's vision, national service needed to be a broad, national commitment, not just a showcase for a few lucky applicants. But by February, national service looked more like a pilot program than a defining initiative. That month, Clinton asked for $7.4 billion over four years— "hardly the scholarships-for-all he had initially promised," wrote Steven Waldman in *Newsweek*. "So before Clinton's plan was even introduced to Congress, it had been radically scaled back." Congress scaled it back still further, approving, in the end, only $1.5 billion over three years. In the end, the program looked more like a new ornament than a New Covenant.

Explaining why it settled for something so unrevolutionary, the Clinton administration at one point brought forward R. Sargent Shriver, John F. Kennedy's brother-in-law and the first director of the Peace Corps. "With the shortage of money now," he said, "one has to be satisfied with achieving modest goals." Imagine—a "poorer" nation than in Kennedy's day, when the federal government's budget, in constant dollars, was only a third the size of today's!

Within the administration's ranks, the reality of demosclerosis soon sank in. "You either look for fundamental structural reforms or you settle for smaller and smaller quantities of the same old programs," one of Clinton's domestic advisers told me. "Those are the only two choices." I asked him what he thought would happen. "If I had to make a bet," he said, "I'd say that, nine times out of ten, the defensive forces of the same old programs will be stronger than the offensive forces advocating new programs."

His conjecture was correct. Paul C. Light, a political scholar at the Brookings Institution in Washington, has compared presidential agendas going back to the Kennedy years, and the results speak plainly of what I call demosclerosis and what Light calls the "derivative presidency." Presidents Kennedy, Johnson, and Nixon all produced copious agendas, with two or three times as many initiatives as Clinton. "Clinton's first term," says Light, "produced just thirty-three proposals, the smallest Democratic agenda in thirty years." More telling, however, is that roughly two-thirds of the Kennedy and Johnson and Nixon agendas consisted of new programs, whereas two-thirds of Clinton's consisted of fine-tunings or enhancements of old programs—an increase in the earned-income tax credit, immigration reform, a minimum-wage increase, reauthorization of the water-pollution laws, "and a host of small adjustments to existing programs."

Clinton admired JFK and spoke of emulating FDR. In fact, Light concludes, Clinton's first-term agenda did resemble that of an earlier president: Gerald Ford. "Despite their very different political circumstances, not the least of which were 116 more House seats working in Clinton's favor, the two presidents ended up with remarkably simple derivative agendas."

And so it was that this ambitious young president emerged, by the end of his term, as a recognized master of the "microinitiative." He would deliver long State of the Union speeches in which he would reel off lists of tiny new tax credits, little enhancements of this or that program, and other marginalia. As Light notes, Clinton argued zealously for school uniforms, guaranteed overnights for hospitalized mothers, safety locks for handguns, a national registry of sex offenders, and a national tutoring initiative. As a candidate in 1992, he had ridiculed President Bush for smallness of vision, and he had sworn to change the government. By the end of his term, it was not the government that had changed, but the president.

Here, There, Everywhere

In America, sclerosis is furthest advanced within the federal government. That isn't surprising; as a general rule, the larger and more centralized a government and the more redistributive power it commands, the more it is beset by parasites and gold diggers and professional favor-brokers. But the disease is in no sense unique to the federal government.

Look, for example, at California, the largest state government. Dan Walters, a *Sacramento Bee* columnist who has been covering California state government for years, says, "The process has slowed and slowed and slowed. In terms of major policy stuff, absolutely nothing gets done." On education, health, tort reform, and other major issues that energize interest groups, there are "no major policy decisions whatever. This is a total lock-up situation."

Barry Keene, a Democrat representing the northern coast, was the state Senate majority leader when he quit in disgust in 1992. "I came to the Senate to make policy, and the legislative body stopped doing that," he said, when I spoke to him. "It was like glue in the engine. It just gradually started slowing and slowing and then came to a virtual stop." After leaving, he became president of an interest group (what else?) called the Association for California Tort Reform. When I spoke with him, he acknowledged that he had joined the problem, but what could he do? The interest groups in California, like the ones in Washington, knew they were choking the system, but none could stop lobbying until all the others did. "There is a general recognition among the interest groups that the thing is not working very well," said Dan Walters, "but as long as it is the way it is, they're going to protect whatever interest they've got."

Many Californians, like Washingtonians, blamed sclerosis on divided control of the government: Republicans in the governor's mansion, Democrats in the statehouse. But that couldn't be the whole story. In California, divided control has been common for decades, yet sclerosis steadily worsened. Others pointed to California's sagging economy, which reduced the flow of taxes in the early 1990s, making legislators' jobs nastier and more contentious. But, again, demosclerosis became glaring well before the economy sank, and it did not depart when the economy revived. So other factors must have been at work.

If you examine California's official biennial directory of full-time lobbyists, you find that, between the mid-1970s and the early 1990s, the number of companies and groups employing lobbyists more than doubled. "Our directories have been getting bigger every year we publish them," says David Hulse, a political reform specialist in the California secretary of state's office. In 1989, that office registered 783 full-time lobbyists (all of whom are required by law to register); by late 1998, less than a decade later, there were 1,279, an increase of more than 60 percent. In the past, California lobbyists worked mainly for interest groups and deep-pocketed companies. More recently, many have gone into business for themselves, as free-floating entrepreneurs. "Now you have lobbyists coming in without a client," Hulse says. Career-minded entrepreneurs register as lobbyists and then go hunting for work—and they find it. According to the California secretary of state, the amount spent lobbying the California government almost quintupled between 1980 and 1998.

In fact, the day before I talked to Barry Keene, a brand-new interest group—one representing occupational therapists—had paid him a call. They wanted to know how to lobby legislators. "It's a growing process," Keene told me. "The people who represented interest groups in Sacramento became more professional, they made more money, you had more contract lobbyists, as opposed to in-house lobbyists. You saw law firms opening offices in Sacramento providing lobbying services and appearances before administrative agencies. And that process is still evolving. You had television, you had targeted computer mail, you had phone banks, and you had the introduction of high-paid hired guns, people who knew how to manipulate these things."

Familiar stuff, all of that: the standard paraphernalia of professional parasitism in its high-growth mode. But then came something unexpected. As the legislative process died, the initiative process came alive. In theory, initiatives allow voters to pass their own laws. In practice, interest groups can use initiatives, too. "The initiative process is not truly a public process anymore," Keene said. "So when I say people do things on their own, I don't truly mean the general public. I mean the people who finance initiatives. They began circumventing the legislature. In doing so, they created a body of law that began putting a straitjacket on the setting of priorities by the legislature and the governor." In 1978, antitax activists used Proposition 13 to pass a property-tax cut for themselves, and—a classic anticompetitive maneuver—they did it in a way that favored existing property holders (themselves) at the expense of newcomers. Then came the California teachers' union, which passed an initiative requiring that about 40 percent of the state budget go to education every year.

By the early 1990s, what with initiatives, federal mandates, court orders, and legally guaranteed entitlement benefits, 85 percent or more of California's giant budget was locked in place, according to the state department of finance. Busy lobbies were working to lock in still more.

In New York City, thanks to the political clout of vested taxicab companies, the number of taxi licenses was frozen at Depression-era levels for about sixty years, from 1937 until 1996 (and even then only a few hundred additional licenses were issued). The schools of New York spend more per student than all but a few other big-city districts, yet produce dismal results. Only a third of each education dollar goes to teachers and classroom instruction; hiring a new security guard can take five layers of bureaucracy. "A Soviet-style bureaucracy has enveloped the school system," reported *The Economist*, "and powerful, obstinate unions prevent reforms from happening at anything more than a snail's pace."

Sclerotic local governments like New York's possess a perverse advantage: Their residents can flee and their credit ratings can sink—and then they are forced to reform, at least a bit. Under Mayor Rudolph Giuliani, New York City made some impressive strides. Similarly, after Philadelphia hit the fiscal wall in 1990, it renegotiated its labor contracts, thinned its workforce, and contracted out a few lines of work—for instance, the city print shop. Even so, Philadelphia's leaders couldn't bring themselves to close offices or end old programs. "What they wound up doing was proposing to close one small library in a leased building and one stable for the mounted police," noted Ronald G. Henry, the executive director of the Pennsylvania Intergovernmental Cooperation Authority. "They really have to do much more to try to make some fundamental structural changes."

If reforming a city is hard, imagine how much harder reforming Washington may be. The U.S. government can't go bankrupt, and its citizens aren't about to flee. There is no wall for it to hit, at least in the foreseeable future. And so its slide toward stagnation is that much harder to check.

For conservatives, demosclerosis means that there is no significant hope of scraping away outmoded or counterproductive liberal policies, because nothing old can be jettisoned. For liberals, it means that there is no significant hope of using government as a progressive problem-solving tool, because the method of trial and error has broken down. For politicians, it means tinkering on the margins of public policy. For the public, it means living with an increasingly dysfunctional government, one that gradually turns itself into a sort of living fossil. Only the professionals of the transfer-seeking economy have been consistently happy.

Dysfunction breeds discontent, and discontent breeds backlash, and backlash duly came. Frustrated, even enraged, a series of reformers set out to writhe free of the straitjacket. Their attacks on demosclerosis, alas, showed how little they, and the public, understood it.

7

The Reform Era

To LOOK BACK upon the 1980s and 1990s is to see what appears to be, at first blush, a period of quietude following the social and political storms of the 1960s and 1970s. The Reagan and Clinton years brought fiscal wars over deficits and culture wars over abortion and political correctness, but no Vietnam, no stagflation, no dogs and fire hoses in Alabama, and no chilling confrontations between democracy and totalitarianism. Intellectuals often complained that the Reagan period was complacent and vacuous, and that the Clinton years brought the abandonment of the activist spirit that once had energized American liberalism. The appearance, though, was partly deceiving. If American society was calmer after the 1970s, American government decidedly was not, for discontent with society had been displaced by discontent with government.

 The era beginning in 1981 and ending, perhaps, in 1996 marks the most concentrated period of governmental reformism since the Progressives swept to power in Washington and in the cities nearly a century earlier. There was, however, a difference. The Progressives largely succeeded in breaking the old cronyist machines and replacing them with a class of professional administrators and a "clean government" ethic (with mixed effects, by the way). The reformers in the Reagan-to-Clinton years failed. They did not remake government; it remade them.

For the Progressives, the problem had been corruption and greed and the heavy hands of the bosses, who favored friends and shut out adversaries and thereby (in the view of the day) created political monopolies as damaging to the public good as were the great economic trusts. More openness, more access, and above all more professionalism were the answers. By 1981, when Reagan took office, the Progressive formula had been turned on its head, although at that point few people realized the extent of the change. America's government was easily among the cleanest in the world or, indeed, in history. Endless safeguards of bureaucratic procedure and legal due process ensured that any decision that was deemed arbitrary or unfair could be challenged, first in administrative rulemaking, then in court, and finally in Congress. The civil service had been professionalized—and so, more recently and probably more importantly, had been the political class. It was now not only possible but common to be a full-time, professional lobbyist or political consultant.

And access? It was copious, redundant—so copious and redundant as to transform Washington itself into the site of a bidding war. With the old congressional seniority system weakened by the post-Watergate reformers of the 1970s, Congress now consisted of 535 individual entrepreneurs, each member chosen independently of party and president, each member a canny survivalist who could be asked to follow where the committee chairman or whip led but who could not be required to do so. For the (now) countless thousands of groups that professionally worked Washington, this meant that what you did not get from one member of Congress you could seek from another. The relationship worked the other way, too. When the politicians came calling on the lobbies for campaign money, as they did with growing brazenness, each group knew there were plenty of other lobbies, often competitors and adversaries, eager to help. If the banking chairman did not get what he wanted from the

American Bankers Association, why, the credit union people or S&L people or insurance people or securities people were only too willing to step into the breach. The culture of government, by 1981, was honest and professional and astonishingly transparent; no one hid anything. But the economics of government, by then, was that of a piranha pool, with thousands of small but sharp-toothed and very strongly motivated actors determined not to be the loser at the end of the day. Every actor's activity, of course, drew in yet more actors: that was the transfer-seeking spiral, which by the time of Reagan's election was well established. The Maryland state lottery once ran an ad campaign on the theme "If you don't play, you can't win." By the 1980s, Washington had become a kind of demented casino, whose slogan was "If you don't play, you can't win—but boy, can you lose!" Not surprisingly, everybody played.

The public, of course, was angry and disillusioned by 1980. The "trust in government" barometer had collapsed since the early 1960s. Confidence in government had been replaced with cynicism and suspicion. Among conservatives, a reform movement had arisen, in tandem with the change in the government itself. The movement was not progressivism so much as regressivism, but it was equipped with a powerful and sweeping critique of government and with a grand architecture of reform. Some liberals, too, dreamed of sweeping change. Ironically, however, although the liberal reformers and conservative reformers vied to pull Washington in opposite directions, they would soon discover they were trapped together like antagonistic prisoners thrown into the same cell. Both were mostly helpless.

If you view Washington's problems as superficial and transitory—the result of having elected this or that president, or of divided partisan control of government, or what have you—then the answer should be to elect some new leader or to consolidate power. If you think the problem is that the politicians are all the same, all empty suits wedded to the status quo, then the solution should be to elect some revolutionaries who will shake things up. If you think the problem is that reform in one direction simply goes the wrong way, then the right approach should be to try reform in the opposite direction.

As it turned out, the era of reform proved to be a uniquely useful natural laboratory for diagnosing government's condition, because many of the available permutations were tried. First the Republicans enjoyed effective control of both Congress and the White House, then the Democrats controlled both branches, and then control was divided. Far from electing empty suits, the voters on three occasions brought in strikingly fresh and energetic leaders, leaders who fervently believed in reform and who spared no effort to make it happen. And far from standing pat in moderation, the reform efforts lurched in two opposite directions.

Yet, by the end of the 1990s, the reform era had subsided into exhaustion. The voters seemed to have given up, and there was no viable reform movement anywhere in sight. The battlefield was empty, the Bastille untaken, and the adversary little more than inconvenienced. In fact, the Washington establishment was fatter and happier than ever. In this chapter I review what happened, briefly and with an eye on general patterns rather than moment-to-moment detail. In the next chapter I try to explain those patterns.

Birth of a Notion

If you wanted to identify a date when the modern attack on entrenched government was born, a reasonable choice would be September 18, 1952. That was the day when a young man named Barry Goldwater formally opened his campaign against no less a personage than Ernest W. McFarland, the majority leader of the U.S. Senate. Goldwater was, in those days, a first-rate photographer and pilot, a second-rate businessman, and a minor political figure in what was still the third-rate city of Phoenix. He set out against the odds—but, given President Truman's unpopularity, not altogether quixotically—to unseat one of the capital's leading lights. That he upset Washington by winning seemed appropriate, for Washington upset him. Goldwater pledged, on that September day, not to accept Washington but to change it, to stop the "expanding governmental bureaucracy, government-created inflation, and . . . the highest taxes ever extracted from the American citizen."

That the campaign to reform government emerged from the right was not historically inevitable, but it also was not particularly surprising. Liberals in those years—like many liberals now—were mostly content with incremental expansion of government. They were happy to put new things on top of old things, as the ideas and opportunities arose, and in those years that was still easy to do. Time, it seemed to them, was on their side. Replacing old things that worked poorly or choked off better things was never on their agenda—a fact that did more than anything else to discredit both the resulting government, which often didn't work very well, and the liberal movement, which seemed more interested in building its empire than in ensuring real-world success. Conservatives, on the other hand, realized that the longer they waited, the harder their job would be. And so the first and main postwar agenda to reform Washington was a conservative agenda.

It was Goldwater who popularized the agenda and gave it an edge of righteous anger. In 1960, he published what quickly became the blueprint, in a book mostly compiled from his speeches and written for him by a *National Review* magazine editor named L. Brent Bozell. *The Conscience of a Conservative* electrified conservatives then and inspired two generations of reformers. To read it four decades later is to be struck, almost astonished, by the extent to which it laid out a map for all the subsequent waves of conservative reform, from Goldwater himself through Ronald Reagan and right on to Newt Gingrich.

"The federal government has moved into every field in which it believes its services are needed," Goldwater wrote. "The result is a Leviathan, a vast national authority out of touch with the people, and out of their control." Change could come only when voters elected politicians who would say: "My aim is not to pass laws, but to repeal them. It is not to inaugurate new programs, but to cancel old ones that do violence to the Constitution, or that have failed in their purpose, or that impose on the people an unwarranted financial burden."

And so, Goldwater argued, powers and duties should be returned to the states, which were closer to the problems they were dealing with. (This held for civil rights, too—race relations were best handled locally.) Agricultural prices should be left to markets; he called for "prompt and final termination of the farm subsidy program." Welfare should be a private concern, since public welfare transforms its recipient "into a dependent animal creature without his knowing it." For education, the answer was not more money but higher standards. Across the board, the federal government should pull back:

> The government must begin to withdraw from a whole series of programs that are outside its constitutional mandate—from social welfare programs, education, public power, agriculture, public housing, urban renewal and all the other activities that can be better performed by lower levels of government or by private institutions or by individuals. I do not suggest that the federal government drop all of these programs overnight. But I do suggest that we establish, by law, a rigid timetable for staged withdrawal.

Goldwater's electoral collapse in the 1964 presidential race proved seminal, in two ways at once. On the one hand, the Democrats and Goldwater himself ("Extremism in the defense of liberty is no vice" and "In your heart you know he's right") succeeded in stigmatizing the conservative reform agenda as nutty and heartless, for years to come. Liberals and Presidents Johnson and Nixon were freed from any respectable intellectual counterweight to their own agendas, which vastly expanded both the reach and the shape of the government. Goldwater's failure also, however, both foreshadowed and ignited the fury of two generations of conservative activists, who were enraged at what they regarded as government's infringements on their liberties and who were now, if anything, still more enraged at the liberal establishment's contempt for them. And so began the era of sporadic assaults on "big government" that constitute, together, the best evidence on the possibility of comprehensive reform.

The reformers had a notion of what to do. To begin with, they assumed they enjoyed the support of a large portion of the public—a "silent majority," even—who shared their disgust. So they would rally their sympathizers against Washington's self-serving elites. Doing so, of course, would require bold and visionary leadership. The key was to find the general to lead a charge uphill.

They found and elected such leaders, not once but twice, both of them extraordinary men who swept to power on what appeared to be an outpouring of public support. Yet things went badly wrong—not once but twice.

The Stockman Cometh

In 1981, I arrived in Washington for the first time to do an internship at *National Journal* magazine. I had lucked into the job, not only by getting it but by alighting in Washington during the remarkable "Reagan summer"—the peak of the so-called Reagan Revolution. And the time did seem revolutionary, not only to me but to everyone. Rolling through the corridors of Congress, like a giant watermelon (as David Stockman once put it), was a reform agenda unlike any known to Capitol Hill: a big tax cut; a giant defense increase, literally more money than the Pentagon knew what to do with (the Reagan people picked a big number, doubled it, and later figured out what to buy); and, of course, the attack on the "social pork barrel" that Stockman had denounced so vividly in his *Public Interest* article six years earlier.

At the end of that legislative season, Ronald Reagan had accomplished more than anyone had thought possible. He brought about a historic shift in Washington's priorities: lower taxes, higher defense, domestic restraint. By 1984, an analysis by the Urban Institute found at the time, the Reaganites had cut taxes (relative to the projected increases they had inherited) by about 3 percent of the gross domestic product, increased defense spending by about 1 percent of GDP, and reduced nondefense program spending by about 1.5 percent of GDP. You'll notice, if you add the numbers, that something is missing. Reagan had persuaded Congress to cut domestic spending by about 10 percent in real terms, but he had originally sought reductions of twice that magnitude. Impressive as the 10 percent reduction seemed in a Washington accustomed to incremental change in only one direction, it was wholly insufficient to pay for the administration's defense increase and tax cut. In fact, the not-so-secret dirty secret was that even Stockman's original budget had failed to propose nearly enough spending cuts to do the job. Desperately, Stockman inserted a stopgap "magic asterisk" into the budget: "additional savings to be proposed." The result, famously, was the dizzying deficit that for a while turned America's government into a fiscal basket case, and that took fifteen years of turmoil to subdue. Indeed, by Reagan's second term, Congress's frantic efforts to control the deficit nudged taxes right back to the norm that had prevailed ever since Eisenhower. Nonetheless, remarkably, Reagan's policies had about doubled the national debt by the end of his first term, and had about tripled it by the end of his second.

Still, the deficit was not, perhaps, the Reaganites' most telling failure, though it was certainly their most conspicuous. Although Stockman had not managed to find the dollars he needed, he did make a respectable run at the social pork barrel. He proposed closing a number of programs—the Economic Development Administration, the Legal Services Corporation, the Appalachian Regional Commission, and so on—and reducing by about half the budgets of many others. Yet at the end of Reagan's first year, and at the end of his eight-year tenure, the programs were virtually all still there, and the money was still flowing. By the mid-

1980s, as Stockman himself complained, the Reagan administration's transportation budget (after adjusting for inflation) was 15 percent higher than Carter's, 40 percent higher than Johnson's, and 50 percent higher than Kennedy's. The subsidies for big oil, the bailouts for timber companies, the government-sponsored agricultural cartels, the command-and-control dairy program—those and all the other pillars of the social pork barrel stood tall and proud, with Reagan himself rejecting many of Stockman's proposed reductions. "We can't cause an honest business to lose money," the president would say.

What began as a revolution became a sort of annual guerrilla theater. Every year the Reagan administration would demand the elimination of the Economic Development Administration, the Legal Services Corporation, the Appalachian Regional Commission. Every year Congress would simply ignore the requests. After eight years, the government was spending relatively more of its budget on defense and debt service (especially debt service) and relatively less on ordinary domestic programs. Those were important changes in relative budgetary priorities. But Reagan left the *structure* of the government pretty much as he had found it.

Partly that was because the Democrats held majorities in the House and, after 1986, the Senate. But this could hardly have been the whole story, since Reagan enjoyed *effective* control of both chambers in his crucial first year or so (conservative Southern Democrats voted with the Republicans), and the Republicans held the Senate for most of his presidency. More of the story had to do with the dynamics of change in Washington. Cutting taxes is fun, no matter a politican's party affiliation. "There was never any doubt that a tax bill very much like the president's would pass," observed the late Herbert Stein, one of Washington's wisest and most experienced economists. "It is, after all, one of the hoary axioms of political life that a congressman should and will vote for every tax cut. When the tax cut provides some relief for all taxpayers, and when it is certified as essential by the most conservative president in fifty years, its adoption is assured." In fact, once the tax cuts got rolling, an appalled Stockman looked on as the Democrats strove to outbid the Republicans in giving away tax breaks to friendly interests, until the total tax reduction was almost double what the supply-siders had originally envisioned. As for the defense increase, it wasn't the Democrats' first choice, but it caused them no pain, and in fact it spilled a lot of gravy on its way through their districts. But chopping domestic programs out of the budget—that was no fun at all.

To begin with, the enraged lobbies rose from their roosts and flew up in Congress's face, beating their wings and shrieking—a point I won't belabor. More important, the Democrats, on principle, abhorred what Reagan (really Stockman) was trying to do. Not only was the administration out to gut, say, Legal Services on ideological grounds, thereby "defunding" what the Reaganites viewed as nests of liberal activism, but worse, the Reagan people seemed to go out of their way to violate Stockman's credo that weak claims, rather than weak clients, would be attacked. In fact, Reagan's early budgets particularly took aim at means-tested entitlements and at aid to state and local governments— the poor and city governments being notably Democratic constituencies. The big middle-class entitlements were spared. "Reagan Won't Cut Seven Social Programs That Aid 80 Million," proclaimed a *New York Times* headline in a February 1981 article announcing that the large programs for the elderly, such as Social Security and Medicare and veterans' benefits, would be off-limits to Stockman's scissors. Indeed, those programs thrived under Reagan. So what Reagan was offering wasn't even a Goldwater-style principled conservatism; it was more like "More for our people, less for their people."

Facing relatively clear sailing for tax cuts and defense increases, versus implacable Democratic opposition to reforms targeted disproportionately on Democratic constituencies, Reagan didn't have a hard time seeing what to do: win what he could, and give up the rest. In order to win his defense buildup and his tax cuts—which were always what he cared most about—he traded away the shrinking of government and the fiscal balance, which were what Stockman cared most about. The short-term result suited practically everyone. Reagan could stand opposed to big government without actually hurting anyone. (Being both tough and genial isn't really so hard, if you don't require anyone to do anything painful.) Congress, rejecting Reagan's annual laundry list of program eliminations, could ride every year to the rescue of damsels in distress, which was good politics and good for raising money from the damsels' patrons. The lobbies, like the fire department in a town full of arsonists, were strengthened by Reagan's attacks, which made buying protection, in the form of several well-paid lobbyists, more important than ever. The Defense Department got its planes and battleships, the taxpayers got their tax relief—and their grandchildren got the bill, in the form of $1.4 trillion in new national debt. The Reagan Revolution upset the old entente in Washington but replaced it with a new one—plus, of course, a $200 billion fiscal crater.

And so, in the end, pretty much everyone was happy, except Stockman, who had imagined doing something quite different. "In the final analysis, there has been no Reagan Revolution in national economic governance," Stockman wrote ruefully in 1986. "All the umbilical cords of dependency still exist because the public elects politicians who want to preserve them." The attempt at comprehensive reform had sought, he said in a metaphor that vied to outrun his deficits, to "peer deep into the veil of the future and chain the ship of state to an exacting blueprint. It can't be done. It shouldn't have been tried."

There is a classic graffito that states "God is dead.—Nietzsche. Nietzsche is dead.—God." By 1986, five years after the Reagan Revolution, the social pork barrel was still in place, and David Stockman was gone.

In a way, Reagan had never been the man to lead an attack

on big government. "He always went for hard-luck stories," wrote Stockman. "Despite his right-wing image, his ideology and philosophy always take a back seat when he learns that some individual human being might be hurt." In that respect, Reagan was just like the public. In any event, Reagan had never prepared the public for anything like what Stockman intended to do. Just the opposite, actually. In 1960, Goldwater—being Goldwater—announced that "as a practical matter spending cuts must come before tax cuts. If we reduce taxes before firm, principled decisions are made about expenditures, we will court deficit spending and the inflationary effects that invariably follow." Reagan took the same line in 1976, when he failed in his bid for the Republican nomination, and in 1978 he was still saying, "Frankly, I'm afraid this country is going to have to suffer two, three years of hard times to pay for the binge we've been on." Then, however, the supply-siders appeared on the scene, persuading themselves and Reagan that tax cuts should be the top priority. Meanwhile, Reagan scrupulously avoided talking about any specific or even troublesome reductions in programs. He was trying to persuade the public that he was sensible and sane, no mad nuclear bomber or wild-eyed budget slasher. It is no wonder that, when the time came to take action that might have made some real-life constituency unhappy, the public was unsympathetic and Reagan was half-hearted.

If at First . . .

Newt Gingrich was, if anything, even more remarkable than David Stockman, and was probably, at his peak, more powerful. At the height of his influence, in 1995, Gingrich eclipsed even the president, who was reduced to mewing that "the president is still relevant." Gingrich was a genuine visionary. He was always full of grand strategies, plans, ambitions, all of which would redefine the terms of debate or change the paradigm of government. In his early years in Congress, he spoke with blazing eyes and dizzying rhetoric of space exploration as America's next new frontier. He was a leader of a group of conservatives who championed market incentives and economic growth and supply-side optimism as an alternative to the (they argued) oppressive welfare state. The "Conservative Opportunity Society," they pointedly called their club. They set themselves up in conspicuous contrast with the grumbling negativism of traditional penny-pinching conservatives and the parched puritanism of the Religious Right. In those years, Gingrich would speak of his plans to any reporter in sight. Once, in 1988, on the way through National Airport in Washington, another reporter and I spotted "Newt," who promptly invited us to kill time at a bar where he fed us stratagems and theories while we fed ourselves beer and cocktail mix.

But he was ruthless, too, and politically agile, and among the paradigms that he intended to smash were the old and, so he believed, corrupt ways of Congress, with its deference to Old Bulls (read: Democrats' political machine) and its premium on "comity" (read: everybody scratches everybody's back). The Republicans, he and others of the young Turks believed, had settled into the part of well-fed lackeys, kept docile by Democrats who dropped scraps from the table. Only by smashing complacency could his party, and his vision, break through.

Thus Gingrich set out to take down a Democratic House speaker, and he succeeded; and then he set out to take down a Democratic majority, and he succeeded again. And then, in 1995, with President Clinton walloped and wounded, Gingrich set out to do what no House speaker had done in the twentieth century: defy the hallowed truism that the president proposes and Congress disposes. To lead the country from Capitol Hill is like trying to steer a canoe from the front. Congress is a squabbling mob of egos. It can't normally make quick decisions; it can't collectively explain itself to the public; it can't readily develop a unified agenda. Gingrich set out to do all three, by becoming the very personification of the revolutionary 104th Congress.

Gingrich was Reagan's admirer and heir, but his revolution was of a different complexion. He had no Cold War or—therefore—defense buildup to worry about, and, unlike Reagan, he was not inclined to accept half a loaf and then blithely claim victory. Even when he was inclined to compromise, his troops, notably the seventy-three newly elected Republican "freshman" representatives, were not. They detested Washington and its ways, and made no secret of their determination not to be bought off or seduced. Unlike Reagan, they were prepared to go down fighting. Cut government, cut taxes: that was all they cared about. Their zeal and radicalism gave them unbounded energy and unusual group discipline, which they placed at Gingrich's disposal. Still more important, their "Contract with America" gave them an agenda, a flag around which to rally.

Gingrich, for his part, combined realism with millennialism in a peculiar but potent mixture. Not everything would change that month or that year, he warned as he officially assumed the speakership in January 1995. But, he believed, the new Republican ascendancy marked a turning point. "These are the early stages of a genuine revolution," he told the *Washington Times* that January. Gingrich would use his new House majority as a battering ram to break through the old power structure and so open the way for the long march backward from big government. "What I can do between now and Easter," he said then, "is break up the Washington logjam, shift power to the fifty states, break up all the liberal national organizations—and make them scramble to the state capitals in Texas, Georgia and in Missouri." At that electrifying hour, it seemed possible that he might succeed once again.

Say Good Night, Newt

To say that Gingrich and his troops failed altogether would be wrong. They completely overhauled the country's welfare system, which had been dysfunctional for so long. They put recipients on time limits, they revoked the program's status as an open-ended "entitlement" that paid for as much welfare as was demanded, and they returned many of the decisions to the states, which were supposed to move recipients into jobs. For the welfare reformers, a few things went right. First, the issue had risen to the "top of the mind" of ordinary voters, who cared enough to notice what the politicians were doing. Second, both parties were promising change, with Clinton himself having promised, in his 1992 presidential campaign, to "abolish welfare as we know it." Third, welfare recipients are a weak lobby. The reform that emerged from the Republican Congress, with its time limits on benefits and its "cashing out" of what had been an open-ended entitlement program, may not have been perfect (what is?), but it was a genuine landmark.

Also a landmark, in a smaller but still notable way, was the Republicans' reform of several major farm programs. Goldwater had griped about them. Stockman had griped about them. But no one could touch them. In 1996, however, the Gingrich Congress was able to bring off a coup. Many grain farmers, especially younger ones, were chafing under the old-style program, with its heavy-handed rules about how much they could plant and its occasional payments for *not* planting. Moreover, farm prices were high, which meant that federal support payments were low. The Republicans figured out that they could afford to buy off the farmers by offering them more subsidy money in the near term in exchange for structural reforms. Instead of trying to manipulate or second-guess market prices, the government would offer wheat and corn farmers straight cash in generous quantities. (The payments were supposed to dwindle over time but—surprise!—didn't.) "I think what finally happened is those old boys in the commodity groups said, 'That's just too much money to leave on the table,'" a farm lobbyist told me at the time. The result, though modest in breadth (it applied mainly to wheat and corn), was a model of creative reformist thinking. The government continued spending on farmers, but it bought a more flexible, less intrusive program.

In any ordinary Congress, reforming welfare and the largest of the farm programs would have amounted to a sterling record. But this, of course, was no ordinary Congress. The Republicans had set their sights on *comprehensive* reform, which is what made their effort so interesting from my point of view. They planned to cut taxes *and* kill whole cabinet agencies *and* overturn burdensome regulations *and* return powers to the states. It was the entire Goldwater litany.

And so, in spring 1995, Gingrich's budgeters proposed eliminating about three hundred programs, including some big ones, and three cabinet agencies (Commerce, Education, Energy). Then came the months-long war of attrition. To pass his budget without the Democrats' help, Gingrich needed the support of nearly all his troops—and even for this "revolutionary" Congress, the temptation to rescue damsels in distress was irresistible. By the time the budget had been passed by the House, it killed only about thirty of the original three hundred, according to Stephen Moore of the Cato Institute, a Washington think tank. The House Budget Committee chairman had hoped for about $15 billion in reductions in subsidies for business—the "corporate welfare" that brighter Republicans, such as Stockman, knew had to be attacked if the Republicans were to seem principled in their attack on the welfare state. There is no particularly good way to figure what counts as "corporate welfare," but a reasonable guess would be $50 billion or more at that time; so $15 billion was a fairly big bite. But the House's final budget reduced this box of goodies by only about $1.5 billion.

That was what happened just in Gingrich's House, before the argument shifted to the less radical Senate. The Senate declined to revoke even a single major government commitment to any powerful constituency. Even after the Senate was done, still to come were Clinton's veto, the Republicans' disastrous shutdown of the government, and their final collapse. So, at the end of the day, what was the score?

The Appalachian Regional Commission, the Corporation for Public Broadcasting, the Tennessee Valley Authority, the National Endowment for the Arts—all were longtime objects of conservatives' scorn, and all survived. So did the Economic Development Administration, Amtrak, and the Legal Services Corporation. So did the federal peanut program, that 1934 "temporary assistance" requiring, sixty years later, that farmers have licenses to grow peanuts. The Republican House couldn't muster a majority to kill it, partly because the leadership feared that the whole farm bill, with those cherished grain reforms, would collapse if the peanut diehards deserted. "It just affirms that getting rid of farm welfare is much harder than getting rid of social welfare," said a dejected Representative Christopher Shays, the Republican who led the fight against peanuts. The Commerce and Education and Energy Departments lived on. Cato's Moore noted that, by 1997, spending had actually *risen* by 1.3 percent for the thirty-eight biggest programs the Gingrich people had slated for demolition.

It's interesting, in this connection, to plot eliminations as a sort of fever chart of demosclerosis. I mentioned that, in eight years, the Reagan administration managed to kill all of four major programs, and that in fiscal 1993, the Bush administration tried to get rid of 246 small items (most of them not full-scale programs but projects and grants and the like) and speared only eight. President Clinton's hard-won 1993 budget deal managed to eliminate only forty-one small programs, worth a total of about $1.3 billion, or less than one-thousandth of the budget—even though Clinton, unlike Bush, was working with a Congress that his party controlled.

The Gingrich Republicans tried much harder than Clinton or than Bush—harder even than Reagan. In their "revolutionary" mode, they excised just over two hundred items, according to my count based on congressional figures. That was a better score than Clinton's forty-one, and a handful of the dead were worth noticing: the Interstate Commerce Commission, the

Bureau of Mines, the U.S. Travel and Tourism Administration, and the congressional Office of Technology Assessment. Most, however, were akin to the Interior Department's $1 million locomotive fuel-cell program. Better than nothing, yes; but the grand total was about $4 billion, or a quarter of 1 percent of the budget, so Gingrich's revolution was in fact operating only in the narrow margins at the edges of the government. And junking even those gewgaws had thrown the revolutionaries into pitched battle against the dug-in lobbies and the White House and the congressional Democrats, all of whom lost no chance to portray Gingrich as driving a cleaver through the marrow of the government.

The reform effort was exhausting, thankless, and mostly futile. Understandably, the Republicans soon subsided into torpor. For fiscal 1997, they managed to eradicate twenty-seven items, according to congressional data. For 1998, the figure was something less than half of that; the dollar figures, microscopic. "Every year it gets tougher to get program terminations," one Republican congressional aide told me in 1998. The Republicans were spent, and the programs they had attacked were, if anything, more deeply entrenched than ever.

In political terms, the Gingrichites' efforts bought them much less than nothing. Their shutdown of the government and their take-no-prisoners rhetoric alienated the public and rehabilitated a sagging Clinton. The second Gingrich Congress learned its lesson. Whimpering, humiliated, in 1997 it signed an utterly conventional budget deal with Clinton, making no pretense of reform. In 1998, it passed a laughingstock $216 billion highway bill, so bloated with goodies—bike paths, hiking trails, bus museums, parking garages, research grants, and much more—that Bill Clinton called it fiscally irresponsible (before, that is, he signed it). "This bill is the best indication that the Republican Revolution is over," Shays, the Republican congressman, told *The Washington Post*, as it became clear that most Republicans were supporting the monster. No one argued with him. Soon afterward, the House Republicans got busy impeaching the president. Soon after that, Gingrich was gone. Reagan had projected at least the illusion of conservative success in the war on big government, by surrendering while declaring victory; but Gingrich had been simply annihilated.

"Courage"

One day, at a conference a year or so after the Gingrich "revolution" collapsed, I found myself sitting in the audience next to a senior aide to one of the fiercest antigovernment conservatives of the Gingrichite class of 1994. At the front of the room, a panel was talking about reasons the attempt to grab the government by the horns and wrestle it down had resulted in such an ugly impaling. The man next to me, a true believer, wasn't buying the clever political analysis he was hearing. "Courage," he kept saying, like a man rubbing worry beads, "courage." The problem, he told me, was that Gingrich and his crew had lost their nerve. In the winter of 1995 and 1996, when the government was shuttered during the impasse with President Clinton and public opinion turned against the Republicans, Gingrich had given way instead of fighting on.

Who, I wondered at the time, could possibly believe that? If there was one attribute that Gingrich manifestly didn't lack, it was courage. He had shown far more of it than had the conservatives' hero, Ronald Reagan. The problem wasn't soft leadership, and so replacing Gingrich wasn't the solution.

Maybe the problem, then, was the conservative agenda. The public didn't like what it saw, or what it was told it saw. Hadn't Gingrich steered too far to the right, misreading his mandate and so careening into the gutter? No doubt. Moreover, Gingrich controlled only half of one of three branches of the government. So maybe a real test of demosclerosis would be for a president and a Congress to try a dramatic reform together. And maybe this reform should try not to take things from the people but to give them things, things they said they wanted. As it happens, that experiment, too, was essayed.

The Liberals Try

On September 23, 1993, President Clinton took the unusual step of summoning both houses of Congress to a joint session. From the House rostrum he looked out over the Congress, and beyond it to the public, to announce what would be by far the most ambitious policy initiative of his presidency. "Those who do not now have health-care coverage will have it, and for those who have it, it will never be taken away," he said—a breathtaking promise. "So let us agree on this: whatever else we disagree on, before this Congress finishes its work next year, you will pass, and I will sign, legislation to guarantee this security to every citizen of this country."

A universal federal health program had been on Democrats' agenda for a long time. President Johnson had gotten as far as creating the Medicare program for the elderly. That was a step of momentous importance, but it brought the liberal dream of universality no closer and possibly even pushed the dream further away. By increasing the demand for medical care and pouring in federal money, Medicare helped drive up health-care prices. Then, when the government tried to reduce its burgeoning costs by cutting its Medicare payments, doctors and hospitals made up the difference by shifting costs to private customers—businesses and insurance companies. The private customers reacted by banding together to cut costs—that was "managed care" and its variants—and also, of course, by raising health-insurance rates, to the point where tens of millions of Americans couldn't afford the insurance or weren't offered it by their employers. By 1993, when Clinton presented his program, 35 million people were uninsured. Most of them did get health care—for instance, from emergency rooms—but that only put more pressure on the rest of the system.

Clinton responded with a 1,342-page health bill that was fantastically complicated. It set up an entity called the National Health Board. This "would have many difficult tasks to perform," noted the Congressional Budget Office (CBO) in its analysis of the plan: "establishing a national program for managing the quality of care, developing a national information system for health care, establishing the initial target for the per capita premium for each regional alliance, determining the inflation factor for each regional alliance, estimating the market shares for each health plan in each regional alliance, developing risk-adjustment factors, and recommending modifications to the benefit package."

That was just one entity's portfolio. The proposed regional health alliances would have had "an even broader, and possibly more demanding, set of responsibilities." They would have to be purchasing agents, contract negotiators, welfare agencies, financial intermediaries, payment collectors, and more. Students of government found no example of any existing agency administering a portfolio of responsibilities as dense and as internally conflicted as was envisioned for Clinton's health alliances. "Any one of these functions," said the CBO dryly, "could be a major undertaking for an existing agency with some experience, let alone for a new agency that would have to perform them all."

In 1994, a proposal that required the government to do so much at once might as well have been written on Mars. It was an extravagant gesture of denial, a proposal that seemed serenely untroubled by such details as government's actual condition on the planet Earth in the 1990s. It risked straining an already overstressed, overextended government to the breaking point, and in doing so it risked dragging Washington's already low credibility to fathomless new depths. If people hated government before, imagine their ire when they could blame it for whatever they didn't like about their health care. Whether the program would have damaged the health-care system was a contentious question, but in any case it would almost certainly have wrecked the government.

The health-care effort was, of course, a legislative debacle. As *Congressional Quarterly* noted at the time, five major committees and a flock of secondary committees struggled trying to draft bits and pieces of the overhaul bill. "In the end," reported the magazine, "none of the bills both met Clinton's requirement for universal coverage and had enough support to pass." In August 1994, the Democratic Congress simply gave up, humiliating itself and Clinton. Worse, the plan so frightened voters that it played perhaps the leading part in the public's gut-punch to Democrats in the 1994 elections, which handed Congress to the Republicans and thereby put Newt Gingrich in business.

I'm the first to agree that placing the health-care fiasco side by side with Stockman's or Gingrich's Goldwaterian revolutions is putting an apple with two oranges. Ideologically, ClintonCare could not have been more different from the conservative reform efforts. Cutting back government was the last thing the liberal reformers wanted to do. Still, the debacle is worth examining in the context of demosclerosis. As a natural experiment in the dynamics of reform, it makes a useful complement to the Reagan and Gingrich efforts. If the problem was merely the particular direction in which the Republican reformers wanted to take the country—well, here was a different direction, to put it mildly. No Republican root-canal politics this time! No vampire Stockman lunging with a dagger at the country's farmers and pensioners and students! Moreover, here again was an attempt at *comprehensive* reform. The plan was primarily aimed at reforming the private sector, not the government, but its passage would have required a vast array of changes that would all need to be held together through the legislative process. As the Medicare problems had shown, and as the architects of the Clinton health bill were well aware, reforms that modified only one part of the system could simply transfer problems elsewhere.

Finally, for believers in the "gridlock" view of the world, this time the stars really did seem right. Gingrich ran into Clinton's veto. Reagan enjoyed effective control of both chambers of

Congress in 1981, but after that the Democrats reasserted themselves. In 1993, by contrast, the president held a majority in both houses of Congress, and he thought he held a mandate. Indeed, in 1993 and much of 1994, practically everybody expected some sort of grandiose health plan to pass. Given the public's annoyance and businesses' distress with the system as it stood, the Republicans couldn't simply fold their arms and say no to everything, nor were they inclined to. "For the first time in this century," Clinton told Congress in his September 1993 speech, "leaders of both political parties have joined together around the principle of providing universal comprehensive health care. It is a magic moment, and we must seize it."

So why did Clinton fail? The reasons, it turns out, were not altogether unlike the reasons for the very different Gingrich and Stockman failures.

To begin with, Clinton failed to prepare the public to make some choices that weren't altogether pleasant. Actually assembling a health plan involved some trade-offs that could be ignored while merely electioneering for one. In fact, like Reagan in 1980, Clinton did the opposite of preparing the public. In that speech of September 23, he promised "a comprehensive package of benefits over the course of an entire lifetime, roughly comparable to the benefit package offered by most Fortune 500 companies." He promised to make the system simpler: "simpler for the patients and simpler for those who actually deliver health care." He promised less red tape and paperwork. He promised to cut down on fraud and abuse. He promised to increase the quality of care, of medical research, and of health information. And he promised to do all of that at effectively no cost. "The vast majority of the Americans watching this tonight will pay the same or less for health-care coverage that will be the same or better than the coverage they have tonight. That is the central reality."

Reality? With those words, the president attained a pinnacle of unreality that was positively dizzying. Coverage for everyone forever, complete with Fortune 500 benefits—at lower cost! Increased accountability, less fraud, better quality control—all with less red tape! Although a good program might have squeezed some waste from the system, over the longer term no program of any sort can increase quantity, increase quality, and decrease cost simultaneously. Clinton was promising to defy the economic laws of gravity. It was supply-side health reform, and when, inevitably, the real-world details began seeping out, they weren't what the public had expected. With the quiet support of the Republicans, the Health Insurance Association of America launched a $14 million ad campaign in which a young professional couple, "Harry and Louise," were seen examining the health-care bill and finding, as an appalled Louise said, "This plan forces us to buy our health insurance through these new, mandatory government health alliances." That wasn't what Clinton had promised.

Meanwhile, by spring 1994, it was becoming clear that the same process of piecemeal dismemberment that had torn apart Stockman's budget package, and that would later dismantle Gingrich's, was doing the same to Clinton's health plan. I've said several times that lobbies aren't evil—or if some are, no one can agree on which. They are doing their job, which means both stirring the pot for new benefits and making sure they don't get left behind as others mobilize. When Washington cranks up an effort to reform a seventh of the economy at a single blow, every group in the country is potentially affected, and so every lobby faces the same stark choice: get in or get trampled. The Center for Public Integrity, a Washington research group, did some counting and concluded that Clinton's health-care reform was, as of that time, "the most heavily lobbied legislative initiative in United States history." Hundreds of groups spent cumulatively more than $100 million to influence the reform effort, according to the center's rough estimate; about a hundred law firms, lobbying firms, and public-relations companies were retained; dozens of former officials of at least three administrations went to work for health-care interests. Political donations from health groups grew by a third, reported Citizen Action. Exemplifying the Newtonian law of transfer-seeking (on average, every lobbying effort provokes an equal and opposite lobbying effort), when the Clinton administration staged a "Health Care Security Express" bus tour, a coalition called Citizens Against Rationing Health mounted a counteroffensive bus tour of its own. Groups scrambled desperately, and expensively, to be included in the package of government-assured health benefits. The chiropractors' lobby spent $2.8 million on advertising and lobbying and nearly tripled its campaign contributions, reported Jim Drinkard of the Associated Press. It "also produced videos for its members to show in waiting rooms to their patients," Drinkard wrote. "And it compiled a massive database of 350,000 patient names in twenty congressional districts and four states."

For the parasite economy, the health mobilization was a shot of adrenaline straight into a vein—or a splash of gasoline onto a fire. The reform effort launched dozens of groups and fed hundreds (thousands?) of lobbyists. A dozen large companies formed the Corporate Health Care Coalition; a coalition of health insurers and business associations formed the Voluntary Purchasing Cooperative Coalition; sixteen big-city hospitals formed the National Association of Urban Access Hospitals. In preparation for the fight, health-related political action committees sprang up. Two hundred of them were active in the 1991–1992 election cycle, of which about four dozen were new; in the six months following the election, at least another ten health PACs registered with the Federal Election Commission. The pathologists formed a political action committee, as did the plastic surgeons, the anesthesiologists, and others. The initiative was a veritable jobs program for lobbyists. "The players in the [health-care] reform debate seem afraid not to hire scads of consultants," wrote Julie Kosterlitz in *National Journal*, adding that "consultants, naturally, are ecstatic." "It's unmanaged competition," crowed one overjoyed public-relations executive.

Unfortunately for the Clinton plan, or for any suitable substitute, passing a coherent reform—as opposed to a random one—required holding the parts together at least long enough to get it passed. Instead the knobs and buttons and screws were being pulled off left and right, and every time the bill lost a working part, there was less consensus on how to fix it. The committees on Capitol Hill were overwhelmed and submerged by the complexity of the task and the chaos of the teeming interest groups. After a time, as the effort on Capitol Hill continued, the health reform was like the car that keeps rolling after its engine falls out. The thing went for a while on momentum and then suddenly, shockingly, collapsed. A few months later, in the congressional elections, the Democrats collapsed with it. The winners were the Republicans, who would do plenty of their own losing in the following year, and the parasite economy, which maintained its perfect record of winning no matter who else loses.

Common Elements

Taken by itself, the Reagan failure or the Gingrich failure or the Clinton failure can be attributed to particular circumstances of this or that sort. Reagan had other fish to fry; Gingrich seemed overzealous and his agenda was too right-wing to pass; Clinton overpromised and his agenda was too left-wing to pass. And so on. Certainly the American system was designed to make wholesale reform difficult and to put brambles in the path of radical leaders. Political theorists have suggested that the founders understood that their system would run, so to speak, in two quite different political modes. Normally government's activities would be fragmented and transactional, and the public would pay only spotty attention, if it paid any at all. Only occasionally, and under unusual circumstances, would some major issue rise to the forefront of public debate and engage the country's attention, and thus only occasionally would some large change of direction be produced. In that case, perhaps Stockman and Gingrich and

Clinton were all expecting too much, more than the system was ever designed to deliver.

Yet the surprise in the stories of the two Goldwaterian reforms and, to a lesser extent, Clinton's massive health-care effort was not their failure to change the world overnight. The surprise was the completeness of the reformers' destruction, given the mandate they seemed to have enjoyed. The public was unhappy with its government. It elected leaders who promised "change." On several occasions, the public appeared to have voted for large-scale, nonroutine change—delivering precisely the sort of mandate that is supposed to be capable of overriding Washington's "business as usual" mode. But then the public seemed to turn against the reformers, not just disaffectedly but savagely, and the reforms were blocked. So maybe the particularistic explanations, though true as far as they go, aren't enough. Taken together, the three big reform efforts present enough general similarities to warrant some further explaining—in fact, some rethinking of the standard picture of how government works, and what to expect from it.

8

Government's End

IN THE SUMMER 1989 issue of *The National Interest* magazine, an obscure State Department functionary named Francis Fukuyama proclaimed the end of history. One way to achieve renown is to be audaciously misunderstood, and Fukuyama certainly achieved that. Obviously, history had not come to an end; not even the sort of great-power geopolitical history of which Fukuyama was writing had come to an end. Fukuyama, however, was using the word "history" in a particular and rather curious sense. He was a thinker in the tradition of G.W.F. Hegel, the early nineteenth-century German philosopher who viewed history as a steady progress through successive stages of human organization, with freedom gradually increasing. In the Hegelian tradition, history itself could be seen as unfolding through a dialectical process, as conflicts between and within governmental and economic regimes worked themselves out. Thesis, antithesis, synthesis.

But what if there no longer was any coherent, sustainable alternative to the Western system of liberal democracy? What if the last big conflict had been resolved? Then history, in Hegel's peculiar sense, was over. True, there continued to be feudal states, monarchies, tyrannies, military governments, dictatorships, theocracies, and even, here and there, the odd spot of lingering communism. The great ideological battle over how best to manage a human society, however, was finished. "The exhaustion of viable systematic alternatives to Western liberalism," Fukuyama wrote, had led to "the end point of mankind's ideological evolution and the universalization of Western liberal democracy as the final form of human government."

In effect, he was saying that if you want to know how the most successful, sustainable sort of human society will be organized in the future—well, look around. This is it. True, there will be plenty of variations on the theme, many local and regional differences, and many struggles and much change. The mixture of elements within the structure of liberal societies will be constantly in flux, and there will be more than enough worldly events to fill the history books of the future. But the big question, said Fukuyama, the (literally) history-making question, had been settled.

Fukuyama's idea made a splash partly because it was audacious and partly because, with the fall of communism and the Berlin Wall, its timing was good. But partly it also quite aptly captured the common feeling that something had changed fundamentally in the world: that the arrow of history had, with the evolution of liberal capitalism, reached a point from which there would be no turning back. Having emerged from many millennia of struggle for control of human society, Western liberalism had now established itself as not just a phase in that struggle but as its one really successful outcome.

I am no Hegelian, and I take sweeping claims, including Fukuyama's, with a grain of salt. Still, by the time Fukuyama's thesis had aged a decade, it seemed to have worn pretty well. It also served as a useful reminder. History is turbulent and change is constant, but deep social forces can conspire to produce long periods of equilibrium, from which radical change in any direction is difficult, perhaps even impossible without the stimulus of some outside shock or catastrophe (shades, here, of Mancur Olson). And it is possible, even probable, that, in the structural sense, the American government has reached such a stage: a kind of steady state from which it may be dislodged by some powerful outside force but from which it cannot dislodge itself.

In other words, it is possible that the government has reached its end, in a sense somewhat like Fukuyama's concept of "end." No, government isn't dead, as is clear to anyone who pays taxes or draws Social Security. But its overall scope and shape are no longer negotiable. They have evolved to a state from which they cannot, if you will, unevolve.

True, there will be change in the mix of programs and in the claims on the federal purse of various needs and functions. As baby boomers age, pension spending will grow as a share of the total, and education spending may diminish. Defense will rise and fall and rise and fall. Washington will change, sometimes wrenchingly, and will face difficult choices between quite different sorts of policies. Politicians and activists and interest groups will tussle and shout as though the very future of democracy were at stake. There will be sound and fury aplenty. But signifying how much? If you want to know basically how the American government will look for the indefinite future—well, look around. Taxpayers will not allow the government to do a great deal more than it does. Sorry, liberals. The client groups, however, will not allow the government to do much less than it does. Sorry, conservatives. Goldwaterian reformers who dream of making Washington a small town again, or even a significantly smaller town, might as well leave the pumpkin patch and go home. Above all, politicians and the electorate can tinker with parts of the government, but they cannot make it coherent or rational, and only now and then can they reform it more than marginally. Sorry, voters.

In effect, having passed through a minimalist stage in its first 150 or so years and then an expansionist stage in its next fifty years, Washington has trapped itself in a new equilibrium. It has become a sort of sprawling organism, its many parts not particularly good at solving social problems but extremely good at surviving from year to year and at serving assorted clients. And this evolution *cannot be undone*.

This is, I'm the first to agree, a fairly strong claim. It is certainly not the only reading of the situation, and if it is true, it seems bleak. Actually, it's not so bleak, but I'll get to all that in Chapter 10. Here, let me focus on the elements of the case for government's end, in that particular evolutionary sense of "end."

Dinner at Mancur's

Start with a thought experiment, one that goes back to Mancur Olson's problem of collective action, in which, for reasons as fundamental as arithmetic, large and diverse populations have trouble working together even when doing so is strongly in their interest. You are one of, say, four people eating together at a restaurant. The four will share the bill equally. The bill is presented, and everyone is horrified. It seems that you noticed that if you ordered a $10 appetizer of snail-darter soup, you could eat the whole thing while paying only $2.50 for the privilege. But the other three made the same calculation, so everybody indulged. And so everybody ordered dessert, and wine, and aperitifs, and entrees of beer-fed, hand-massaged beef, and more.

This problem is not hard to solve. The four diners could talk to one another as they order and exchange information about what they'll have. If someone suggests something very expensive, someone else might cough or frown. They might reach an understanding of about how much their dinner should cost and tailor their choices accordingly.

Now, however, change the scenario in only one respect: Put the dinner under, say, the New Orleans Superdome, and put, say, 10,000 diners around the table. Each diner knows what he orders, can see what the five or ten people to either side of him order, and can talk to those people and maybe a few others. Now the problem is greatly magnified—so greatly, in fact, that it becomes a different sort of problem, in two ways.

First, the incentive to overdo your order is, arithmetically, much larger. If you order an extra dessert that costs $10, you pay only an additional tenth of a cent ($10 divided by 10,000 diners). No one who isn't paying special attention to your order will notice the difference. In fact, for a tenth of a cent, no one would even bother to find out what you're ordering. Second, not only is the problem much more serious, but the solution is much more elusive as well. If you wanted to deter dessert ordering, what would you do? Giving up your own dessert, if that's all that happens, is unsatisfactory: You lose your dessert, but your share of the bill falls by only a tenth of a cent. Maybe you can persuade the five people on either side of you to give up dessert. If all eleven of you do so, each of you saves 1.1 cents. Congratulations. If you stand on the table and shout, maybe you can persuade a hundred people to skip dessert. Now you're getting somewhere: Each of these heroic sacrificers will lose his dessert while reducing his dinner bill—and everybody else's—by a dime.

Note a further problem. The more people you try to persuade, the more patchy the results will be. If I make a dessert-skipping deal with the man to my left and the woman to my right, chances are that I've had some friendly chat with them over appetizers and have established at least some rudimentary level of trust. Plus, of course, each of the three of us sees what the others are ordering, so we can verify that all three of us have kept the bargain. But for a cluster of a hundred to know or even watch each other is much harder. You might have to set up some sort of monitoring process, and even then the incentive to cheat would be large, because if Jones breaks the deal and orders dessert while others keep their promises, Jones gets dessert *and* saves a dime on his dinner tab. So saving even this one dime each by organizing a dessert boycott among a hundred diners, though possible, is difficult. And, of course, a hundred diners are still only 1 percent of the total, and a dime is still only a dime.

Now try to imagine overcoming the dessert problem around the whole table of 10,000 diners, half of whom (say) cannot even clearly see the other half. To make the situation challenging, add a further condition. Rather than being limited to 10,000, this dinner is open to anyone who pays a small—and, proportionately, shrinking—gate fee. (Remember, setting up a pressure group or hiring a lobbyist becomes relatively easier every year, as technology improves and communications costs fall and so on.) In fact, more and more diners are attracted to the meal, because if you don't join in the festivities you may not eat. (Remember, failing to play the lobbying game against your competitors can cost you dearly.) So the dinner grows and grows, and the newcomers are strangers to everybody present. Why trust them? Under the circumstances, there's no very compelling reason for anyone to do anything except order the best meal he can.

Remember, what you're up against here is arithmetic: If you sacrifice, you know what you lose, but you may gain nothing or next to nothing, because you can't be assured that more than a handful of others will follow suit. No, correction: You *can* be assured that most people will *not* follow suit. Most people will look around the table and, being patriotic or communitarian but not blind or feebleminded, make the same calculation: Ms. Patriot's sacrifice is unlikely to be emulated by more than a few other people. After all, everyone understands the arithmetic. Even if you sacrifice, the gesture is likely to be wasted, because many other people won't. What would have been your dessert will end up on someone else's plate. Not being in the business of making futile gestures, you decline to sacrifice. Because everybody else makes the same calculation, the prophecy is self-fulfilling.

By now you no doubt see where this analogy is going. Government is the dinner table, and its client groups are the diners. I've often emphasized that lobbies aren't evil, and now that point comes more sharply into focus. In fact, viewing lobbies as rapacious or unpatriotic completely misconstrues the situation, by turning a very difficult arithmetical problem into a facile moral one. To reach the bad result in which collective action fails, you don't need to assume the diners are greedy or selfish or out to hurt their fellow citizens. You need only assume they're *rational*.

In the example of the Superdome dinner, the alert reader may have recognized a case of the problem that Mancur Olson worked through in 1965 in *The Logic of Collective Action*—the same problem I discussed briefly in Chapter 2. As Olson himself put the case, "The fairly small (or intermediate) group has a fair chance that voluntary action will solve its collective problems, but the large, latent group cannot act in accordance with its common interests so long as the members of the group are free to further their individual interests."

Another useful way to think about this lamentable situation is in terms of a classic economic conundrum that economists have called "the tragedy of the commons." The problem appears where you have a limited resource that's open to all comers. Suppose, for instance, you have a common forest and many independent loggers. Each logger will rush to cut down and sell as many trees as possible, before everyone else takes all the lumber. The forest is badly overlogged. In fact, chances are that it will soon be destroyed. This problem arises again and again: The overhunting of the buffalo was a classic and devastating case; a more recent one was the overhunting of elephants in Africa. In a common-resource situation, if everyone tries to win, everybody loses. Note the apt use of the word "tragedy" for this situation instead of "conspiracy" or "immorality." Most people in the commons are acting not out of greed or depravity, but out of the impulse to survive in the world as they find it. Good intentions, or at least honest intentions, breed collective ruin.

Something similar happens with a run on government, which is what the Olsonian problem creates. The universe of public policies is a kind of commons. If you see others rushing to lobby for favorable laws and regulations, you rush to do the same so as not to be left at a disadvantage. But the government can do only so much. Its resource base and management ability are limited, and its adaptability erodes with each additional benefit that interest groups lock in. In fact, the more different things it tries to do at once, the less effective it tends to become. Thus if everybody descends on Washington hunting some favorable public policy, government becomes rigid, overburdened, and incoherent. Soon its problem-solving capacity is despoiled. Everybody loses.

So what is the answer? There is no answer. In the Superdome-dinner situation as I've set it up, or in the forest situation, the combination of rational actors and Olsonian arithmetic is not beatable by any quantity of good intentions. Asking all the world's fishermen to please, pretty please, voluntarily limit their catch may help a little around the margins, but, as we know, it cannot save the world's fishing stocks. Instead, you need to change the situation.

Leadership and Followership

Mancur Olson, needless to say, appreciated this problem. He understood the difficulty of reforming a government consisting of countless thousands of programs and benefits and transfers "owned" by countless thousands of clients. A couple of years before he died, I asked him what to do. Well, he said, each of the tiny minorities represented by a client group can be easily beaten by the *united* opposition of a large majority. The trick was to assemble the majority. To do that, you would need two things. First, members of the broad public—the people supporting the lobbies around the dinner table, so to speak—need to understand the trap they're in, so that they appreciate that there really is a general problem and a collective payoff if everybody gives up dessert. Second, you need a leader with the vision to assemble a reform package, and with the political skills to sell the deal and keep it together.

In effect, you need to add a new element to the Superdome dinner: the possibility that somebody with a megaphone will have either the authority or the prestige to lead the diners in making a deal to forgo dessert. Ideally, this leader would also be in a position to enforce the deal or at least to offer some general assurance that it would stick. "I won't rescind dessert until I have a written commitment from at least 90 percent of our diners," this leader might say, "and then I'll appoint monitors who will report to me on what everybody is ordering."

Consider the case again from a slightly different angle: Escaping the tragedy of the commons requires that some person or institution or group would assume ownership or stewardship of the common resource. For a forest, that could mean ownership by a private party or stewardship by the Forest Service; for the fisheries, it could mean some sort of treaty commitment (as with whales). For the government in Washington, it means giving reformers enough political power to "own" the government, as it were, long enough to assemble a reform package and make it stick. With committed leadership and committed followership, getting a handle on the government should be possible.

Now some good news. We know, for a fact, that a reform along those lines is possible, because it has been done.

In 1986, Congress (then split between a Republican Senate and a Democratic House) and President Reagan did what many old-timers in Washington said could never be done: They pushed through a wholesale cleanup of the tax code. Jimmy Carter, in the 1970s, called the tax code a disgrace to the human race. If that was true, then by the mid-1980s the code was also a disgrace to chimpanzees and hyenas. It had become a microcosm of the government as a whole: a sprawling mess of handouts and favors and gimmicks and shelters, a deluxe condominium for parasites. As the code descended further into incoherence and overcomplexity, enlightened Democrats began calling for reform. Republicans, not wanting to lose the issue, jumped on board. In 1985, the Reagan administration proposed sharply curtailing loopholes and using the money to reduce tax rates. In 1986, with a hard push from the president, the tax-reform bill passed. At one blow, it swept away years' worth of accumulated tax breaks that had distorted the economy and acted as a full-employment program for tax lobbyists.

Before the reform, there were so many tax shelters that people with $100,000 incomes were paying only half the official 50 percent marginal rate on their last dollars earned. After their loopholes had been plugged and their rates reduced, they paid as much as ever, and the poor paid less. On balance, tax reform was a takeaway from the lobbying industry, not a giveaway to the rich. With tax rates lower, people had less reason to lobby for loopholes. After all, once your top tax rate is cut from 50 percent to 25 percent, a tax shelter is only half as valuable to you—so a tax lobbyist is only half as much worth hiring.

In all, the 1986 tax reform was the most brilliant antiparasite stratagem of its time (incomparably more successful than Stockman's budget efforts). True, lobbies never give up and go home, and politicians can never resist buying votes by offering tax breaks to favorite lobbies. In 1988, George Bush promised fistfuls of tax breaks in his election campaign—for capital gains, for oil and gas, for rural development, you name it. Bill Clinton was even worse, proposing bunches of new tax breaks. In fact, nobody could resist using the tax code as a pork barrel. In 1997, the Republican Congress passed a "Taxpayer Relief Act" that added 800 amendments to the tax code, 290 new sections, and 36 retroactive provisions. Over time, the 1986 tax reform eroded. Nonetheless, it proved a point. Politicians can do a big housecleaning.

There is a "but," however: Some things need to go right. With the 1986 tax reform, Republicans in the White House, led by Reagan, and Democrats on Capitol Hill, led by the chairman of the House Ways and Means Committee (Dan Rostenkowski), were in broad ideological agreement on what to do. The Republicans liked reducing the rates, and the Democrats liked closing the loopholes for the rich. Well, if they closed the loopholes, they could reduce the rates. Consensus helped neutralize the partisanship that could have blown apart a deal. With both sides in general accord, the party leaders could act as monitors and disciplinarians.

Moreover, both sides realized they needed to develop and enact a big package that would bestow large, visible, and thus politically attractive rewards upon ordinary voters. Going after only this loophole or that one was a sucker's game, because no one would care or even notice except the lobby that was offended. But the tax reformers rounded up whole herds of loopholes and pushed them over the cliff, and then used the money to buy highly visible rate cuts. The promise of a pot of gold at the end of the rainbow—but only if the deal held together—sufficed to neutralize the voters, who might otherwise have been rallied to opposition. The voters were never particularly enthusiastic about the tax reform; they tended to be suspicious of anything Washington did. But they assented to it or decided they didn't care.

There were still the lobbies to worry about. But the reformers realized that by cutting rates they could turn the lobbies against each other, because for every group whose taxes rose, there would be another whose taxes fell. In fact, many lobbies found themselves neutralized by a dilemma: Keeping a loophole by killing the tax bill might also mean losing the benefits that would come with lower rates. With the politicians united, the voters apathetic, and the lobbies divided, the job got done.

It worked once. It ought to work again. So what keeps going wrong?

The flaw isn't lack of leadership. I made clear in the previous chapter that, whatever else may have been missing in the reform era of the 1980s and 1990s, creative and energetic leadership was on hand. For all their various shortcomings, Reagan and Stockman and Clinton and Gingrich were not lacking in talent or vision. Popular cynicism notwithstanding, the American system is good at cultivating and bringing forward leaders of quality and substance. Something else keeps going wrong. The problem, it turns out, is not poor leadership but poor followership. Consider closely, in this connection, the case of Newt Gingrich, and how the transfer-seeking game, which he sought to subvert, subverted him instead.

A Revolutionary's Blueprint

In hindsight (always the most discerning kind of vision), Gingrich seems to have been an overweening idealist who pushed his luck too far. But defeat appears inevitable only after the war. Gingrich did not enter office as House speaker without a plan. He explained it in January 1995, and it was not a stupid plan.

He was no newcomer. Like David Stockman, who was himself a former House member familiar with the "iron triangle" (bureaucracy, client lobby, congressional patrons) that protected every program, Gingrich went in with his eyes wide open. The power structure on Capitol Hill, he told the *Washington Times* as he assumed the speakership, had "ossified into a straitjacket. That is not partisan or ideological—these guys and their staffs had networks of power and networks of relationships and habits and things that they weren't going to break for a mere president. They'd ignored Nixon, Ford, Carter. They had blocked Reagan and beaten Bush." Moreover, "every time you mention something which ought to be shrunk or zeroed, twenty-five people who are making money off of it jump up to explain why it is a wonderful institution and they should continue to make money off it."

Gingrich's response, his battle plan, is instructive, because on paper it was plausible. First, he would mobilize his supporters, the fiery voters who had demolished Democrats and tossed out a reigning House speaker to put Gingrich and his reformers in charge. "The point we're going to make to people is, you'd better call your representative and tell them you want them to help pass the constitutional amendment to require a balanced budget—with a tax-increase limit. We're going to use every bully pulpit we have. . . . And we're going to tell every conservative group in the country and every group that wants smaller government, you'd better talk to your representatives." The intensity of the government reformers was high, Gingrich knew, so they could mobilize some of the same merciless spot pressure as the interest groups.

As for the Democrats, the 1994 election had thrown them into disarray. The president sounded chagrined, humbled, the wind knocked out of him. "I agree with much of what the electorate said yesterday," he said the day after the election. "They still believe that government is more often the problem than the solution. They don't want any party to be the party of government. They don't want the presumption to be that people in Washington know what's best. . . . I accept responsibility for not delivering to whatever extent it's my fault we haven't delivered." This humbled president would still wield a veto, but he would be presented with a stream of bills passed on the Republicans' terms in the wake of an election that had given them a mandate. If he refused to deal, he would risk seeming obstructive and deaf to the voters' demands. Anyway (said the Republicans to themselves), this was not a president who had shown a lot of backbone.

The lobbies, of course, could be counted upon to try to block or emasculate everything. Gingrich's response: swamp them. Attack so many programs at once that the Democrats and liberals and establishmentarians would have to choose the programs they wanted to save. The rest, the Republicans would knock off. The Democrats would have to "figure out which fights to stay and fight," Gingrich said. Gingrich was hoping to invert the usual Washington pattern, in which reformers were required to focus their energies on a few programs and let the rest of their program slide away. By attacking on a broad front, he would force the *defenders* to concentrate their fire. The Republicans would not get everything, but they would get a great deal.

Finally, Gingrich knew that at each stage of the process —

House deliberations, Senate deliberations, House-Senate conferences, negotiations with the White House, presidential vetoes—he would lose bits and pieces of his agenda. A month or a year wouldn't be enough, a point he went out of his way to emphasize. Instead, he would start in 1995, running a flying wedge through the Washington power structure, and then come back again and again after that, widening the breach. There could be no "Mao-style revolution," he said. "I want to get to a dramatically smaller federal government. I think you do that one step at a time, but you insist on steps every year. . . . The reason I keep telling people to study FDR is if you take fourteen steps successfully you're a lot farther down the road than this guy next to you if he's trying to get all fourteen steps in one jump."

The trouble was, of course, that he never got to the second step. Why?

The Paradox of Particulars

Voters in the polling booth vote for "change" in the abstract. But presidents and members of Congress can't. "In Congress, we don't get to vote on the abstraction," Republican representative Vin Weber told *Time* in 1992, shortly before retiring from office. "We have to vote for or against actual programs." That means confronting actual constituencies. Gingrich's hope to invert this equation foundered on the fact that in the case of any *particular* program or subsidy or perquisite of whatever sort, there is almost always far more energy on the defensive side than on the offensive side.

Say someone in Gingrich's position as a House leader hoped to reform or abolish a thousand programs. No one of those programs is essential to his effort. If he must, he can always drop twenty or thirty or even a hundred or two. There is no overwhelming incentive to go after any particular constituency. To the defender of the subsidy for left-handed screwdrivers, however, only *one* program matters: his own. He will spare no effort.

For that defender, and for each of the others, it's life or death.

Gingrich understood this but thought he could count on his zealous Republicans to hold the line across a broad front. The discipline he was expecting, however, was superhuman. The temptation to help out this one group, or that one, was not Democratic or liberal; it was universal. After all, the clients understood that if one congressman would not help them, another might. Every congressman understood this, too. Why let someone else do the rescuing and take the credit? And every congressman also understood that every other congressman understood. And so, at every stage in the process, Democrats *and* Republicans demanded that this or that program be let off the hook. "I'd love to support you, Mr. Speaker, but I tell you, I am just taking a beating from those left-handed screwdriver people in my district—you've got to cut me a break." Facing this inevitable onslaught, Gingrich found that it was he, not the Democrats or the liberals, who was swamped.

Stockman had run into the same problem, and had reacted with contempt for the gutless Republicans who were all for cutting government except the bits they wanted to save. Stockman, however, missed the point: Given the calculus of the game, the gutless Republicans were doing the only rational thing. The same sort of calculus had wrecked Clinton's health-care package. In fact, what was remarkable in 1995, arguably, was not how much the reform package was watered down in Gingrich's House (with significant program terminations shrinking by a factor of ten) but how large a tattered remnant actually survived.

Gingrich understood the importance of public mobilization. He counted on it to push his program past the Democrats and Clinton. Clinton's bus campaign for health care was a similar attempt to go "over the head" of Congress. In Gingrich's case, and also in Stockman's and Clinton's, the reformers depended on the public to rally around when political hackery began to prevail over the spirit of reform. And, sure enough, the public always did rally—but *to the wrong side.*

It turns out to be surprisingly easy for the protectors of programs to spook the public by screaming bloody murder. The public wants the government to be leaner, but not at the expense of students, farmers, bankers, workers, veterans, retirees, homeowners, artists, teachers, train riders, or cats and dogs. The people cannot abide the ghoulish shrieks and moans that are heard the moment the reformers' scalpel comes out. The same narrow focus and intense commitment that make lobbies so adept at defending themselves on Capitol Hill also make them good at alarming the public with "red alert" mailings and scary television ads (as with "Harry and Louise"). When all else fails, there is the old "Don't hurt our children" ploy. In 1993, when Congress managed to abolish the wool and mohair subsidy, the reformers were all the more courageous for having faced down pleas like the one from Nelda Corbell, whose parents raised mohair in Texas: "I am eight years old and I want to know why the government wants to take away our living." What kind of monster would hurt little Nelda?

Now and then, politicians manage to turn public opinion against a particular lobby, or at least they manage to exploit a change in public opinion, as the tobacco lobby found out. But usually they can't even do that. In his 1996 presidential campaign, when Bob Dole tried to mobilize public sentiment against the teachers' unions, he was judged quixotic. The public is nervous, often rightly, when politicians try to demonize some faction or other. Public nervousness makes the climate of opinion flammable; all that remains is to light a spark.

Rational Paranoia

In May 1981, President Reagan, on Stockman's advice, proposed a package of modest reductions in Social Security: reduced benefits for early retirees, a three-month delay in the cost-of-living adjustment, and so forth. The result was what *Congressional Quarterly* described as a "tempest in Congress." The Democrats until then had been helpless against Stockman, but they knew that this time he had stumbled onto vulnerable ground. The House Democratic caucus promptly and unanimously passed a resolution denouncing Reagan's "unconscionable breach of faith" and swearing not to "destroy the program or a generation of retirees." Democrats in the Senate promised to use "every rule in the book" to stop the proposal. "Democrats waged their assault with obvious glee," said *Congressional Quarterly*, and they kept waging it through the 1982 elections, when they gained twenty-six seats in the House and regained effective control there. Painting Reagan and the Republicans as scourges of Social Security received a good deal of the credit (the economic recession received most of the rest).

In 1995, Newt Gingrich's Republicans, responsibly and courageously, undertook to propose some modest but significant reforms of the Medicare program for the elderly. That the program's finances were in trouble, and that reductions would have to be made one way or another, were facts known to everybody in Washington, including President Clinton. He proposed reducing the growth of Medicare's costs from more than 4 percent a year for six years to 2.7 percent. The Republican plan, in not exactly sharp contrast, proposed reducing the growth path to 1.5 percent, with some larger structural reforms than Clinton preferred. In dollars, the difference between the plans was about 7 percent in the last year, 2002. But that was enough for the Democrats. Through the 1996 campaigns, they hammered the Republicans for "cutting" Medicare. "The Republicans are wrong to want to cut Medicare benefits," a voice-over intoned in one Democratic ad, as the faces of Bob Dole and Newt Gingrich danced on the screen. "And President Clinton is right to protect Medicare, right to defend our decision as a nation to do what's moral, good, and right by our elderly." The campaign became known as Mediscare, and it was accounted a great success. The public was quite willing to believe that Gingrich and his crew were out to gut Medicare. Despite their pleas of innocence, the Republicans never recovered.

In 1993, Bill Clinton proposed a health-care reform package. In 1994 came Harry and Louise and plenty of others like them. But you know that story. The point is that the trick works for both parties.

It works, you may say, because the public is ignorant and easily frightened. That explanation is true, to some extent. But it fails to give the public quite enough credit, because the public's suspicions were rational in each case. When the Gingrichites tried to make changes in Medicare, they plausibly argued, just as someone might argue to overeaters at the Superdome dinner, that the (small) pain they were imposing on one group would be more than offset by the benefits to everybody from lower deficits, lower taxes, and a solvent Medicare program. But at that stage, the Democrats and the lobbies, acting as a swing vote, did exactly as the playbook suggests. They recast the debate as group versus group rather than as group versus nation. They stood on a box with a megaphone and warned: "Don't believe those Republicans! They're not going to give anything back to you once they've cut Medicare. They're financing tax cuts for the rich! They're just taking from you to give to their friends!"

Most Americans will sacrifice for a larger public good, but few will sacrifice for a competing group. The larger public loses interest in reducing Medicare, or in reducing anything else, if it believes that the only result will be to shift resources from one group to another. By kindling suspicions that the Republicans were acting in the interests of their favorite clients rather than of the nation as a whole, the Democrats and their allied lobbies had no trouble sinking the Republicans' Medicare deal. On health reform, the Republicans and the plan's other opponents used the same tactic against Clinton and the Democrats. "This plan doesn't mean more care at lower prices," they said. "It means poorer care for you and better care for other people, with huge new bureaucracies in the bargain."

Alas, this trick of kindling mistrust can almost always be used by somebody, because the charges, though overdrawn and often misleading, are usually plausible and partly true. The Republicans *were* trying to cut Medicare while also reducing taxes for better-off citizens. The Democrats *were* relying on bureaucratic controls to constrain choices for the middle class and expand health access for the poor. In 1981, the Reagan administration *was* trying to use Social Security reductions to help pay for upper-class tax cuts. In a democracy, parties do not get things done (or win elections) unless they favor their supporters, which means that the other side of any argument can always cry foul. And the voters' cynicism, which admittedly is often justified, makes them quick to believe charges that the system will double-cross them. The cynicism, of course, is self-fulfilling.

So here is the final conundrum of collective political action. If you assume that everyone else will act in his rational self-interest, you have every reason to support politicians who put dollars or benefits or protections in your pocket, and little or no reason to support politicians who remove them. Although it is certainly possible to neutralize the opposition party and divide the lobbies and win the public's support, no sensible politician or voter ought to expect it to happen. Far more likely is the fate of the reformers of the 1980s and 1990s, who found themselves, after starting out well, suddenly staring at a coalition of opponents that comprised the opposition party, the lobbies, and the broad public. Against that array of forces, there is simply no hope. Reformers are crushed.

I have described in this book many dynamic asymmetries, forces acting in lopsided ways on complex systems—groups, governments, societies—that are themselves in constant motion. There is Olson's asymmetry of collective action, giving narrow groups such large advantages in furthering their common good. There is Olson's asymmetry of group-formation, as groups prove hard to form but much harder still to eliminate. There is the asymmetry of demosclerosis itself, in which *programs* likewise are hard to form but nearly impossible to excise. To that already rather daunting pile can now be added one more: For all the rea-

sons discussed in this chapter, it is quite easy to mobilize political support for "reform" in the abstract but much easier still to
mobilize political opposition to reforms in the particular. Reform,
sure. But not *this* reform! Not *that* reform! Some other reform!
Something less hurtful to me, or to my friends, or to any deserv-
ing party, or to anybody at all.

In the movie *The African Queen*, a famous scene has the pro-
tagonists' boat hopelessly stuck in a marsh—only a few yards, it
turns out, from open water. Today's government is in a similar
plight. Dissatisfaction ought, by rights, to open the path to comprehensive change. But it does not. The *African Queen* was lifted
from the quagmire by the tide. But in the case of the American
government, the boat cannot be lifted. The government is, of its
nature, inseparable and inalienable from the million commitments it has made and the million interest groups it has
spawned. They now form its environment. It cannot lift itself
above them. With the replacement of Carter with Reagan, Bush
with Clinton, and Clinton (for a while) with Gingrich, the restive
electorate outside Washington showed that it could still radical-
ize politics, at least temporarily, and shake the very ground of
the capital. Notwithstanding all the little gray groups and politicians and lobbyists and claques that occupy and ossify the government, the broad electorate proved more than able to coil itself
and strike back. What was lacking in the system was not energy
or leadership but the ability to focus reformist energy on any
particular program of reform. Converting the electorate's shud-
dering waves of discontent into the hundreds or thousands of
alterations to programs affecting specific groups is like converting earthquake energy into steam power: possible in theory but
elusive in practice.

Hey! That's Mine!

So far, I've kept the discussion at the systemic level: the level of
the game, so to speak, in which the politics of reform finds itself.

The game problem, of course, is the Olsonian arithmetic of collective action, inasmuch as the broad public never cares about eliminating any given program remotely as much as its beneficiaries care about saving it. But that mechanical imbalance is rooted in, and compounded by, an attitudinal imbalance. Consider what I have come to think of as the entitlement mentality.

At the core of the entitlement mentality is this presumption: Whatever benefits me (or my group) belongs to me. Programs are property. Maybe, in a pinch, I'll let you reduce my benefits. But if you cut my program without my permission, that's theft. I have every reason to be outraged.

I'm not saying that entitlements have no place in government. One reason we have government is to offer security in an uncertain world. I also am not saying that entitlement thinking is always wrong or inappropriate. Social Security should not be overhauled twice a year in hopes of making it perfect. On the other hand, though, the politics of entitlement should not become so prevalent as to obliterate the politics of experiment. But that is exactly what has happened.

In Washington, a standard and generally useful distinction is between entitlement programs and discretionary ones. In the argot of budgeting, entitlements are permanent grants written into law; unless the law is changed, you automatically receive your benefits every year. Discretionary programs are the ones that come up for annual review; unless the law is renewed, the programs stop spending. Anyway, that's the theory. With it goes the conventional wisdom that the big entitlements—the federal social-insurance programs, like Social Security and Medicare— operate on a different level of politics from the many smaller subsidies that serve smaller groups. And this conventional wisdom is largely true. In my effort to schematize, I've tended to treat the politics of Social Security (say) as interchangeable with the politics of maritime subsidies (say). In reality, a broad social-insurance system engages the public's attention and pushes political hot buttons in ways that quiet little programs can never do. Cutting Medicare is difficult because it inevitably becomes a national political issue, whereas cutting the peanut protectorate is difficult because it inevitably does *not* become a national political issue.

I don't want to dismiss this distinction, which is important. Yet to settle for it is to breeze past a curious and underappreciated truth. The politics of broad programs and the politics of narrow programs, for all their differences, finally converge to a pronounced similarity at the operational level, because, in the real world today, *every federal program is an entitlement.* Not every program technically is an entitlement, of course, but every program behaves as though it were. It lasts forever, and it's viewed as a right by the people who benefit from it. Some constituencies are very large, and others are very small, but they all claim and exercise ownership rights over whatever piece of the government "belongs" to them.

If the collective-action problem is the mechanism of sclerosis, then the entitlement mind-set is the morality. The collective-action arithmetic induces everybody around the table to hold onto whatever he possesses, since, after all, nothing any one actor can do by himself will have any discernible effect on the overall situation. Meanwhile, the entitlement mentality provides moral support for this same tendency. After all, no one should be required to give up what is rightly his, at least not until everyone else has agreed to do the same. If others get to keep theirs, I get to keep mine! Of course, since everybody knows that everybody else feels equally entitled, no one has any sane reason to be the sucker who sacrifices. Checkmate. And so the entitlement mentality and the Olsonian obstacles to collective action merge, finally, into a single seamless problem.

The result is a peculiar, though entirely understandable, sort of disconnect. The American public is made up of good and patriotic people who want the best for their country and are more than willing to sacrifice—okay, not too much sacrifice, but within reason—in order to make things better. But they do not see why any *particular* person or group, least of all oneself, should be singled out to give.

In a particularly revealing vein, in 1994 pollsters for ABC News asked people what politicians should and should not do. Predictably, a heavy majority (77 percent) blamed "special-interest groups" for Congress's failure to get more done; an almost equally heavy majority (63 percent) piously said that their representative should be more interested "in doing what's best for the country" than "in doing what's best for your own congressional district where you live." No surprise. People forever demand that politicians push the special interests aside and do what's best for the country as a whole—which is what politicians forever promise to do. But generally people decline to believe that there may be a conflict between their program or district and the national interest. Pressing on, the ABC pollsters asked again what it is that members of Congress should be doing, but this time they did not imply a conflict between parochial interests and the larger good. In effect, they asked the question the way it is asked in the voting booth, without an "either-or." ("For each item I name, please tell me if that's something your own representative in Congress should or should not be doing.") Should your representative be "trying to direct more government spending to your congressional district"? Yes! said 58 percent. Should he be "trying to bring federal projects to your district"? Yes! yes! said 73 percent. And should he be "trying to help create jobs in your district"? Yes again! said 90 percent.

"I don't feel the people of this country have any control over what's going on, even if we voted in the person we wanted," a thirty-five-year-old Indiana woman told *The New York Times* in 1994. By the 1990s, Americans increasingly had come to believe that Washington was in business for itself—which, increasingly, it was. But they spoke as though Washington was in business *only* for itself rather than brokering endlessly escalating conflicts between ever proliferating groups—as though the people themselves had nothing to do with this. Here, then, was the central paradox of American democracy as the century turned: The public was, at one and the same time, deeply implicated and utterly alienated.

Survival Skills

What to conclude, then? First, what *not* to conclude.

From the beginning, I have emphasized that this book tries to be a *dynamic* analysis of government. The problems in modern government don't have to do with the system's standing inert or producing a paucity of new laws and regulations, because government emphatically does not stand inert or produce a paucity of new laws and regulations. Rather, it is in a constant state of frenzied motion. To suppose that the combination of unbalanced forces that I've described allows no change or reform would be altogether wrong. The significance, rather, is in the *nature* and *direction* of the changes that get made, and—what this argument is headed toward—the implications of that sort of change for political control of the government.

To see this, begin by recalling something I said in Chapter 6: "In a Darwinian sense, the collectivity of federal policies is ceasing to evolve." Because almost no program can be ended, the *collectivity* of government activities becomes like a company producing every product it ever made, with the government as a whole sclerotic and incoherent and the parts often working at cross-purposes. The message of this chapter and the previous one is that comprehensive, top-down change—change that attempts to reshape the government according to some sort of coherent plan or set of principles—is inherently much harder to accomplish than a casual glance would suggest. Even coherently reshaping some piece of the government (grain subsidies, welfare, banking laws), though possible and from time to time successful, is difficult and requires a burst of energy and some good luck.

Here, however I want to deepen the evolutionary metaphor.

We know that every year Congress and the White House review and reauthorize and readminister thousands of programs that are lovingly tended by thousands of client groups. All these people and groups are not keeping themselves busy all the time by doing nothing. We also know that every so often, for ideological or political reasons, some program is attacked by a president or a congressional committee chairman who sees a need to do things differently, or who wants to stir the pot and generate some lobbying activity that will generate some campaign contributions, or both. Of course, almost invariably the program survives, but it may be cut (or expanded) or changed. Its lobbyists may need to scramble to accommodate the new skeptical Californian who replaced the friendly Ohioan on the House Left-Handed Screwdriver Committee.

In this process, adaptation unquestionably occurs. But this is adaptation with a difference. The peanut program, as you'll recall, was a temporary program that turned out not to be temporary. It was designed to cope with a transitory problem in the 1930s agricultural marketplace, using the heavy-handed market controls in fashion at the time. Its original purpose—to keep family peanut farmers in business through Depression-era turmoil—became archaic, as agribusiness replaced family farms and as economic and marketplace conditions changed. The original problem, to the extent it was a problem, went away, or at least became less pressing than any number of other problems. The program, however, turned out to be very well adapted—not well adapted to meeting any pressing national need in any particularly efficient way, mind you, but well adapted *simply at surviving*.

In other words, the subsidies and programs and their client groups adapt, all right, but they do so in a way that makes them more tenacious and helps them to lock out other, possibly better ventures that might work better or be more important. The government as a whole stagnates, failing to relinquish the old and thus failing to evolve toward solving problems in any effective or coherent way. From the top-down point of view of someone who wants to use national programs to solve national problems, the trial-and-error process, and therefore evolution, fails. But from the bottom-up point of view of each client group, government evolves constantly. To be specific, *it evolves to keep its collection of client services intact from one year to the next.*

To see what I mean, it helps to consider an example from life: a federal program known, these days, as the Market Access Program. I say "these days" because it is now on its third name. But I'm getting ahead of myself.

How to Become an Eel

The creature was born in 1985, popping into existence pretty much out of nowhere. No plan was laid out, nor was there any clearly identified national problem to be solved. There was, however, a political problem. That year Congress was passing a budget-busting farm bill for the Midwest, which was in a deep agricultural recession. "Hey, what about us!" said the fruit and vegetable and nut and processed-products industries, many of them based in California. They argued that foreign subsidies were giving them headaches in export markets overseas, and they persuaded a California senator to throw them a bone. And so, to buy the California interests' support for the farm bill, what was then called the Targeted Export Assistance program was born.

The program was, in effect, a subsidy for advertising. The money was given to agricultural groups and agribusinesses, which used it to market their products overseas. Typically, the federal government required companies or groups to apply for funding and put up some money of their own (anywhere from 10 percent to half). Of course, advertising their products is something that businesses typically do in the ordinary course of things. But they argued that farm products were different, since so many of them were sold generically. No one cotton farmer could begin to finance a campaign hawking, say, American cotton in Turkey. So a government subsidy could be justified.

Or not. To conduct such campaigns on behalf of their members was exactly why trade associations and farm co-ops existed in the first place. Why the Wine Institute (granted about $3.8 million from Washington in 1998), the USA Dry Pea and Lentil Council ($554,000), the Popcorn Institute ($342,000), Ocean Spray International ($247,000), or the American Jojoba Association ($89,000) needed taxpayers' help to do their job was never quite clear. Moreover, a significant share of the program's budget went to advertise *branded* products, for which there was no problem of free ridership, even in principle. Through the Poultry and Egg Export Council, McDonald's got $465,000 from the taxpayers in fiscal 1991 to promote Chicken McNuggets. No one offered a very good reason why, if promoting Chicken McNuggets made economic sense, McDonald's needed a subsidy to do it. Other recipients ranged from small players (Southern Pride Catfish) to some of the biggest names in American corporate agriculture: Sunkist, Ernest and Julio Gallo, Tyson Foods, Sun Maid, M&M/Mars. The sorts of promotions being funded sometimes seemed, let us say, picturesque. In 1997, Welch's Foods, a big grape-growers' cooperative, received $800,000 (reported National Public Radio) to pay for newspaper supplements and free juice samples at supermarkets in Latin America and Asia. In 1996, the government (reported the *Fresno Bee*) "paid about $21,000 to fund a California winery tour for nine English wine writers and buyers." Forty British journalists tasted American wine at a posh London hotel, courtesy of American taxpayers. And so on.

Most programs, the vast majority, labor in welcome obscurity. They are under little evolutionary pressure and remain much the same over time, as the scorpion and shark have done. But helping advertise Chicken McNuggets or sponsoring wine-tasting tours was bound to attract attention. As you might gather from the news stories just cited, almost from its inception this subsidy was a whipping boy, not only for free-market groups but for environmentalists and urban Democrats and, not least, populist liberal opponents of "corporate welfare." People who needed "wasteful" government programs to denounce made this one their first stop. Year after year, the program was spotlit by groups with names like Citizens Against Government Waste and Taxpayers for Common Sense.

Perhaps a good way to think of this program is as a big, juicy crawdad sitting in full view in shallow waters. It needed survival skills. In the real world, of course, a crawdad is a crawdad; but in Washington, a crawdad can, within only a very few years, become an eel, lean and slippery and elusive.

How? First, the program's supporters and its administrators in the Agriculture Department poured forth a cascade of studies purporting to show how subsidies for marketing had increased American farm exports by untold billions of dollars. When outside experts looked at the studies, they noted, as any good economist would, that simply counting up the exports flowing from subsidized products revealed nothing at all. Congress's General Accounting Office, on at least two occasions, sifted through this mass of paper and unearthed nothing worthwhile. In 1997, the GAO said it "found no conclusive evidence that these programs have provided net benefits to the aggregate economy. Government export programs largely reallocate production, employment, and income among sectors." In other words, the program gave to farmers and took from taxpayers and consumers, making a deposit with the politicians and lobbyists along the way. But this was less important than the fact that the program's friends could wave studies touting jobs created and the like.

Second, the program enjoyed plenty of support in both parties. The California delegation—Congress's largest—loved it and teamed up with farm-state Republicans, who had their own subsidies to protect. Enough recipients received enough money in enough states so that Congress was liberally salted with friends. Free-market Republicans and urban Democrats who tried to get rid of the program inevitably ran into opposition from both parties.

Third, and most important, the program adapted. It underwent a series of reforms that made it smaller, to be sure, but that also greatly narrowed its profile. Its annual budget grew from the initial $110 million in 1986 to $200 million by the early 1990s, then fell to about $90 million, where it stayed. This reduction of more than half—from a temporary peak, of course—was touted endlessly as evidence that the program had already given its "fair share" (the entitlement mentality, again). The program also changed its protective plumage. In 1990, the name was changed from Targeted Export Assistance ("assistance" sounded like handouts) to Market Promotion Program. In 1996, the name was changed yet again from Market Promotion Program ("promotion" sounded like corporate welfare) to Market Access Program. Who could be against access to foreign markets?

Other, more significant changes took aim at those headline-making horror stories about "corporate welfare" flowing to giant companies. In 1993, Congress gave some preferences to small companies and nonprofit groups. By 1998, the brand-name promotions by big companies were cut out of the program altogether.

Politically, this move made sense. It would reduce the outrageous "corporate welfare" headlines. But, to the extent the program had any rationale at all, the idea was to use tax dollars as efficiently as possible to push American products into foreign markets—and, of course, bigger companies tend to be the *most* efficient at marketing, overseas or anywhere. "The ability of small companies to spend their branded money is nowhere near that of the larger companies," grumbled an official of the Wine Institute to the *Bee*. True enough: If the goal was to open foreign markets, then a bulldozer would work better than a garden trowel. Big companies like McDonald's could sell a lot more chicken or beef overseas than could Pop Granger's chicken farm. But it was the big brands that were winnowed. Meanwhile, the promotional money continued flowing to huge trade associations and co-ops, like Sunkist, the giant citrus group, which posted annual sales of more than $1 billion and received about $10 million from the Market Access Program just from 1994 to 1998. No one should be surprised to learn that the said recipients gave reliably to their supporters in Washington.

In short, to become more politically rational, the program became less economically rational. It became more about keeping the money flowing and keeping the press away, and less about doing the job in the most efficient way possible.

In 1992, the Democratic chairman of the House Budget Committee, Leon Panetta, looked at the (then) Market Promotion Program and said, "You almost have to consider eliminating programs like this one." The next year, Panetta was President Clinton's new budget director, and he didn't dare touch the program. In 1992, Richard Armey, a free-market House Republican, denounced the (then) Market Promotion Program as "a completely outrageous case of corporate welfare." By 1995, Armey was the House Majority Leader—Newt Gingrich's second-in-command. Still, the Republican Congress pondered all those votes in California and decided that it, too, would take a pass.

After that, matters degenerated into kabuki warfare. Every year the opponents would introduce an amendment to kill the Market Access Program. Every year the defenders would rise to say, as the chairman of the Senate Agriculture Committee said in 1997, that the program had already been "reformed, reformed, and reformed." Out would come the studies showing jobs purportedly created, and again would be heard the recitations of unfair trade practices abroad. At least one congressman simply made more or less the same speech every year. Others added the odd dramatic touch. A New York Republican said that the program was vital to apple growers in his own Hudson Valley. "We are up there, and the temperatures drop down to 30 or 40 below zero. It is tough enough to make a living as it is." Deeply moved, every year a compassionate majority of both parties, in both chambers, reaffirmed support for the Market Access Program.

What, you may wonder, was the end being served? Remember,

this particular program was not created to solve any particular social problem. It was created to solve a political problem (getting a budget-busting farm bill through Congress in 1985). There were never any firm criteria by which to measure its performance, even if the partisans could have agreed on how to do the measuring. But on one criterion it performed well: It learned how to stay alive. It evolved to become less conspicuous and to lose protuberances that predators could grab. And that is how a crawdad becomes an eel.

As I mentioned, the Market Access Program was under more pressure than most, so it had to be particularly agile. Still, evolutionary feats of this sort are not uncommon. You may recall that in Chapter 6 I mentioned the venerable Rural Electrification Administration, still alive and well sixty years after it was created and forty or more years after its original mission had faded to a memory. By the 1990s, it had become what amounted to a government-aided system of utility cooperatives, competing with private and municipal utility companies (which were themselves subsidized in various ways). In 1993, President Clinton proposed eliminating the rural electric subsidy. To lobby for it, three thousand rural citizens descended on Washington, where they were briefed by the National Rural Electric Cooperative Association's staff, armed with information packets and buttons, then sent up to Capitol Hill to buttonhole members. After a horde of them circled the desk of Representative Melvin Watt, a North Carolina Democrat, he said, "It's certainly powerful to see this many people visit you on an issue. It's got to have an impact on you." Something else doubtless had an impact, too. In December 1993, only a few weeks after Congress rescued the rural electric program, the National Rural Electric Cooperative Association announced the name of its new chief executive officer: none other than Representative Glenn English of Oklahoma, who, as chairman of the subcommittee on rural development, had been the program's leading protector in the House. ("Throughout his congressional career," sang the association, "he has shared our goals.") Apparently in a hurry to slip through the revolving door, English left halfway through his term to work for the group whose program he had just saved—a cheeky move even by Washington's slippery standards.

Still, the program was reduced by 40 percent, and, for the first time in its long history, larger subsidies were aimed at needier borrowers—on the whole, meaningful reforms. Then, in 1994, the anachronistic-sounding Rural Electrification Administration was renamed (does this sound familiar?) when it was conjoined with some other Agriculture Department programs. It was called the Rural Utilities Service, with a mission that included financing water, wastewater, and other such local facilities. All of this was done with the support of the subsidies' recipients, who knew they needed new pastures to graze.

At one level, the change was to the good. Here was an archaic program being gradually modified to go where the need was. If the program was to exist, better it should undertake activities that the relevant lobby and members of Congress agreed were suitable. Yet the change could just as rightly be viewed as what old Washington hands call "mission creep," which is when a lobby and a bureaucracy go in search of new ways to secure funding. Both views, in fact, are perfectly correct.

But the larger point is that two simplistic—but opposed—views of the situation are wrong. On the one hand, it is not the case that things stay the same in government. To the contrary, things survive by changing all the time. On the other hand, however, it is equally wrong to think that adaptation of this sort is directed in any coherent way, or solves any particular social problem, or comports to any vision of what government should or shouldn't do, or even notices what's going on in any other part of the government. Rather, what's happening is that particular programs are changing to cling to particular niches. The Rural Utilities Service, as the General Accounting Office noted in a 1997 report, still directed much of its subsidized credit to places that were neither notably rural nor notably needy. Once a utility cooperative qualified as serving a rural area, it didn't need to requalify; for instance, said the GAO, one electric company that qualified for loans in 1945 was still borrowing in 1996, by which point, with 140,000 customers in areas that were now part of a big city, it was hardly "rural." Spreading around subsidies to plenty of congressional districts, including urban ones, offered good political protection. The program evolved to survive by flinging its seeds everywhere.

Law of the Jungle

"Well," you say, "of course! So what else is new?" Fair enough. As long ago as 1969, in his influential book *The End of Liberalism* (whose title, like Francis Fukuyama's, I tip my hat to), the political scientist Theodore J. Lowi noticed how groups and their programs entrenched themselves as independent fiefdoms — microcosmic regimes or, so to speak, duchies. "Each administrative organization becomes a potent political instrumentality," he wrote. In agriculture, for example:

> Each of the self-governing local units becomes one important point in a definable political system which both administers a program and maintains the autonomy of that program in [the] face of all other political forces emanating from other agricultural systems, from antagonistic farm and nonfarm interests, from Congress, from the secretary, and from the president.
>
> The politics of each of these self-governing programs is comprised of a triangular trading pattern, with each point complementing and supporting the other two. The three points are: the central agency, a congressional committee or subcommittee, and the local or district farmer committees. The latter are also usually the grass-roots element of a national interest group.

Lowi's commentary on the results was scathing. These self-propagating little units of government, he said, are worrisome for at least three reasons. First, since only an expert could ever understand or even know about any of the minigovernments, they shut out the public, resulting in "the atrophy of institutions of popular control." Second, the little duchies "tend to create and maintain privilege," favoring insiders and tight-knit groups over outsiders with greater need or better ideas. Third, and by the same token, this insiders' world is deeply conservative, inasmuch as the established clients can be counted on to resist any attempts to upset their cozy arrangements. In consequence of all of this, "Liberal governments cannot plan." (Here he used "liberal" to refer to what he called interest-group liberalism, the giant collectivity of duchies.) "Liberalism replaces planning with bargaining," Lowi said. "In a pluralistic government there is, therefore, no substance. Neither is there procedure. There is only process."

Around the time Lowi was writing those words, in the late 1960s, Mancur Olson's thinking on the arithmetic of collective action was beginning to win attention, and the American government was at the high noon of its dramatic postwar expansion. The years from 1966 to 1976 brought, to name only a few, the National Highway Traffic Safety Administration, the age-discrimination laws, the Consumer Credit Protection Act, the Clean Air Act, the noise- and water-pollution laws, the Environmental Protection Agency, the Occupational Safety and Health Administration, the Consumer Product Safety Commission, the Equal Employment Opportunity Act, and many more. If anyone, back then, had managed to integrate the ideas of Olson and Lowi and then to draw out the implications, he might have seen trouble ahead. In retrospect, what happened is all too clear. The sudden and enormous expansion of the government's reach—often for the best of reasons—led, as a side effect, to the wild proliferation of groups trying to get and stay on Washington's good side. Those groups, as Olson's theory predicted, proved mostly impossible to root out or circumvent, and they established countless new principalities in government—all, of course, on top of the many old ones. By 1981, a reformist president was finding himself almost powerless to reshape the system—if "system" is actually the right word—that resulted. After that, each successive reform wave (Stockman, Clinton, Gingrich) fared worse than the last.

In fact, "system" is not quite the right word. "Ecosystem" is a better word. "System" implies control. But, just as Lowi predicted, today's government is shaped mainly by its own internal dynamics and by the occasional outside shock (war, mass demographic change) rather than by anyone or anything in particular. In Chapter 6, I spoke of the government as a city in which every house has to be built on top of some existing house. From the point of view of an outside problem-solver, that's an apt metaphor. If, today, you set out to build a sensible health program for the elderly, or you decided to provide some kind of public insurance for farmers, no one would dream of creating anything like Medicare or the Agriculture Department's termite nest of subsidies. However, for the people who actually need to work the government, whether as politicians or administrators or lobbyists, there *is* no "outside the system": no pristine vantage point from which to assess and redesign. From this operational point of view, a better metaphor for government in the age of demosclerosis is, I think, a jungle.

I was brought up believing that American government was something like an airplane. The voters were the passengers, and the politicians were at the controls. Maybe the airplane wasn't easy to turn on a whim; in fact, it was designed to be hard to turn. But there was a chain of command. If the politicians didn't do what the electorate wanted, they would be fired and other, more responsive politicians would take their places. And, one way or another, the whole of government worked that way. It was, in that sense, democratically accountable through and through.

That civics-book view is, of course, not all wrong. But the implication of Olson and Lowi and the rise of the parasite economy, with all that they imply, is that at any given moment only the most public, the most controversial, or the most dangerously dysfunctional bits of the government are accessible to coherent reform or direct public pressure, never mind who the reformer happens to be. Once in a while, perhaps once or occasionally twice in a decade, a piece of the government—welfare, say, or maybe Social Security—rises to the forefront of politics, and then a big-picture reform guided by the election returns is, at least, possible (though hardly assured). Nearly always, though, almost all of the government goes its own way. Politicians talk, and think, as though they are pilots in a cockpit. In fact, they are more like elephants in the jungle: highly visible and capable of throwing their weight around or toppling the odd tree, but mostly at the mercy of the intricate ecology that surrounds them. It is the aphids and earthworms and dung beetles and termites and algae, the busy little creatures all in their niches—the farm lobbies and veterans' lobbies and real-estate lobbies and education lobbies and a million other species—that shape the jungle's topography. They are neither evil nor benign, and their unimaginably variegated activities have all sorts of effects on all kinds of things, good or bad depending on your point of view. They are merely doing what they do.

As for the voters, they too are simply a part of the landscape. They are, of course, important, but not in any consistent or reliable way. They are an unpredictable force that once in a while generates an inchoate upheaval, like a flood or a fire. Facing such an upheaval, the bugs and worms and mice and (of course) elephants scurry to adjust; whereupon, after an interruption, all settle in again to the familiar patterns. No, the voters are not helpless. Politicians are not helpless. They just matter, most of the time and in most decisions of ordinary governance, much less than they suppose. Voters and politicians influence the governmental ecology, but they do nothing like control it. No one controls it. In the universe of government, there is no God.

In *The End of Liberalism*, Theodore Lowi said that interest-group liberalism in America had so transformed governance as to have established what he called a new regime, a Second Republic of the United States. The First Republic lasted through the early years of the twentieth century and was marked by a relatively weak and limited federal center. With the rise of interest-group pluralism beginning around the time of the New Deal, the government became increasingly a collection of subsidies and guarantees parceled out to groups, giving rise at last to the Second Republic. Just what he meant by that term is not altogether clear to me, but never mind: His language is interesting and suggests a way of looking at things.

In ideological terms, conservatives see government as properly a guarantor of individual rights, and possibly also as a watchman for the interests of enterprise. For 150 years or so, American government conformed largely to their vision. By today's standards, it was very small and very weak, and the country's many associations were of the voluntary, nonlobbying kind that were familiar to Tocqueville. Call that (this is me, now, not Lowi) a First Republic.

Liberals see government as properly a solver of national problems, and possibly also as a builder of a more nearly ideal society. For thirty or forty or fifty years, beginning around the time of the New Deal, the liberals had their day: The government was ambitious, undertook all sorts of commitments to pensioners and veterans and students and consumers, and seemed often successful in meeting them. But with the growth of the programs came the jungle, the burrowing and flying and stinging creatures; and with the growing perception of failure—with farmers being paid not to grow food, the welfare culture expanding, the tax code becoming spaghetti, lawyers and lobbyists overrunning Washington, inflation, deficits, bureaucracies—came the backlash and the era of reform. Call the expansionist period and the accompanying backlash the Second Republic.

And now, at last, comes this, what you see around you: the perpetual stalemate of evolutionary equilibrium, in which the clients and the calculus of collective action will not allow the government to become much smaller or to reorganize its basic functions, while the taxpayers will not suffer it to grow much bigger. The borders of the jungle are more or less as they will be. From a distance, in macrocosm, the jungle seems an immovable mass, unchanging from year to year and impenetrably dense, whereas up very close, in microcosm, it is a constant turmoil of digging and scurrying and eating and mating. But it exists primarily to survive from year to year and to feed its clients. Its clients—we—draw sustenance from it but yield control. Call that the Third Republic.

In the end, it is not the conservative vision of government or the liberal vision that prevailed. It is no vision at all that prevailed. The client groups prevailed. And that is the end of government. To see the future, look around.

9

Adjusting the World

"THE END of history," wrote Francis Fukuyama in 1989, "will be a very sad time." But the end of government will not, I think, be a sad time. It may indeed be a cheerful, resolute, politically healthy time. Whether it in fact *will* be cheerful and resolute and politically healthy, as opposed to morose and fitful and politically impotent, is another question. To a large extent, the answer depends on whether Americans make some changes in the world, and whether they make some other changes in themselves.

I often notice how people who take good care of themselves and lead vigorous, engaged lives not only live well (and, often, long) but also age gracefully. They know that human beings live along time's arrow, but they also understand that a directional life in which the past cannot be undone is not necessarily a life that gets worse and worse. When they receive their first membership solicitation from the American Association of Retired Persons, they react with a chuckle instead of an anxiety attack. I've noticed, too, how people who cling to youth—facial tucks, comb-overs, adolescent mannerisms—often end up being resentful and decrepit. Instead of becoming graceful and vigorous old people, they become angry and sometimes spiritless ex-young people, too concerned about what they can't do to get on with what they can do.

The analogy between an aging person and an aging democracy (America's, remember, is the oldest in the world) is flawed in some obvious ways, the most obvious being that human aging is a directional process with predictable successive stages and an unvarying destination: death. By contrast, government's arrival at demosclerotic maturity is a whirlwind of activity sustainable indefinitely and leading nowhere in particular. Human aging stops. Democratic government, however, goes on and on, or so one hopes.

Still, the analogy is useful psychologically. It helps explain why, I think, realism and a proper understanding of an admittedly frustrating situation need not lead to despondency or passive gloom. To some extent, in fact, just the opposite. Once you stop banging your head against the wall, expecting to break through at any moment, you can think a little better and maybe try an approach that, though less direct, may be more effective.

This book, as I've said, is about several kinds of dynamic asymmetries in society and government, and how they conspire to shape society and government. Really, though, a simpler way to put the matter is to say that the book is about time's arrow. Underlying the concept of government that I and, probably, you grew up with is a picture of the political system, at whatever level, as a sort of neutral tool—like the airplane. In that standard view, government is time-symmetrical. At any given moment, Washington reflects the people's desires and expands or contracts or changes accordingly. Whether the year is 1900 or 1950 or 2000 or 2050 shouldn't much affect the way government works, except insofar as the voters' preferences change. My objective in this book is to challenge the time-symmetrical view.

Government, like our bodies, is a complex organism whose internal dynamics generate a constant hum of activity and change, and the change flows predominantly one way over time. Governments and groups stimulate each other, change each

other, then react to those changes, and though particular decisions can sometimes be undone, the string of reactions, like the
process that turns an egg into an omelet, cannot be reversed.
New activities in Washington (or, for that matter, in the state
capitals) stimulate new lobbies in society, which in turn accumulate and reduce government's flexibility. As the groups accumulate, and as the collection of programs and policies grows,
the logic of collective action makes it steadily harder for any
leader or coalition or actor to organize any sort of broad reform
effort. And, of course, the economy of transfer-seeking grows in
response to activity of whatever sort.

All of that, I've discussed. What is perhaps most important is
the upshot. None of those asymmetrical processes is repealable:
not the Olsonian dynamic of group accumulation, not the economics of transfer-seeking, not the demosclerotic processes of
program entrenchment and protective adaptation. So, although
the government won't one day have a heart attack and die, it,
like us, is inherently time-asymmetrical. Washington's entire
past, from the eighteenth-century maritime subsidies down to
the latest highway bill, is encoded in the accumulation of subsidies and programs and missions and client groups that define its
present. Never again will Washington be small or simple; never
again will politicians go about their business relatively unmo-
lested by pressure groups prepared to launch instant salvos of
ads or mail or money. And never again (this claim is bolder, but I
think it's almost certainly true) can the electorate exert more
than marginal control over the vast political biosphere that
Washington has at last become.

Aging, of course, can be easier or harder to handle, depending partly on your attitude. The same is true of government's
dotage and its attendant nuisances, disabilities, and dysfunc-
tions. We can live with it well, or we can live with it poorly.
So far, Americans have been living with it poorly, because most
people still imagine government to be like the airplane and can't
understand why its direction won't change. I think, though, we

will come to live with it better. To do that, two broad kinds of adjustments will be needed. We'll need to know what sorts of adjustments we can make to the world, so as to ameliorate the forces of age and time. And we'll need to know what sorts of adjustments we can make to ourselves, so as to approach the government's problems with an attitude that's productive rather than self-defeating. First, in this chapter, the world.

Treatment Without Cure

Begin, first and foremost and most important of all, by giving up on a cure. There is no cure. If you are growing old and fat and frail, a bad solution is to wait on your sofa for a pill that will cure you. But that has been, to a considerable extent, what the public has been doing with government. Prodded by angry voters and encouraged by self-proclaimed outsiders who hold government in contempt (George Wallace, Ross Perot, Patrick J. Buchanan, and so on), politicians trumpet "real change" or "taking back government" or a "new day," and the people cry "Yes! Yes!" and a Gingrich or a Clinton is elected on expectations that explode, leaving the shards and viscera of a reform effort spattered around the capital. The proper lesson of the failed reforms of the 1980s and 1990s isn't that nothing helps. The proper lesson is this: Forget big cures. Go with diet and exercise.

Demosclerosis is like aging in one essential way. Although it can't be cured, it can be *managed*. The prescription is not for a magic elixir but a standing regimen of discipline, with no miracles expected. The key is to be both realistic and persistent. You should not declare yourself cured one morning and stop eating well or exercising. And you also should not declare yourself hopeless and decide never to get out of bed.

How might the syndrome be managed, then? The suggestions that follow—in roughly ascending order of importance—aren't meant to be exhaustive. More thought by more people will generate more and, with luck, better ideas. The suggestions also aren't mutually exclusive; in fact, they tend to reinforce one another, much as exercise, diet, medicines, and reductions in stress can fight heart disease. Just don't expect miracles—and don't give up.

Fixing the Process

For many people, it's an article of faith that political reform is the key to revitalizing government and reducing the power of "special interests." The idea is that if Americans can't stop each other from forming interest groups, then at least we can reform the political process to reduce the groups' influence on our government. We would isolate government from lobbies, as the body might wall off a tumor. The three kinds of reform most talked about are tighter limits on lobbying, reform of the campaign-finance system, and limits on the amount of time that politicians can serve in office.

I don't want to pour cold water on those ideas entirely. Some of them are certainly worth trying. Nonetheless, expectations for process reforms are generally too high and, indeed, tend to miss the point. The process isn't the problem; the problem is the problem.

Consider, first, lobbying restrictions. Disclosure rules have been leaky and should be tightened. But impose actual limits on lobbying, and you tread on the First Amendment's explicit guarantee of the right "to petition the government for a redress of grievances." Reduce that right in any fundamental way, and you compromise the openness of democracy itself.

Anyway, as long as seeking government transfers is a lucrative business, people will invest in it. When your business is at stake in Washington, you *must* find a way to influence the government. You can no more ignore government than you can ignore a fire in your basement. Reforms of the lobbying process may force you to use more devious channels or more open ones. But the millions of ingenious lobbyists and groups whose livelihoods are at stake will always be many steps ahead of reform bills that Congress passes once every ten or twenty years. The more sophisticated the lobbyist, the more ingeniously he can find ways to cope with any limits placed on him. That's his job. In the end, attempts to clamp down on lobbying will mainly place legal hazards in the path of ordinary petitioners while working to the advantage of the professional lobbyists (and their lawyers) who know how to game the system.

Though campaign-finance reform is a more promising route than suppression of lobbying, it faces analogous problems. "I don't think that would affect me one iota," an anonymous but frank "veteran Washington lobbyist" told *National Journal* when he was asked about one leading campaign reform plan. "You can't eliminate the total costs of campaigns for candidates, and there will always be people who want to give. All I need to do is figure out how to get those two together." The more skillful this man is at defeating the campaign-finance limits, the more he'll be paid.

Many cleanup proposals focus on limiting political spending, the theory being that money corrupts the system. It's a weak theory. The truth is that politics is inherently expensive—reaching 100 million voters can't be cheap. "In a vast and heterogeneous society like the United States," writes Norman J. Ornstein, a prominent scholar of Congress, "elections are expensive, and have to be." If you restrict the supply of money without reducing the demand, you just force politicians to search more frantically for cash. In fact, that has been the effect of reforms since the 1970s, which, by making money harder to get, have made politicians more obsessed with raising it. These days, they often seem to have time for little else.

More fundamental is that political money is not the main cause of government's ailments; votes are. You may be able to limit the money that the sugar farmers' lobby can give to a Louisiana congressman. But that lobby can still deliver the votes of the people in its industry; it can still organize get-out-the-vote drives and "we suggest a contribution" campaigns; it can still run phone banks and buy ads supporting its friends; it can still inundate wavering congressmen's offices with mail; it can do a hundred other things. Ornstein suggests imagining, as a thought experiment, that there were *no* interest-group funds flowing to politicians. He doubts that lobbies would work any less hard to defend their interests, or that legislators would be any more eager to enrage constituent groups. In fact, outcomes might not be very different at all. "There simply are no data in the systematic studies that would support the popular assertions about the 'buying' of the Congress or any other massive influence of money on the legislative process," writes the political scientist Frank J. Sorauf. "Even taking the evidence selectively, there is at best a case for a modest influence of money."

The root problem is that the groups with the money represent millions of American voters and are engaging in practices that their members, rightly or wrongly, support. In politics, money is but one kind of political weapon. You need to weaken the groups, or else they simply pick up another weapon.

Advocates of limiting money in politics argue that such reforms can at least make the process more equal. Today, they say, the system favors rich interests that hire slick lobbyists, whereas limits on spending would level the playing field. The trouble with this argument is that it's about three decades out-of-date, and it's backward. Environmentalists, unions, small businesses, veterans, the elderly—those groups and the multitudes like them are not "the rich," and they are all busy lobbying. In fact, it's partly because the fat cats *lost* control that the lobbying process has entered its debilitating spiral. For just that reason, limiting donations from interest groups or political action committees may actually tilt the playing field toward the fat cats and insiders. Groups such as unions and environmental organizations are agglomerations of little people who become a political force by pooling their money; stop them from collecting and disbursing money, and the advantage may shift toward large companies and Mr. Bigs who don't depend on political action committees for their clout. Moreover, the reformers' attempts to regulate and limit money and political advertising have turned campaign laws into a bewildering tangle of legalese, understood by only a few specialists in the whole country. As a result, it's practically impossible to run for a federal office (or even for a growing number of state offices), or to engage in large-scale political activism (meaning any effort that involves television ads), without the support of high-priced lawyers, accountants, and campaign professionals. Further complicating the system by adding yet more layers of rules would have many effects, but making politics more transparent or accessible to real people would certainly not be among them.

Don't get me wrong: Some money reforms should be tried. Public financing of campaigns won't cure government's ills, but it might give politicians some freedom from the ceaseless search for cash, a change that would make political careers more attractive to people who do not want to be professional fund-raisers, wheedlers, or shakedown artists. Disclosure rules for lobbyists and large-dollar political donors are also a good idea, because they let people know who is seeking what goodies, at what cost, and who is doing the bargaining. But remember that changing the money rules can be, at most, only a very small part of coping. After all, since the early 1970s, at least a half dozen political-finance reforms and lobbying laws have been enacted, and those obviously haven't solved Washington's problems.

Indeed, the original 1970s campaign-finance regime itself became petrified and has thus become part of the problem. Contribution limits of $1,000, which seemed like a lot of money in 1974, became absurdly restrictive as inflation reduced their value, forcing candidates into all sorts of back channels to raise money; but the devotees of the 1970s system became a true-believing lobby that howled at the mere mention of raising the limits. The result was to drive the spending underground, or to replace ad campaigns run by politicians (who are accountable to voters) with ad campaigns run by lobbies (which are in business for themselves). The tale is cautionary. In the modern governing environment, today's innovation is tomorrow's prison cell. Reformers who forget this, and who place their bet on some complicated new set of rules, blink away the very nature of the problem they set out to solve.

Also in the 1970s, "sunset provisions" enjoyed a vogue, and some politicians still favor them. Unfortunately, sunset rules in the 1970s turned out to be disappointing. Legislators would call hearings, at which all the owners of subsidies would tout all the excellent accomplishments of their programs, and no one else would care. The programs would be renewed, with the added benefit, for the lobbyists, of regular fire-drills that helped pay the rent. Sunset provisions probably are not harmful, but they aren't the answer.

People who believe that the root of the problem is the professional political class suggest another kind of reform: term limits. Here the idea is to make the government less beholden to lobbies by reducing politicians' stake in their jobs. Instead of being in business for themselves—pandering to entrenched interests in order to protect their lifetime political careers—politicians would (so the argument goes) be real people with real lives. A different, less careerist sort of person would be attracted to politics: the sort who would think less about the interests of government and the professional political class and more about the folks back home, and who would serve for a little while and then return to his hardware store in Dubuque.

Term limits might help. They might indeed weaken the culture of professional politics, in which politicians and lobbyists and groups run in circles to create jobs for each other. On the other hand, term limits also might hurt. Politicians might enter one office and immediately begin scheming and jockeying for the next. No sooner might a House member be elected than he might begin pandering in order to prepare a Senate bid. Instead of nudging careerists out of politics, term limits might just shorten their attention span. More fundamentally, term limits don't much change the equation that confronts every sitting politician who must decide whether to defy organized favor-seekers: Vote against the lobby and weather a blizzard of hate mail, or vote with it and reap its "Honorary Dairyman of the Year" award.

That is not to say that term limits are necessarily a bad idea. They ought to be tried, preferably at the state level to see how they work. And that is happening. By the time of the 1998 elections, eighteen states had imposed term limits on their legislators. If the limits put a damper on the culture of political careerism, then they will have achieved something worthwhile. At bottom, though, the roots of government's decline lie not in the careerist culture but in the transfer-seeking logic that shapes and drives that culture.

Ultimately, the problem with all the process reforms is that the government-friendly environment of the mid-twentieth century is gone forever. There is no repealing the technologies that have made lobbying so cheap, so accessible, so fast. There is no dismantling the infrastructure of professional subsidy brokers and group organizers and lobbies. You can't isolate a democratic government from its society. If society divides and redivides into more groups seeking benefits, government can't and shouldn't be cut off from those groups' influence. Process reforms might at best add a few buffering layers. Although extra buffering layers might be worth having (as long as they don't make the government numb), in the end they are no solution, and they divert attention from substantive reforms that go deeper and offer more hope.

Locking the Cupboard

We Americans organize into lobbies because government can feed us. Some libertarians and conservatives would solve that problem in the most direct way. They would put the food out of reach. That is, they would make the entire transfer-seeking business illegal.

In advancing their idea, these proponents take up a line of thought that dates to the founders. James Madison was aware of the dangers of transfer-seeking and warned against "speculators" who earn profits by brokering government subsidies and favors. "The sober people of America . . . have seen with regret and indignation that sudden changes and legislative interferences, in cases affecting personal rights, become jobs in the hands of enterprising and influential speculators, and snares to the more industrious and less informed part of the community," Madison wrote in *The Federalist* (No. 44). "They very rightly infer, therefore, that some thorough reform is wanting, which will banish speculations on public measures." Madison's idea was that government should have little power to reassign property, so that "speculators on public measures"—transfer-seeking entrepreneurs—would have little to buy and sell. Thus does the Bill of Rights say, in no uncertain terms, "No person shall . . . be deprived of life, liberty, or property without due process of law; nor shall private property be taken for public use without just compensation."

For decades the Supreme Court more or less held to the Madisonian vision, rejecting government's efforts to move private wealth around. In the last third of the nineteenth century, however, the courts began upholding transfer laws. "From 1877 to 1917 the Constitution was altered in numerous ways that made transfers much easier to obtain," according to Terry L. Anderson and Peter J. Hill. "Except for the income tax amendment [of 1913], all of these changes came through [judicial] interpretation." During the New Deal, after a period of resistance, the Supreme Court yielded more ground by blessing President Roosevelt's interventionist economic program. Since then, constitutional restraints on transfer-seeking have been few.

Suppose the situation were more like the state of affairs before the New Deal. Suppose, that is, government's power to reassign resources were reduced. If Washington took money from someone, or passed a regulation reducing the value of someone's property, or restricted someone's use of his property, it would have to compensate him for the loss. If Smith wanted to put a billboard on his beachfront property or pave over his wetland, the government could stop him only by buying his property or compensating him in some other way, rather than just passing a law. Necessarily, then, the government would have a much harder time giving away favors to people who wanted benefits at Smith's expense.

This is the general approach favored by members of the so-called economic-rights or property-rights movement, who believe that government's ability to grant transfers at will has gotten out of hand. Their approach has a big advantage and a big disadvantage. The big advantage is that it would work. There is no point lobbying a government that can't do anything for you. When Washington loses its power to give favors to groups, groups will stop seeking favors from the government. Those groups' lobbyists will go away and get real jobs.

The big disadvantage is that any plan that restricted the government's ability to subsidize merchant mariners would also restrict its ability to run a Social Security program or enact environmental laws. Everything the government does, right down to such core functions as law enforcement and national defense, requires the power to take tax money from one place and put it somewhere else. To strip government of its power to transfer wealth is to "solve" government.

To libertarians, of course, that sounds like a fine idea. Because this book sees government as a self-interested actor, rather than as merely a transparent representative of the people, the original publication won some praise in libertarian quarters. But then those readers would hurl the book away in frustration, complaining: "Why can't he see that the problem is government itself? Why doesn't he just give up, join our crusade, and fight to repeal Washington?"

One reason is that I think a good deal of what modern government does is worth doing. The more telling reason, however, is that the whole point is that Washington *cannot* be repealed or even reduced much in scope, for all the reasons I discussed in the previous chapter. James Madison might indeed be appalled if he returned and saw today's Washington, but there would be nothing he could do about it except fulminate. The dream of turning Leviathan back into a mouse is just that, a dream, and its persistence blocks acceptance of more realistic measures. So on to more practical suggestions.

Scattering the Goodies

One of the reasons Washington is suffocating under the swarm of client groups is that Washington is an irresistible target. You can go there for almost any kind of benefit you want, and it's the only game in town. There are no other federal governments that might undercut you or favor your competitors behind your back. Washington is one-stop shopping for the parasite economy.

If the central government is so big that it attracts every manner of opportunistic interest yet is too unwieldy to adapt as it should, why not decentralize? Why not devolve whole functions to lower levels of government?

Although states and cities aren't immune to sclerosis, far more of them exist. Decentralization tends to mean that lobbies need to spread their resources across more governmental units. Imagine the problems that lobbies might face as they tried to seek subsidies in each of fifty states. Just as important, different states and localities offer the possibility of running different programs that would compete with one another. If Hawaii discovers a better kind of health-care program, or Michigan a better way to finance schools, it will gain an advantage over less effective states. Variety and competition can give each jurisdiction the opportunity and the incentive to learn from the successes and failures of the others. And if, in the end, a local government does turn sclerotic, people can leave. Even if the government is stuck with all its programs, the people aren't stuck—a big advantage.

Meanwhile, back in Washington, if the federal government is given less to do, then it may be able to do its job better.

A thoughtful plan to rearrange responsibilities was proposed in 1992 by Alice M. Rivlin, an economist at the Brookings Institution who went on to serve as director of the Clinton administration's Office of Management and Budget and then as the vice chairman of the Federal Reserve Board. By the 1970s, Washington "resembled a giant conglomerate that has acquired too many different kinds of businesses and cannot coordinate its own activities," she wrote in her book *Reviving the American Dream*. "The federal government has taken on too much responsibility and should return some of its functions to the states. A clearer division of responsibilities between the states and the federal government could make both levels operate more effectively."

Under Rivlin's plan, the federal government would be in charge of the health-care system and broad social-insurance programs like Social Security. Washington would cede to the states control of most or all programs in education, job training, economic development, housing, transportation, social services, and some other fields. One result would be programs that were better adapted to local conditions and thus more effective. Other results would be clearer accountability and sharper competition. "Once clearly in charge," Rivlin argued, "the states would compete vigorously with each other to improve services and attract business by offering high-quality education, infrastructure, and other services."

Decentralization has been batted around for years; President Eisenhower named a commission to study it, and more than a decade later President Nixon named another. In 1981, Bruce Babbitt, the Democratic governor of Arizona (and later President Clinton's secretary of the interior), called for a rearranging of roles. "Congress ought to be worrying about arms control and defense instead of potholes in the street," he wrote. "We just might have both an increased chance of survival and better streets." Barry Goldwater and his conservative heirs, of course, talked about returning power to the states, though they were more interested in pulling Washington's teeth than in stimulating competition. President Reagan touted a "new federalism." Yet, through it all, nothing happened, except that the federal government's elephantiasis grew worse. The parasite economy and the run on government ensured that everyone came to Washington for whatever he wanted, and then never relinquished anything he got.

A further problem is that no one quite agreed on which functions to strip from the central government or how to rewrite its charter. There, again, is the problem of particulars, in which everyone is stoutly in favor of devolving somebody else's program. And, of course, lobbies will fight to keep their federal holdings. So rearranging local and federal roles is a project that will take decades. But it's also a project worth doing and long overdue, especially for those who want the federal government to succeed in the long run.

In the meantime, we need measures that help in the nearer term. So, again, skip ahead, this time to what I think is the most promising class of options.

The Olsonian tendency for groups and perquisites to accumulate cannot be reversed. But it can be weakened. The trick is to attack the Olsonian forces themselves. We can't stop each other from forming interest groups and fighting to preserve subsidies. We can't shut groups and activists out of politics. But what if we can subject them to forces that soften them up? What if we expose them to a kind of chemotherapy, which weakens their grip? I believe it can be done. And there are a number of ways to do it.

Cut the Lobbies' Lifelines

By now, one prescription should be obvious: Wherever and whenever possible, eliminate subsidies and programs, including tax loopholes, which are subsidies that are administered through the tax code. Get rid of things to make room for things. Cut entire programs loose and pitch them overboard.

Killing low-priority programs and entrenched subsidies strengthens government, by freeing up space for innovation. At least as important, it also weakens the parasite class, by shutting off the money that sustains lobbies. When the subsidies stop flowing, the lobbyists seem less worth paying, and their clients have less money to pay with. Why is there a sugar lobby? Because it defends a sugar subsidy. Get rid of the subsidy, and although the lobby perhaps won't vanish overnight, it will be weakened.

To get the job done requires at least three ingredients. First, there must be leadership from the very top. The president is the one politician with a stronger professional interest in the whole government and the whole country than in any particular piece of either. Second, determination and realism are essential. Instead of expecting to launch a giant, world-changing assault on government, you need to come back year after year, never expecting to revolutionize Washington but never ceasing in the search for opportunities to clean house.

Third, and not least, you need liberals. As long as the government keeps doing everything it ever did, and keeps trying to do every possible sort of thing at once, it cannot function well, and so the public will continue to resent it. That means people will continue to resent its champions, who happen to be liberals. What the political writer Kevin Phillips once called "reactionary liberalism"—liberals' tendency to cling to every governmental mission and program as though it were their patrimony—has been the death of the American left. Reactionary liberalism tells the voters that liberals care more about preserving an empire in Washington than about making government actually work. To change the political culture so that housecleaning becomes a routine part of governing, *liberals* will need to take the lead in scouring for programs to eliminate, rather than merely launching the occasional symbolic attack on "corporate welfare" and blowing raspberries at conservatives. *Liberals* should put their shoulder to the work that, until now, has been discussed mainly by antigovernment types.

As they seek to frame their message so as to fortify the public's resolve as client groups shriek, reformers should remember that the reason to prune and chop is not to kill government, or even necessarily to shrink it, but to restore some of its flexibility and effectiveness. Voters of the political center, let alone the left, won't believe this if they hear it from right-wingers, but they may believe it from liberals. Liberals ought to remind themselves and the public, at every turn, that the point is to break the stranglehold of entrenched claimants and to clear ground for new ventures. Making room for adaptation and unloading an over-burdened system are steps toward making government likelier to work. And that is good for liberals, above all.

Domestic Perestroika

Lobbies live to lock money in and competition out. Their fondest love is a monopoly claim on public funds or private markets. Insurance companies defend rules keeping banks out of the insurance business. Fruit growers defend rules letting them limit the number of lemons that can be sold. Cable television companies defend regulations keeping phone companies out of the entertainment-transmission business. Peanut farmers defend a licensing system that lets them shut out new growers. Taxi companies defend rules that prevent the number of cabbies from increasing. Public-school employees, postal workers, and welfare administrators fend off competition from private providers of services.

How to weaken them? Strip away their anticompetitive protections and let competition hammer them. Competition not only helps make the economy more efficient but also weakens entrenched lobbies. It forces transfer-seekers to sink or swim according to their skill at producing goods or services, rather than their skill at lobbying in Washington.

Domestic perestroika starts with removal of government restraints on competition. Jimmy Carter's deregulation of transportation industries and interest rates, though imperfectly executed, was an antiparasite tonic to set beside the 1986 tax reform. Deregulation created some turmoil in the marketplace (which was, of course, just the point), yet it produced better deals for travelers and small savers, greater efficiency in the transportation and financial markets, and, for the most part, better service. After the passage of the Air Cargo Deregulation Act of 1977 and the Airline Deregulation Act of 1978, airfares fell (after adjusting for inflation) by more than 20 percent, the number of passengers doubled, and air accident rates fell by almost half (with, yes, more nonstop service). A Brookings Institution analysis estimated that consumers saved roughly $100 billion in the first decade of deregulation. The railroad deregulation of 1980 saved shippers as much as $5 billion a year, with lower accident rates. After trucking was deregulated in 1980, the number of carriers more than doubled, trucking jobs increased by a third, and the economy saved on the order of $8 billion a year. Such are perestroika's blessings—not unmixed, to be sure, yet more than worth the trouble.

Deregulation isn't always wise, and each case needs to be judged on its merits. But the point is to hunt aggressively for opportunities to tear out anticompetitive franchises, and thus to pursue what the writer James Fallows has called the reopening of America.

No less important than exposing coddled private interests to competition is to expose coddled *government* interests to competition. Today, the public sector, not the private sector, is the biggest haven for monopolistic franchises. In the private sector, monopolies are the exception, but in the public sector they are the rule. In America there are dozens of ways to send overnight mail and packages but only one way to send a first-class letter.

In each city there are thousands of places to get groceries but only one place to get a welfare check. In most places, if you want your household trash collected, you have to pay the government's rate. And so on.

A blind spot of postwar American liberalism has been its failure to understand that a monopoly or cartel administered by a public authority is at least as likely to be backward and abusive as one administered by a private company. "It is one of the enduring paradoxes of American ideology that we attack private monopolies so fervently but embrace public monopolies so warmly," write David Osborne and Ted Gaebler, the authors of *Reinventing Government*. Both kinds of monopolies are likely to produce high prices, poor service, slow innovation, and entrenched arrogance. Both kinds breed lobbies whose mission is to see that the coddling never stops and that newcomers never enter. And just as private cartels and monopolies stultify the economy, so too do public cartels and monopolies stultify the government.

By creating havens for lobbies, monopoly power weakens the government over the longer term. Moreover, because government monopolies are notoriously careless about their customers' welfare, they arouse ill will among the public, weakening government still further. "Our public sector can learn to compete," Osborne and Gaebler remark, "or it can stagnate and shrink, until the only customers who use public services are those who cannot afford an alternative."

Wherever possible, then, bring perestroika to the public sector. Force government providers to compete against other government providers or against private competitors. To cite one well-known example, the city of Phoenix forced its trash-collection agency to compete with outside bidders, with notable success. Various studies, note Osborne and Gaebler, show that "on average public service delivery is 35 to 95 percent more expensive than contracting, even when the cost of administering the contracts is included."

Bringing competition inside the stale confines of government agencies is no longer a radical idea in America. In one of its first initiatives, the Clinton administration glowingly talked up the idea in a 1993 government-reform report (which David Osborne helped write): "By forcing public agencies to compete for their customers—between offices, with other agencies, and with the private sector—we will create a permanent pressure to streamline programs, abandon the obsolete, and improve what's left." Unfortunately, the Clinton people, not keen to alienate the public employees' unions, brought much more enthusiasm to talk than to action. Still, by the mid-1990s, at least fifteen states had passed laws letting private operators run roads and railways. Abroad, Britain, New Zealand, and other countries forced various of their government bureaucracies to provide services competitively.

Allowing competition within government is a promising path. But it is no substitute for the kind of public-sector perestroika that counts the most. Where possible, government monopolies should be swept away altogether.

The schools are a good example. In Washington, D.C., a truant boy told his grandmother he was afraid to go to school: "They have guns and knives at school." In Boston, where four in ten graduates of public high schools could not read at ninth-grade level, students were stabbed and principals threatened. In Houston, a poll found that 85 percent of parents said their kids were unsafe in school. In Chicago's housing projects, children will go live with relatives in other neighborhoods or states, or even try to flunk eighth grade, to avoid the terror of the public high schools. The wealthy can flee dysfunctional and dangerous public schools and have been doing so for years. The poor are left behind to take their chances, all in the name of "saving the public schools"—meaning, saving the jobs of the people who run them.

The public-school lobbies—teachers' unions, principals' associations, school boards' groups—argue that their monopoly claim on taxpayers' money is in the national interest. But, like so many monopoly franchises, this one serves its holders better than its captives. It also resembles other monopolies in its black-hole-like ability to suck in money without noticeably improving performance. Over the period since World War II, spending per public-school student, after adjusting for inflation, increased about 40 percent a decade, doubling every twenty years. Meanwhile, average class sizes fell, and the proportion of teachers holding master's degrees rose. Yet test scores sank and stagnated, and horror stories about what students didn't know became legion. Public schools weren't under pressure to perform, because most of their "customers"—students and parents—could not afford to vote with their feet.

If you hand every parent—or, at the very least, every lower-income parent—a ticket applicable toward school tuition and say, "Take your tax money and go find the best school you can," you allow buyers of education to circumvent the interest groups that have overgrown every cranny of public education. You force entrenched providers to fight for their paychecks. Do that, and many of them will rise to the challenge and improve. Breaking the public-school monopoly is bad for some of the people who happen to be running the public-school system at the moment, but it is not bad for public schools—it is good for them. After the initial shock of adjustment, competition from Toyota and Hyundai made American cars better and American car companies stronger. The same would happen, after the same sort of initial shock, to the public schools. It is no coincidence that the strongest and most effective branch of American public education, the state university system, is also the branch that competes against private providers for tax money (in the form of student loans). No one seriously believes that competition with Stanford makes Berkeley any worse. Although competition is not an educational panacea, there is every reason to think that it would make the schools better—in both sectors, private and public, as all schools work to attract students. The benefits would flow especially to the poorest, who are now trapped in the worst schools. And the country would gain politically by prying the education industry loose from the lobbies' grip.

Not every private company or government agency can be forced into competition. Building three private airports in Cincinnati and forcing them into competition might not work (though, on the other hand, it might). Yet the lobby-weakening potential of market-opening moves is large and still largely untapped. A good rule of thumb is this: Where you see a government restraint on private competition, look for a way to get rid of it. And where you see a government agency sheltered from competition, look for a way to expose it. In every case, you will weaken interest groups and stimulate adaptation.

Foreign Competition

Even at its easiest, eliminating a subsidy or opening a protected niche to competition is very difficult, and success comes only sporadically, even if the reformers try mightily. The forces of stultification, however, operate continuously, day and night. The accumulation of groups and cozy deals never stops. To fight back requires a counterforce capable of weakening entrenched interests and cozy deals day after day, year after year. Foreign competition is such a counterforce.

In the 1990s, as Americans pressed the Europeans to open their heavily protected agriculture markets, French farmers— one of the world's most sanctimonious and thuggish lobbies— made their views known by throwing rotten eggs at cabinet members, blocking Paris's rush-hour traffic, dumping fresh produce in town squares, burning American flags, and vandalizing a McDonald's in Paris, among other jolly antics. "Don't kill the French farmer!" they cried. The voracious European farm lobby has mercilessly cultivated the parliaments of Europe, eating tens of billions of dollars a year in direct subsidies and much more in indirect costs to European consumers and American farmers.

What does Europe's farm lobby fear and hate most of all? Foreign competition.

By taking on the French farmers—something that French politicians weren't inclined to do—the Americans do the whole world a favor, but they especially do the French a favor. The Japanese rely so heavily on foreign pressure of this type that they have a word for it, *gaiatsu*. Economic *gaiatsu*, from Japan and other countries, is one of the great progressive forces in America (and the world) today.

People who bemoan the rise of Japanese auto imports in America forget what Americans were driving in the 1970s and much of the 1980s, when the Big Three complacently ran what their critics argued was a kind of loose cartel. Think how much better cars are today, thanks in no small measure to foreign competition. People who worry about the rise of Japanese steel may not realize that Japanese competition and investment sharpened the American steel industry after decades of disinvestment and obsolescence. "Without Japanese investment, technology, and manufacturing organization, we would likely find ourselves with a much smaller domestic steel industry, if any at all," according to Richard Florida and Martin Kenney, two academics who study the industry. "The power of Japanese industry to transform American steel has been astonishing. Major strides have been made in an industry that was viewed by many as an unsalvageable 'basket case' not more than a decade ago."

Trade introduces new actors and new technologies, which help keep the economy flexible and vital. Just as important, because there is no World Congress to lobby, the job of winning anticompetitive goodies on a worldwide scale is almost impossible. When you expand trade, therefore, you almost automatically weaken local interest groups that thrive within sealed borders.

In this context, the best parasite weakener in the world may be the World Trade Organization. The WTO and the periodic rounds of multilateral trade-opening negotiations that empower it are all but unknown to most Americans, yet they are the most effective form of global *gaiatsu* in operation. In global trade talks, more than a hundred countries regularly negotiate to reduce their trade barriers and market subsidies. The standard arguments for the WTO and other free-trade conventions are economic. "Trade makes us wealthier," the economists say: It hones productivity on the whetstone of competition; it lets people anywhere take advantage of economic efficiencies everywhere; it allows larger economies of scale and speeds countries up the learning curve. Although all of that is true, the most important benefits of trade-opening measures are not economic but political. By weakening lobbies, trade can help invigorate democratic government—not just in the United States but all over the world.

That would be impossible if all countries had the same interest groups and the same cozy deals. But they don't. If Europe's farm protectionism is steeper than America's, and if America's maritime protectionism is steeper than Europe's, then the Europeans can attack the American shipping interests, and the Americans can attack the French farming interests—and both can attack the Japanese securities cartels. Even within sectors, countries can engage in mutual cozy-deal disarmament ("We'll open our wheat market if you'll open yours"). Under the WTO, dozens of countries join the circle and attack each other's lobbies. In effect, governments pick off each other's parasites.

The lobbies fight back. They scream, they scratch, they kick and buck. They say that trade liberalization is unfair and that it will be their ruin. They wrap themselves in the flag and sing the national anthem. When the French farmers blocked the streets and trashed McDonald's, they claimed to be representing France's national heritage. Manufacturers insist that defending their markets (and profits) from foreign "threats" is vital to the national interest, to the technology base, the job base, whatever. Unions insist that foreign competition destroys American jobs and reduces American incomes. Green groups protest that competing against dirtier countries undercuts environmental standards at home. Their arguments, being seductive, are worth a moment's examination.

As for environmentalists, they often worry more about trade than they need to. Trade makes nations richer, and richer nations are the ones that can afford environmental standards in the first place. "Studies show that pollution intensity has grown most rapidly in those countries that remained most closed to world market forces," reports the Organization for Economic Co-operation and Development. "In turn, this lends support to the view that openness to foreign competition is more likely to raise than lower environmental standards." Indeed, if you plot countries' environmental records against their incomes, as the OECD has done, you immediately see that countries become cleaner as they grow richer. Yes, a dirtier country may enjoy some advantages in competing with a cleaner one, but it may also suffer from many disadvantages—higher medical costs, a sicker workforce, inefficient resource use, and so on. There is no empirical or historical reason to think that dirtier countries "win" in trade and cleaner ones "lose"; if they did, then it would be hard to account for America's continued economic dominance since the 1970s, when the Environmental Protection Agency first opened for business.

Moreover, the discipline of foreign competition helps keep environmental rules economically sensible. If you know that General Motors must compete with Toyota, you'll be more careful to reduce GM's tailpipe emissions in a relatively efficient way, and not past the point where tailpipe emissions aren't worth reducing. You can focus your environmental energies where you get the most bang for the buck. That is good for the environment, and it is good for the economy—though it is not good for extremist activists and single-issue lobbies, because it restrains the demands they can attain at the expense of the economy as a whole.

Unions' calls to save American jobs and wages are appealing but misguided. True, trade puts painful pressure on unions—*if they are uncompetitive.* Effective and flexible unions can make their companies more productive. The unions that need to worry are the ones that defend archaic work rules, engage in featherbedding, block productive cooperation with management, or try to fix wages at levels that markets won't support (thus feeding inflation and currency devaluation). But this is exactly the boon of trade: It puts competitive pressure on cozy arrangements that benefit entrenched groups but rigidify the economy as a whole.

The impassioned 1993 debate over the North American Free Trade Agreement (NAFTA), and the subsequent attacks on trade from both the left and the "economic patriots" of the right, brought front and center one of the most common objections to foreign competition—namely, that it reduces employment in America. That charge is flat wrong—no more sensible than claiming that Illinois loses jobs by trading with New York and California. The period after World War II was marked by trade liberalization, yet it brought dramatic increases in employment, in the United States as well as abroad. Imports have more than doubled as a share of the American economy from the early 1970s to the late 1990s, growing faster than exports, but over that same period the economy added more than 50 million new jobs, and the percentage of the population that was employed rose rather than declined. And that stood to reason. Suppose you buy a foreign car that is just as good but $1,000 cheaper than the American equivalent, or that costs the same but saves you $1,000 in repair costs. You have "earned" an extra $1,000, which you will spend or invest elsewhere in the economy, putting people to work and giving yourself what amounts to a raise. Meanwhile, foreigners selling in the U.S. market earn dollars, which they spend by buying American exports and (especially when there's a trade deficit) investing in the American economy. Either way, trade is a win-win game for the economy as a whole.

The problem isn't that foreign competition destroys American jobs on net, but that it often shifts jobs from one sector to another in ways that benefit the economy as a whole but sting specific groups, which organize lobbying efforts to block the change. And that, again, is the point: Foreign competition hurts entrenched interest groups. Sympathize with them, help them with adjustment when necessary, but *expose them to competition*.

Companies and business groups that argue for protection from foreign competition, whether in steel or agriculture, never fail to invoke the national interest and the threat that foreigners will "take over" some important sector. What they do not say is that protection of one American industry necessarily comes at the expense of many others. Protect American carmakers, and their higher prices hurt thousands of American businesses that buy cars; protect American manufacturers of flat-panel computer displays, and higher display prices hurt the competitiveness of American computer makers, who need the best displays at the lowest cost; protect American sugar growers, and higher sweetener costs hurt food manufacturers of every description. Every business lobby claims to be especially vital to the economy or the nation, but you can't protect them all. When the reshuffling game is over, the winners are the ones with the sharpest lobbyists.

If you want to keep barnacles off your boat, head for white water. Americans should seek at every turn to expose lobbies to foreign competition rather than shelter them. They should exploit every chance to tear down trade barriers (of which America has plenty), and they should welcome foreign investment.

I don't want to oversell foreign competition. It is not a magic potion. Interest groups that aren't directly involved with trade — the veterans' lobby or the seniors' lobby, for instance — aren't much affected by foreign competition one way or another. Still, of all the countermeasures in the arsenal, foreign competition may offer the best combination of effectiveness and accessibility. We know it helps, and we have the means to pursue it. Above all, it works every day. As the tax-reform experience showed, if you scatter parasites only once, they soon reassemble. But foreign competition pounds them all the time. It is a sentinel that never sleeps.

Not Enough

At this point in the discussion, after I have put my stack of suggestions on the table, you may feel unsatisfied. After all, the medicines seem a little weak, compared with the scope of the disease. On the one side, there are powerful ossifying forces that well up from deep within society and that operate on the entire government constantly. And on the other side is yet another call for free trade. America does a lot of trading already, you say. Will doing more of it solve the problem?

The complaint, alas, is just. I began this chapter by trying to banish the expectation of cures, and now is the time to reemphasize the point. The sorts of measures I have discussed are not a list of solutions; they are a list of treatments. A country that tries to follow the path of openness will not be immune to the buildup of lobbies and the calcification of government. In the long term, openness will probably not even stop the process. But it will *slow* the process, and in a good year, when America wins a major international trade agreement or scrubs the barnacles from its tax code, the country can recover some lost ground. Here the analogy with exercise is apt. Exercise will not stop you from growing older. But every hour of exercise helps. No developed country in the world is as overrun with cartels and sweet deals and cozy arrangements between government and special interests as Japan. For a while, Japan looked to have beaten the world, but in fact its relative closure to competition, foreign and domestic, turned out to have made it too rigid to adapt either economically or politically, with depressing results. America's relative economic vigor comes from America's relative economic openness. An open country is, in the long run, almost invariably better off than a closed one, even though it will have its share of problems. The same is true of government. Measures to open it are difficult and painful and cannot cure the disease. What they can do, however, is make the difference between coping well and coping poorly.

Now arises a second objection, one that goes deep. In this chapter, it seems, I propose to deal with the Olsonian forces by recommending the very measures that those forces block. If we could wave a magic wand and get rid of well-protected programs or trade barriers or tax breaks or any of the rest of it, then this book wouldn't be necessary in the first place. The lobbies fight subsidy reductions, tax increases, decentralizing moves, trade liberalizations—they fight everything I advocate. Just how are we supposed to use competition to weaken lobbies when the whole problem is that the lobbies are blocking competition? Isn't this book like the doctor who prescribes running for a paraplegic?

No, not quite. And here the attitude of the patient—of the American public and its political leaders—becomes particularly important. David Stockman and Newt Gingrich and (though differently) Bill Clinton decided to build Rome (or sack it, depending on your point of view) in a day. They attempted to gather up the whole system in their arms and rearrange it. But that is not the right way. The right way is a little bit at a time, steadily, constantly. If you're weak and overweight and unfit and have a bad heart, you don't go off to a spa for three weeks and expect to come back a new person. You go to a weight-loss camp, maybe, but to learn new habits, new ways to live. You eat a little better every day, walk a little every day, and reduce stress where you can. And you *keep at it*. You don't expect to have the heart or body of a twenty-year-old. But you do not view this as failure.

These attitudinal points, no doubt, seem small. But in fact they are important, for they contain the seeds of a healthier, more mature relationship between the people and their government.

10

Adjusting Ourselves

ALTHOUGH I have never been to a bullfight, several people have told me that the event is mostly a stupefying exercise in choreographed cruelty, in which what is mainly interesting is the outlandish dumbness of the bull. The picadors and toreros stick the beast with darts and jab him with lances, and still he charges, to receive still more torments. The matador taunts him, and he charges some more, until he is near death as much from exhaustion as from bleeding. A British journalist I know, who reported on a bullfight in Mexico, was particularly startled to see how the matador, to demonstrate his mastery, would at intervals turn his back on the bull and strut slowly, arrogantly away. But the bulls, said this correspondent, "are bred more than anything for surpassing stupidity. While the guy with the sparkly costume and the insufferable airs is swaggering off, bum waving practically in the creature's face, it never once occurs to any bull that this is the time to summon up a bit of strength, lower those horns, and transform his tormentor into a swivel chair."

The famous 1974 fight in Kinshasa, Zaire, between Muhammad Ali and George Foreman was a fight that Ali was supposed to lose. Foreman was nine years younger than Ali, bigger, stronger, fiercer. No one had withstood the elemental force of his punches. At the age of nineteen, in 1968, he was an Olympic gold medalist; by the time of the Rumble in the Jungle with Ali, he was the undefeated world heavyweight champion, having knocked out Joe Frazier in only two rounds in 1973. Yet Ali beat Foreman. As the audience looked on gasping, Ali went to the ropes, covering his face while letting Foreman pummel him with blow after blow and taunting him to punch some more. Some spectators thought Ali had lost the will to fight. And then, at length, Foreman was exhausted, punched out. Ali's superior agility and tactical genius could come into play, and Ali took down Foreman in the eighth round.

When I think of the American electorate's spasms of discontent and fury at government over the last few decades, I sometimes think of that bull in the arena. When I think of the ability of all the little transfer-seekers to prevail against headstrong reformers ostensibly supported by the broad electorate, I think of Ali's rope-a-dope. It is true that every now and then, in the bull-ring, a matador is gored; and every now and then, in Washington, the public overturns some furniture. But at the end of the day, the bull is still stew, and Washington is still Washington.

If you believe the old civics-book view of the world, then the rise of the transfer-seeking economy represents the interpolation of a meddling class of intermediaries and jobbers standing between the people and their government. In that case, the mission is to sweep the intermediaries away, or, at least, to drive straight through them with a bulldozer. You could then show the crowd in Washington who's boss, sending it fleeing before the majestic power of the people's will. If that is your plan, you may well be as successful, give or take a little, as George Foreman or the bull.

On the other hand, if you understand the forces that have brought America's government to its present end, then you are likely to realize that the transfer-seekers are no more separable from government than trees are from a forest. You may also realize that the arithmetic of transfer-seeking can't be revoked as long as government has enough power to serve its citizens. The clients and their protectorates are no mere interlopers or appendages or transitory afflictions. Like the species that occupy and shape a coral reef, they are the government's inhabitants, cultivators, fabricators. As Theodore Lowi realized, to a very large degree they *are* the government. You cannot get around them, past them, over them, or under them. And you cannot just punch furiously at them, or you get rope-a-doped.

If Americans want to be less like the bull and more like Muhammad Ali, the future belongs to a governing philosophy that I think of as "radical incrementalism": the determination to foment revolutionary change over the geological time scale. That means looking every day of every year for opportunities to push policies in the procompetitive directions that I discussed in the previous chapter. But it also means nudging ourselves toward accepting government as it is. It means replacing immoderate expectations and sporadic, convulsive reform efforts with moderate expectations and determined, unceasing incremental change. For liberals, for conservatives, above all for the broad public, the time has come for some attitude adjustments.

Why Liberals and Conservatives Will Be Unhappy

As the reality of government's irreversible (but manageable) sclerosis sinks in, many traditional liberals are bound to start squirming uncomfortably. "It can't be!" they'll say. American liberals tend to believe that government's problem-solving capacity is large and expandable. Programs solve problems; more problems require more programs. Many liberals have long assumed that Washington can do almost anything it puts its mind to, if only the right people are in charge.

I hope this book has persuaded you that the liberal assumption, however natural, is wrong. Instead, there is a necessary and inherent trade-off between what government tries to do and what it *can* do. By initiating programs that create lobbies that lock in programs, government chokes on its own output. And this problem can't be wished away. Like a careful doctor meting out drugs thoughtfully, liberals need to stay constantly aware of the natural limits on how much Washington can do, and they need to respect those limits. As a rule, they have failed to do that.

Some liberals will dismiss sclerosis as conservative cant: just another attack on government (and on liberalism). "More defeatism from the people who have always told us to give up. Well, forget it!" That reaction would be unfortunate, a counterproductive act of denial—as, again, I hope the preceding arguments have suggested. Another, more common, form of denial is "Yes, but never mind." A few weeks before Bill Clinton first took office, back when changing everything was a foregone conclusion, I met with a Clinton adviser who advocated fistfuls of targeted federal investment programs and industrial policies (and who went on to play a leading role in the administration's inauspicious health-care effort). Demosclerosis implies that it's impossible to insulate such programs from interest groups that capture the benefits and then hoard them. How, I asked, would you get around that problem? He shrugged, then replied: "We *have* to make this kind of thing work."

That's "Yes, but never mind" thinking: "Yes, organized interests take over programs and turn them into permanent fiefdoms, but we'll keep on acting as though they didn't, in hopes that maybe this time they won't." At government's end, "Yes, but never mind" won't do. Liberals who want to start a new program or expand an old one ought, at least, to design their program with the realities of demosclerosis in mind. That may mean, for example, channeling services through providers who compete with each other for the "business" of the program's end users, rather than running programs through government bureaucracies or monopoly contractors whose main imperative is to keep the service providers, politicians, and bureaucrats cozy. It is no coincidence that the G.I. Bill (education vouchers for veterans) and the food-stamp program (grocery vouchers for the poor) have been among the most successful programs of their kind.

By a similar token, liberals need to understand sclerosis as a byproduct of Washington's own activities and not as a product of obstructionist corporate baddies. Washington is like a town whose factories are poisoning its water supply: At some point, the town needs to stop building new factories and start cleaning up the water. In the future, if liberals really care about making government better, as opposed to just making it bigger or more ambitious, they'll need to see cleaning up the accumulated muck as part and parcel of the *liberal* agenda rather than as a concession to conservatism.

Until they do, their hope of using government in ever more creative ways is fanciful and, ultimately, self-defeating. Visions of technocratic activism—sharp-eyed government entrepreneurs making cutting-edge investments, agile officials fine-tuning innovative social programs, successful local experiments turned into equally successful national programs—are mirages. Government's effectiveness is naturally self-limiting, and those who deny or defy the limits are invariably making the situation worse, not better.

Government's end thus spells the end not of liberalism but of liberalism without limits. If politicians and the public pick their shots carefully, they can solve a handful of problems pretty well. But if they try to solve every problem at once—which is what they have done—they energize every possible lobby and every potential group, thus feeding the very process that destroys government's ability to adapt.

My frustration is that too few liberals are yet ready to understand this premise. Many cling to a kind of unlimited governmentalism that, for example, undertakes to restore rural economies, revitalize inner cities, and shore up suburbs all at once. In a sense, they're loving government to death, which really means loving liberalism to death, because liberalism relies on government to solve problems. When government fails, liberalism fails. And that is the story of the last twenty or more years. Liberals would do themselves a favor to stop assuming automatically that cutting programs is an antigovernment move. It isn't, any more than revising product lines is an antibusiness move.

Conservatives are more comfortable than liberals with the notion of natural limits on what government can do. But they have some adjusting to do, too. Demosclerosis turns government into more and more of a rambling, ill-adapted shambles that often gets in the way but can't be eliminated. From a conservative point of view, decrepit government just sits there, like a big boulder in the middle of the road. If it fails to serve a liberal agenda, it is equally likely to block a conservative one. Liberals may not get new job-training programs that work, but conservatives also can't get rid of archaic regulations or pointless programs.

Conservatives would thus be foolish to think that government's end is a victory for them. They, too, need to fight it. That means throwing coddled business lobbies out into the cold. It means saying no to financiers and insurance executives and manufacturers and farm-bureau members and many other subsidized interests who are important parts of the conservative political base—and who don't at all mind subsidies and cozy deals that inure to their benefit. Above all, it means telling the voters the truth.

For decades, the American conservative movement has been founded on two promises. One of them, it kept: Soviet communism was not just contained but defeated. The other promise, however, was to reverse the onslaught of big government. And that promise was built on an evasion. Conservatives kept saying: "It's those *liberals* who keep building up Washington!"

What the conservatives did not say was that the average American government-basher reaps a golden harvest of tax breaks and subsidies. Government transfer payments are a sum equivalent to about a quarter of all wages and salaries earned by Americans—and that's before counting such massive tax breaks as the deduction for interest on mortgages. "As far as federal expenditures are concerned," wrote Herbert Stein, who was the chairman of President Nixon's Council of Economic Advisers, "[the] welfare state for the not-poor is about five times as big as the welfare state for the poor." Tax breaks and regulatory protections are even more heavily skewed toward the not-poor. By the early 1990s, noted former commerce secretary Peter G. Peterson, an average household whose income was over $100,000 collected almost twice as much in government entitlement and tax benefits as did a household earning less than $10,000. (If the government's goal is to equalize incomes, he said, "it would do a better job if it . . . simply scattered all the money by airplane over every population center, to be gathered at random by passersby.") No one is off the gravy train—certainly not conservative politicians and their antigovernment constituencies.

Newt Gingrich's 1994 Contract with America was full of poll-tested bromides and bumper-sticker favorites (term limits, balanced-budget amendment, middle-class tax cuts, anticrime measures). What it did not contain, even in broad outline, was any attempt to lay the groundwork among conservative voters for any unpleasant reduction in government's scope. Ronald Reagan, in his successful 1980 campaign, told the people that smaller government meant cutting "waste." Even Barry Goldwater flinched. As his biographer Robert Alan Goldberg has pointed out, when Goldwater first ran for the Senate in 1952, he promised to halt the expansion of the federal bureaucracy and cut taxes. Indeed, he described FDR's New Deal and Truman's Fair Deal as "a devilish plan to eventually socialize this country." But he also hastened to reassure his listeners that his opposition to government did not mean actually eliminating any federal programs. "No responsible Republican has any intention or desire to abolish any one of them." Why do you suppose the conservatives failed?

The reluctance of conservatives to sell themselves to the public as the party of pain—the root-canal party—is understandable. Nonetheless, as long as conservatives are unwilling to level with the voters about what smaller government actually means— less stuff for *you*—they will be enablers of the public's addiction to transfer-seeking. In their eagerness to make government-cutting sound easy and fun, conservatives have helped persuade the electorate that there is no reason to support any actual hard work of cutting anything except "waste" (read: somebody else's programs). Thus has American conservatism become hand-maiden to the "big government" that it so stridently condemns.

Can either side adjust? It's not easy, partly because the conservative and liberal ideologies stymie each other. Conservatives hate to say no to their subsidized friends because they believe liberals will take the money and spend it on new benefits for big-city mayors and welfare bureaucrats. Liberals hate to say yes to program reductions because they believe conservatives will take the money and spend it on tax cuts for the rich. Both sides compete for the affections of a middle class that would just as soon not be told it's part of the problem. So neither side gets anywhere. Government stays too big for conservatives and too inflexible for liberals. It neither solves problems nor goes away.

How Moderates Can Help

Well, politicians are always going to overpromise, and activists are always going to try to bite off more than they can chew, and the left and right will always be dogmatic and stubborn and opposed to all of each other's best ideas. That's life. In fact, having some unrealistic reformers around is all to the good, because they generate energy and ideas, and over the long haul—sometimes even over the short haul—they change the boundaries of the politically possible. (All of the major reforms of the 1970s, 1980s, and 1990s—Carter's deregulation, Reagan's tax reform, Clinton's welfare reform—began as gleams in the eyes of unrealistic people with odd ideas.) No, hope lies less with the activists at either side of the spectrum than with the much larger group of ordinary voters in the middle. Those of us who live in the broad middle, and who devote our everyday lives to life rather than to politics, are the ones who bear the real burden of adjustment.

The adjustment begins with mature expectations. If the public is going to reward politicians who chip away at the empire of the entrenched interests, then it will need to appreciate what the politicians manage to do, which means, above all, not expecting too much. For decades, the public has been holding politicians to unrealistic standards. To no small extent, of course, that is because the politicians made unrealistic promises. But that's what politicians do. What the rest of us should not do is to let the politicians' blustery rhetoric define what it is we mean by success.

Radicals promise a new era of popular government or smaller government or whatever because they believe it is achievable (otherwise, why be radical?). Politicians promise similar new eras because they find it to be expedient (otherwise, why elect them?). In 1999, one Republican presidential candidate (former Tennessee governor Lamar Alexander) made a habit of promising to "cut federal regulations exactly in half." He named only one regulation to be cut, an Environmental Protection Agency rule having to do with propane storage on farms. The other thousands and thousands of regulations to be swept away would presumably be identified after the election. This sort of rhetoric is not helpful. It sets ludicrous expectations for success and proposes entirely fanciful reforms. It amounts to a wishing away of government, a blithe denial of what government is.

At government's end, success comes in dribs and drabs, often unglamorously. The transportation reforms of the 1970s and the tax reform of 1986 and the World Trade Organization agreement of 1993 were all very powerful and important antisclerotics. The farm bill of 1996 may prove to be another, and so might a major reform of the banking laws (to their credit, the politicians kept failing but kept trying to and are trying again as I write this). But none of those measures did or could transform Washington into a City of the People. No really effective antisclerotic medicine ever will. For Americans of the broad center, it's important not to expect miracles. Otherwise, we'll fail to reward politicians who come through with real-world reforms. Real-world success means not "returning government to the people" (or whatever) but simply putting additional pressure on particular lobbies at every opportunity, a less dramatic but far more attainable goal.

That is what I was getting at when I said, in the first chapter, that it's not enough to accept the natural limits on government's ability to change society, an adjustment that is already grudgingly under way. Equally or even more important is a willingness to accept the natural limits on society's ability to change government. There will be no "revolution." The future is not an emergence from a dark wood into a flowered vista of the Emerald City. It is instead an unceasing struggle to clear paths through the jungle, hacking down weeds and beating back swamps, but never either winning decisively or losing. If we work at it, every decade or so there might be one or two major programmatic reforms, like the farm and welfare bills of the 1990s or the tax reform of the 1980s or the transportation deregulation of the 1970s—something fundamental that brings fresh air to a dank and moldy chamber of the government. Plus, no less important, there would be a constant opportunistic hunt for smaller ways to expose protected lobbies to competition: charter schools, subsidy reductions, what have you.

One or two major programmatic reforms in a decade, plus a constant drizzle of smaller, incremental reforms along the way, seem to be small potatoes if you're used to hearing politicians promise (as, for example, some of the Gingrichite Republicans did in 1995) a 40 percent reduction in government's size. But incremental change on a steady course can be surprisingly powerful. In the mid-1980s, the federal budget deficit looked intractable. It seemed to dwarf each of the deficit-reduction plans that Congress passed every couple of years or so. Yet patience and persistence paid off. True, the high tax receipts generated by a glowing economy made a critical contribution. But so did Ronald Reagan's reluctant tax increases of 1982 and 1984, George Bush's antideficit deal with the Democratic Congress in 1990, and Bill Clinton's smaller but still noteworthy budget agreement with Congress in 1993. None of the agreements made lasting structural changes in the government, and all of them were derided at the time, by me among others, as inadequate to the scope of the problem. But each of those many attacks on the budget deficit involved some degree of real political courage on the part of politicians. (Bush's 1990 budget deal, when he broke his "no new taxes" promise, was especially notable in that regard. The deal probably cost Bush his presidency, but it also probably did more than any other single policy measure to control the deficit.) Sure enough, the increments added up. The moral of the story is also, I think, a good motto for smart reformers in the new century: At government's end, the small potatoes *are* the big potatoes.

Why a Dream Must Be Buried

The sort of radical incrementalism I'm suggesting amounts to accepting a different and, for many people, discomforting view of the public's sovereignty. Voters and politicians are not absolute lords of the realm or a court of highest authority; they are more like kings in the age of Magna Carta, constrained on every side by powerful barons who can be cajoled but not commanded. Washington, we have all grown up being assured, is our servant. We command it! But in fact, at government's end, we must negotiate with it. And if we do not negotiate cleverly, it gets the better of us. Learning to live with this sort of government is, for many Americans, a shock. That is maybe the hardest adjustment of all.

Not so long ago, the promise of American government seemed boundless, at least if you were anywhere to the left of Barry Goldwater. The federal government seemed the most promising social tool ever invented. In practice, of course, Washington still often fell short. But most of us assumed that the governmental tool kit would be refined to make more and more problems soluble. Government, like technology, would improve rather than decline with age; it would learn how to run programs that would solve poverty, dampen business cycles, and so on. Even today, many people are unwilling to give up on the idea that government can be the tool of their dreams. They call upon it to fix low productivity, high hospital bills, teenage pregnancy, and cable-television rates. But instead of becoming stronger, government became feebler. Instead of improving its grip on national problems, it lost traction.

The great expectations of a sweet but fleeting era are difficult to relinquish. But there is no point indulging fantasies. Government's debilities are not temporary. That doesn't mean that government is dead. It does mean that the government of our dreams is dead.

In truth, this demise is no disaster. The Social Security checks will still go out, the budget will still be passed (most years), and patchwork reforms and emergency bills will still be approved. When a program goes totally haywire, it will be stopped from exploding altogether. When Medicare costs began running willy-nilly in the 1980s, Washington was able to tinker with the program to tame the worst excesses. True, the government has become less agile and effective. But that's a prescription for frustration, not death. And frustration with government, as Americans know from experience, is something they can live with if need be.

In some ways, in fact, the death of the dream may be to the good. Americans tend to be obsessed with government. Liberals hunt for a governmental solution for every problem; conservatives hunt for a governmental cause for every problem. Liberals scheme day and night to expand government; conservatives, to shrink it. All of them are governmentalists, in the sense that they define their ideologies and social passions in relation to government. In fact, many people's first impulse is to think that if American government calcifies, so must American society.

It isn't so. One way or another, social change finds ways to flow around obstacles and obsolescence. Technology and ingenuity work to undercut anachronisms and monopolies. The postal service's monopoly on first-class mail has not stopped the onslaught from fax technology, to say nothing of e-mail and the Internet. American sugar interests managed to restrict sugar imports, but they couldn't fend off NutraSweet.

Besides, there are many ways to solve problems, many tools besides government. It's a shame when government gets rusty, but people won't wait around sitting on their hands until Washington turns into a creative dynamo. When General Motors found that its workers couldn't read and add well enough to run a new high-tech plant, it started teaching them. Today, many corporations are delivering education that the public schools are not. Others are providing child care and family services for their workers. Haggar Apparel discovered that premature births among its employees were contributing to its rising health-care costs. The company began offering prenatal health classes and took steps to encourage preventive care, with good results. Black & Decker did something similar. Sunbeam-Oster Appliance Company set up a program offering free pregnancy testing and bimonthly maternity classes. The American litigation system has become increasingly clotted with opportunistic lawsuits, pursued in many cases by aggressive lawyers who are themselves one of Washington's most powerful (and wealthy) lobbies. That's not good. But when I signed the papers to revise this book, I also agreed to use binding arbitration to settle any disputes with the publisher. Instead of going through the courts, I'll go around them.

People who need to solve problems are inventive. Blocked in one direction, they will try another. Environmentalists are no strangers to the arthritic pace of government bureaucracy and the excruciating cost of litigation. "The legislation-regulation-litigation sequence is painfully slow," as Jessica Mathews of the World Resources Institute has pointed out. The Center for Resource Economics, an environmental research organization, conducted a study of the Environmental Protection Agency and found that the agency had been so hobbled by underfunding, mismanagement, and outside political intervention that it "has been unable to accomplish its mission [and] cannot ensure that American communities and industries are in full compliance with a single federal environmental law." So environmentalists have begun going around the transfer-seeking swamp. "Environmentalists and industries have recently been looking for alternatives to the regulatory straitjacket," notes Mathews, citing "notable instances of cooperation," as when McDonald's and the Environmental Defense Fund worked together to reduce the company's production of solid wastes.

Such ad hoc arrangements may not be ideal, but the point is that government calcification does not necessarily mean that problems don't get solved. Other institutions can compensate, at least to some degree. To a large degree, they probably will. If government's condition deteriorates instead of stabilizing, we'll just need to think harder about nongovernmental ways to solve problems.

On Beyond Government

In a way, if Washington had to succumb to old age, it could have picked a worse time than now. Although America's government is decreasingly flexible and adaptive, America's leading problems are increasingly nongovernmental. Strangely, government's debilities may bring the perverse but useful side benefit of forcing Americans to focus less on Washington at a time when our problems have become singularly unresponsive to Washington solutions.

A few years ago, at an embassy party on a sticky summer day, I chatted with a man whom I regard as one of Washington's leading analysts of public policy—a scholar and (at that time) government official who leans liberal and Democratic but is well respected by members of both parties. (I keep his name confidential here because public officials aren't supposed to talk as honestly as he did.) We began talking about the country's social problems and how his outlook had changed over two decades, since the 1970s. Even back then, he considered himself a realist: He thought well-designed government programs might be able to improve social conditions by—oh, maybe 40 percent. And today? He pondered a minute, sipped his drink, and ventured: probably more on the order of 5 percent. Although he was well aware of government's weakening record of solving problems, at that moment he wasn't thinking about government. He was thinking about a profound change in the nature of the country's problems.

As a rule of thumb, large, central governments are best at four kinds of missions. First, they can wage or prepare for war—something no other institution can do. Fighting two world wars and then the Cold War was easily the federal government's most important project in the twentieth century, and also the most successful. Second, governments can build big national infrastructure projects: giant, one-shot bricks-and-mortar programs that are designed to leave tracks or roads on the ground for years. The federal government built the interstate highway system, ran the Manhattan Project, and flew astronauts to the moon. Insofar as those were focused, do-it-once projects, they succeeded. (By contrast, when the government tried to convert NASA to an ongoing concern, expecting it to adapt without giving it a clear mission, the space program ran into trouble.) Third, although government is poor at providing services or manipulating human behavior, it is good at writing checks. By doing so, it set up the basic safety-net programs, such as Social Security and unemployment insurance. Finally, government is good at setting minimum standards of political and social freedom. Thus it struck down local barriers to opportunity for blacks, something that no other institution could have done.

On balance, Washington did all those things quite well. Then, having done them, it looked at itself and found that it had been transformed, and it looked around and saw that the world, too,

had been transformed. Today we meet the result of both trans-
formations: Washington's golden age, a roughly thirty-year period
beginning with the New Deal, is over, for good.

Government was transformed partly by its prior successes; it
was a victim of its own brand of imperial overstretch.
Encouraged by the successes of a relatively flexible government
doing relatively manageable tasks, people began to say things
like "If we can send a man to the moon, then by God we can
solve [here insert favorite unmet social need]"—as though
because government can do some things well, it should be
expected to do all things well. People didn't see that a government adept at mailing Social Security checks is not necessarily
adept at running a health-care system, nor did they see how they
might calcify government by demanding too much from it. A million intricate social and human missions were heaped on
Washington's docket, each to be accomplished by many programs defended by countless constituencies—all at a time when
Washington's adaptability had been gravely diminished. That, of
course, is the story of demosclerosis.

Meanwhile, however, the world was changing. Much as
viruses mutate to resist vaccines, so the country's problems
changed in ways that have defeated the postwar toolbox of centralized government programs. By the 1990s, America's leading
problems—not the only problems but certainly the most important ones—related not to the physical infrastructure but to the
social and moral infrastructure. The murder rate doubled
between the early 1960s and the early 1990s, and would have
been higher still if not for improved medical care (a homicide
occurs only if the victim dies). A young black man in Watts or
the South Side of Chicago was likelier to be killed in violence
than was a soldier during an average tour in Vietnam. American
high-school students performed less well than either their parents' generation or their peers in other developed countries, and
many of the schools became physically dangerous as well as edu-
cationally bankrupt. Early in the twentieth century, America

saved more than almost any other developed country; by the end of the century, its personal saving rate was at the bottom of the heap. The divorce rate more than doubled between 1960 and 1980; from 1960 to 1995, the illegitimacy rate rose from 5 percent to more than 30 percent. In 1970, one in nine American children lived in a fatherless home; by 1997 more than one in four did (including 60 percent of black children). The link between fatherlessness and pathology—poverty, violence, crime, mental illness, poor education, and other personal and social troubles—is now beyond denying.

The point is not that all these problems are getting worse. Some of the alarming trends have begun to turn around, partly because people began to focus on them. Rather, the point is that the *nature* of the country's most pressing problems changed. In 1960, a teenager was twice as likely to die of cancer as to be killed by somebody else; only twenty years later, the odds were reversed. Not only did cancer deaths decrease, but killings increased. While we developed the medical technology to prevent and treat cancer, we lost our grip on the social technology to prevent and treat violence, which in theory is more preventable. This seems almost crazy. Who could ever have imagined?

Government no doubt had some role in creating or complicating these problems; no doubt it must play some role in reducing or ameliorating them. But in comparison to family, community, church, school, and self, government is the social institution that is least well adapted to solving them. Washington can write a check and build a bomb, but divorce and crime are not the kinds of problems the government can throw money at or solve with a crash development program. Even the most adroit public sector cannot rebuild character the way it can rebuild roads.

As I write these words on the doorstep of the new century, America is enjoying a period of resurgence. Its social and economic problems are not all solved, but many of the trends are going in the right direction. The economy has been performing remarkably well; crime and divorce rates have declined, although they remain well above the levels of the early 1960s and before; people are living longer and staying healthier. No doubt the future will bring setbacks, crises, and always plenty of troubles. Still, the contrast between the government's decline and the republic's vigor serves as a powerful reminder that government's end is a disappointment, but it is not a death warrant. It is less a death warrant, in fact, than it is a ticket to whatever comes next.

On Beyond Blame

When he left office in 1981, Jimmy Carter delivered a warning. "Today, as people have become ever more doubtful of the ability of the government to deal with our problems, we are increasingly drawn to single-issue groups and special-interest organizations to ensure that, whatever else happens, our own personal views and our own private interests are protected," he said. "This is a disturbing factor in American political life. It tends to distort our purposes, because the national interest is not always the sum of all our single or special interests." He was right then, and he is still right.

To hope that Americans will desist from joining groups that advance their interests, or from voting for politicians who grant them favors, is neither realistic nor fair. But to hope that they will understand how their activities contribute to their government's problems doesn't seem so crazy. Understanding isn't a solution (there is no solution), but it is a big help. It can make the political climate more congenial to radical incrementalism by showing people why constant, consistent pressure from the political center can work, and why spasmodic "revolutions" from the political extremes so often fail. It can also, perhaps, make the public a little better aware of how the blame-game, with its "not my fault" mentality, serves the interests of the transfer-seeking class.

The rise of the professional transfer-seeking economy, with its breathtaking ability to mobilize antagonism and neutralize enemies, is, of course, a problem. But behind every transfer-seeking professional is a client saying "Gimme," or at least saying "Protect me." In its mindlessly mechanical way, the transfer-seeking game is clever. Generalized voter discontent and inflated political rhetoric about "change" trouble the transfer-seekers not at all, and often play into their hands. As the people become angrier, the groups and associations and lawyers and lobbyists and politicians tell them, "Those fiendish special interests are behind it! Hire me to protect you before they rob you blind! Vote for me to see to it that *your* interests are represented!" By now, you know where that leads. Blaming some villain for what is in fact a systemic problem is a guarantee that the real problem will not be confronted. It is a guarantee, in other words, that everyone will keep ordering the ten-dollar dessert, and will justify it by pointing to the glutton across the table.

Monkeys ransack the forest for medicinal plants that kill intestinal worms. Dogs gnaw through fur and flesh to rip out ticks or fleas. So the American body politic instinctively flails against the parasite economy, casting votes for politicians who claim to be "outsiders" or who promise to fight the "special interests" that are responsible for all our suffering. No one in politics is eager to repudiate the politics of blame and tell the people the truth: that they—we—are the special interests. Who finances and sustains the parasite economy? Not villainous lobbyists or crooked insiders or crafty foreigners. Look in the mirror.

For the public to get its mind fully around its deep complicity in government's debilitation will, no doubt, be a process of decades. But then, we have decades, and understanding can make a big difference on the margins, which is, after all, where the action is going to be for the indefinite future. In 1982, Mancur Olson ended *The Rise and Decline of Nations* on a hopeful note. "Ideas certainly do make a difference," he wrote. "May we not then reasonably expect, if special interests are (as I have claimed) harmful to economic growth, full employment, coherent government, equal opportunity, and social mobility, that students of the matter will become increasingly aware of this as time goes on? And that the awareness eventually will spread to larger and larger proportions of the population? And that this wider awareness will greatly limit the losses from the special interests? That is what I expect, at least when I am searching for a happy ending."

A year or two before he died, when I last saw him, Mancur Olson was still searching for that happy ending, and he reported being optimistic three days out of five. His spirit was the proper one.

A New Entente

So the end of government is not, after all, a sad time. It's sad, I suppose, if you happen to be a liberal idealist or a conservative revolutionary, for whom nothing less than a new dawn will do. For the rest of us, it is a time of maturely diminished expectations combined with maturely persistent ministrations.

That combination, admittedly, isn't an easy balance to strike, because the two elements are in tension, pulling in opposite directions. One message seems to be "It's all over. You can never win, so give up." The other message seems to be "Keep at it! Open the government and the economy! You'll never finish the job, but every little bit helps!" It's fair to wonder: If there can be no promise of final victory, how can anyone sustain enthusiasm for the fight?

In the end, that is why it's so important to adjust our attitudes to government, as well as to adjust government itself. Like the aging person who knows he'll never be young again but who nevertheless understands why he should stay on his diet and take some exercise every day, Americans need to understand the limits of change without surrendering to passivity. They need to understand what is doable. Then they need to do it.

To some extent, I think, that sort of mental adjustment is under way. It seemed to begin somewhere around the time the second Republican Revolution flared and burned out. The Washington of the late 1990s was a more jaded but also more realistic place than the Washington of the late 1980s or—certainly—the Washington of the late 1970s or the late 1960s. Voters and politicians and activists, especially politicians and activists, all have a long way to go to adjust to government's end. If you squint, however, you can just make out the way ahead toward a new entente between the people and their government: one that deals with government as it has come to be and as it will remain, rather than as we may wish it were or as we imagine it once was.

After half a century of ballyhooed "new deals" in American political life—the original New Deal and then the Fair Deal and the New Frontier and the Great Society and the Reagan Revolution and the Republican Revolution and whatever else—comes a hush, and then a still, small voice, like a rustling of leaves. It speaks, to those who have the patience and maturity to listen, of what is perhaps the most momentous new deal of all. Call it Real Life.

A Note on Sources

To avoid burdening the reader with footnotes and the like, I have generally cited sources in the text. Following are more details on sources used.

Chapter 1

Alan Simpson's Senate speech, which still repays reading, was given on February 22, 1985, while Senate leaders negotiated the confirmation of Edwin Meese III as attorney general. The speech can be found beginning on page S-1797 of that day's *Congressional Record*. Marvin Leath's speech in the House of Representatives was delivered May 23, 1985, and is in the *Record* beginning on page H-3646. The Everett Carll Ladd quotation is from "Why Are So Many People So Pessimistic in So Many Different Countries?" in *The Public Perspective*, March/April 1993. The Putnam, et al., multination survey data on confidence in politicians and parliaments, as well as Martin Wattenberg's figure on decline in voter turnouts, are reported in *The Economist*, July 17, 1999.

Chapter 2

Mancur Olson's *The Logic of Collective Action* was published by Harvard University Press (1965); *The Rise and Decline of Nations*, by Yale University Press (1982). David Grann's *New Republic* article was from November 30, 1998. The American Motors executive speaking in 1976 about General Motors was quoted by John A. Barnes in "A Sad Day for GM Proves that the Market Rules," *The Wall Street Journal*, February 25, 1992. W. Hampton Sides's piquant description of the bicycle couriers Suicide and Scrooge can be found in the December

279

A Note on Sources

21, 1992, issue of *The New Republic*. The Associated Press's story on the Alliance for Safe and Responsible Lead Abatement is from February 17, 1999.

Chapter 3

For the historical material on lobbying, I have gratefully drawn on Jeffrey H. Birnbaum's book *The Lobbyists: How Influence Peddlers Get Their Way in Washington* (Times Books, 1992). It is the best account I know of the life of a lobbyist. Also useful is Birnbaum's article "Lobbyists: Why the Bad Rap?" in *The American Enterprise,* November/December 1992.

For the coinage "the advocacy explosion" and much helpful data on the expansion of lobbying, see Jeffrey M. Berry's book *The Interest Group Society* (Scott, Foresman/Little, Brown, 1989). On the advocacy explosion, another valuable source of data and analysis is Allan J. Cigler and Burdett A. Loomis, eds., *Interest Group Politics,* third edition (CQ Press, 1991). The "typical study" in 1985 of public-interest groups is by the Foundation for Public Affairs and is discussed by Ronald G. Shaiko, "More Bang for the Buck: The New Era of Full-Service Public Interest Organizations," in Cigler and Loomis. The data on growth of environmental groups are from Christopher J. Bosso, "Adaptation and Change in the Environmental Movement," also in Cigler and Loomis.

Robert Wright's quotation is from his article "Democracy's Impending Demise," in *The Sciences,* November/December 1985. Steven E. Schier's thinking on "activation" of constituencies is in *By Invitation Only: Contemporary Party, Interest Group and Campaign Strategies* (forthcoming from the University of Pittsburgh Press). Hugh Heclo's article "Hyperdemocracy" appeared in the *Wilson Quarterly,* Winter 1999.

Dean Robert C. Clark's quotation is from "Why So Many Lawyers? Are They Good or Bad?" in *Fordham Law Review,* Vol. 61, No. 2 (November 1992). On the formation of farm groups in this century, I have drawn on John Mark Hansen's book *Gaining Access: Congress and the Farm Lobby, 1919–1981* (University of Chicago Press, 1991). Terry L. Anderson's *New York Times* op-ed piece discussing the socioeconomics of environmental-group members is from June 28, 1993.

Chapter 4

The estimates by David N. Laband and John P. Sophocleus of investment in criminal transfer-seeking were published in their article "An Estimate of Resource Expenditures on Transfer Activity in the United States," *Quarterly Journal of Economics,* Vol. 107, No. 3 (August 1992). I am indebted to David Laband for the term "transfer-seeking" (among economists, the rather obscure term "rent-seeking" is more common). On the lobbying fight between nurses and anesthesiologists, see Shawn Zeller, "Clamps, Sutures, and Big, Big Bucks," in *National Journal,* March 20, 1999.

A Note on Sources

The quotations in this chapter from Cigler and Loomis are from their introduction to *Interest Group Politics,* cited in the Chapter 3 sources. Marc Galanter's figures on state judicial activity—and much other data on legal activity—may be found in "Law Abounding: Legalisation Around the North Atlantic," *The Modern Law Review,* Vol. 55, No. 1 (January 1992).

The Center for Responsive Politics, whose research I draw upon in this chapter and elsewhere in the book, provides a wealth of information on political contributions, much of it available on the center's website, http://www.opensecrets.org. Louis Jacobson's account of Internet lobbying appeared in *National Journal,* December 19, 1998. For an eye-opener on the interest-group industry, no one should miss *National Journal'*s regular surveys of group executives' pay and perks; I have drawn upon the 1995 data, published April 26, 1997. David E. Rosenbaum's astute analysis of tax-law churning ran in *The New York Times* on December 8, 1992.

Chapter 5

James DeLong's article on the family-leave bill was in *The New Republic,* April 19, 1993. For the maritime lobby's subsidies, see Rob Quartel, a former member of the Federal Maritime Commission, writing on the op-ed page of *The Washington Post,* December 15, 1992.

The RAND overview of tort litigation is by Deborah R. Hensler, Mary E. Vaiana, James S. Kakalik, and Mark A. Peterson, in *Trends in Tort Litigation: The Story Behind the Statistics* (RAND, 1987). The Saul B. Shapiro quotation is from his op-ed article "Clumsy? Sue New York City," in *The New York Times,* September 30, 1992. Peter Huber's book, detailing the impact of litigation on manufacturers of vaccines and small airplanes, is *Liability: The Legal Revolution and Its Consequences* (Basic Books, 1988). The extended quotation from Dan Dobbs is taken from "Can You Care for People and Still Count the Costs?" in the *Maryland Law Review,* Vol. 46, No. 1 (1986). For tort-litigation costs, an important source is Tillinghast's *Tort Cost Trends: An International Perspective;* I drew upon the 1992 edition and the 1995 update.

For estimates of the costs of international farm subsidies, the key source is the Organization for Economic Cooperation and Development; on the total cost of subsidies, I cite the 1997 figure as reported in the OECD's 1998 policy brief *Agricultural Policy Reform.* The RAND estimates of employment effects of laws restricting firing are in James N. Dertouzos and Lynn A. Karoly, *Labor-Market Responses to Employer Liability* (RAND, 1992).

The findings on fancy restaurants in state capitals are from the paper by David N. Laband, Frank Mixon, and Robert Ekelund, Jr., in *Public Choice,* Vol. 78, No. 2 (February 1994). The $1 trillion estimate of transfer-seeking investment in 1985 is from the article by Laband and Sophocleus cited in the Chapter 4 sources.

A Note on Sources

Chapter 6

On the sugar program's costs and beneficiaries, see the U.S. General Accounting Office's report *Sugar Program: Changing Domestic and International Conditions Require Program Changes* (April 1993). Education Secretary Richard W. Riley's renunciation of school-voucher experiments was from his confirmation hearings, quoted in *Education Week,* January 20, 1993. On the rural electrification program, a good sketch of the politics is in James Bennet, "Power Failure," *The Washington Monthly,* July 1990 (to which I am indebted for the quotation from the former government official who said that opposing the program was hopeless). On the peanut program, see the General Accounting Office's *Peanut Program: Changes Are Needed to Make the Program Responsive to Market Forces* (February 1993).

Freeman Dyson's invaluable perspective on finding the right size, along with many other powerful insights, is in *Infinite in All Directions* (Harper & Row, 1988). I also quote briefly from Dyson's *From Eros to Gaia* (Pantheon, 1992).

On Roosevelt's New Deal, I am indebted to Michael Barone, *Our Country: The Shaping of America from Roosevelt to Reagan* (Free Press, 1990). The estimate of investment spending in Clinton's first budget is from Todd Schafer, "Still Neglecting Public Investment: The FY94 Budget Outlook," Economic Policy Institute briefing paper, September 1993. Steven Waldman's report on the national-service initiative's fate is in *Newsweek,* September 20, 1993. Paul C. Light's work on the "derivative presidency" is in *The President's Agenda: Domestic Policy Choice from Kennedy to Clinton* (Johns Hopkins University Press); I draw on the third edition, published in 1999.

Chapter 7

Here and in subsequent chapters, I gratefully draw upon Robert Alan Goldberg's fine biography *Barry Goldwater* (Yale University Press, 1995). The Urban Institute's analysis of Reagan's budgetary impact is Gregory B. Mills's "The Budget: A Failure of Discipline," in the institute's 1984 book *The Reagan Record* (edited by John L. Palmer and Isabel V. Sawhill). David Stockman's book *The Triumph of Politics: How the Reagan Revolution Failed* (Harper & Row, 1986) is a valuable source. Herbert Stein wrote in *Presidential Economics: The Making of Economic Policy from Roosevelt to Clinton* (American Enterprise Institute, 1994).

Stephen Moore's indispensable accounting of the Gingrich reforms is in *Reason* magazine, July 1998. On the Clinton health plan's demands on government, see the Congressional Budget Office's February 1994 *Analysis of the Administration's Health Proposal.*

Chapter 8

Gingrich's discussion of his legislative strategy is in the *Washington Times* of January 4, 1995. The ABC News poll was released on September 16, 1994, and

A Note on Sources

was also discussed by Richard Morin in *The Washington Post* of October 16, 1994 (ABC News informed me that the questions on what members of Congress should and shouldn't be doing were not asked again subsequently).

On the rural electrification program, Representative Melvin Watt was quoted by Kevin Merida in *The Washington Post*, May 8, 1993. The General Accounting Office's report, *Rural Utilities Service: Opportunities to Operate Electricity and Telecommunications Loan Programs More Effectively*, is from February 4, 1998.

I quote from the second (1979) edition of Theodore J. Lowi's *The End of Liberalism: The Second Republic of the United States* (W. W. Norton & Co.).

Chapter 9

Norman Ornstein's quotation is from his article "Money in Politics," *The Ripon Forum*, July/August 1992. Frank J. Sorauf's is from *Money in American Elections* (Scott, Foresman, 1988). On the Supreme Court and transfer-seeking, see Terry L. Anderson and Peter J. Hill, *The Birth of a Transfer Society* (Hoover Institution Press, 1980).

Alice Rivlin's provocative book *Reviving the American Dream: The Economy, the States, and the Federal Government* was published in 1992 by the Brookings Institution. Also on the subject of reallocating federal and state roles, Bruce Babbitt (then governor of Arizona) wrote in *The New Republic*, January 24, 1981.

The Osborne and Gaebler statements are from their book *Reinventing Government: How the Entrepreneurial Spirit Is Transforming the Public Sector* (Addison-Wesley, 1992). For a detailed account of how Japanese investment and know-how revitalized American rust-belt industries, an indispensable source is Martin Kenney and Richard Florida, *Beyond Mass Production: The Japanese System and Its Transfer to the U.S.* (Oxford University Press, 1993). The Organization for Economic Cooperation and Development's discussion of trade and the environment is from the OECD's 1998 policy brief *Open Markets Matter: The Benefits of Trade and Investment Liberalization*.

Chapter 10

My bullfight correspondent was Gideon Lichfield of *The Economist*. On welfare for the not-poor, see Herbert Stein's "Who's Subsidizing Whom?" in *The Wall Street Journal*, September 15, 1993, and Peter G. Peterson's "Facing Up," in *The Atlantic Monthly*, October 1993. Jessica Mathews wrote on the op-ed page of *The Washington Post*, November 9, 1992. The Center for Resource Economics study of the EPA was reported in *The Washington Post*, May 24, 1993.

Index

Index

AOL, 92

Appalachian Regional Commission, 171, 172, 180

Arista Records, 111

Arizona Center for Law in the Public Interest, 49

Armey, Richard, 220

Asians, 40

Authoritarianism, 35–36, 37. *See also* Totalitarianism

Automobile industry, 30, 49, 61, 66, 146–147, 249, 251, 255

Avis Company, 68, 69

B

Babbitt, Bruce, 242–243

Baby boomers, 193

Baha'i religion, 41–42

Bankers, 75, 129

Banking reform, 11, 129–130

Barnette, Hank, 95

Bass Anglers Sportsman Society, 46–47

Bergland, Bob, 136, 137, 138

Berry, Jeffrey, 41

Big government, 3, 6, 10, 59, 148, 170, 174, 177, 182, 263, 265. *See also* Federal government, size/flexibility of

Big Three automakers, 30, 251. *See also* Automobile industry

Bill of Rights, 239

Birnbaum, Jeffrey H., 40, 92

Black, Hugo L., 39

Black and Decker, 270

Blacks, 40, 272, 273

Boston, 218

Bovard, James, 116

Bozell, L. Brent, 168

Brookings Institution, 246

Brown, Milt and Catherine, 78–79

Brownback, Sam, 98

Buchanan, Frank M., 40, 41

Buchanan, James, 39

Buchanan, Patrick J., 232

Budget, national, 153, 158, 171, 172, 173, 180, 181, 216, 221, 268

constitutional amendment for, 202

See also Deficits

Bureau of Mines, 181

Bush, George, 11, 55, 129, 132, 134–135, 144, 157, 180, 200, 202, 210, 267, 268

C

Cabinet agencies, 179

California, 159–162, 216, 218, 220

Campaign financing, 88, 88(fig.), 233, 234, 236–237. *See also* Money in politics

Canada, 16, 55, 105–106

Cancer, 274

Capitalism, 133, 192

Car alarms, 32–33

Car-Rental Coalition, 69, 91

Car-rental companies, 67–70, 77

Cartels, 29–30, 32, 172, 247, 251, 252

Carter, Jimmy, 14, 15, 172, 199, 202, 210, 246

Cato Institute, 179

Caucuses, congressional, 28

CBO. *See* Congressional Budget Office

Center for Public Integrity, 187

Center for Resource Economics, 270

Center for Responsive Politics, 89, 102, 103–104

Change, 125–126, 146, 147, 150, 155, 159, 166, 168, 189, 190, 192, 193, 204, 229, 232, 272–273, 276

incremental, 260, 267–268, 275

and political control of government, 214, 267

See also Federal programs, changing; Reforms; Social change

Chicago, 248

Chicago Tribune, 129

Child care, 11, 270

Children, 206

China, 37

Chiropractors, 188

Cigler, Allan J., 78, 87

Cisco Systems, 92

Cities, 38, 118–119

Citizen Action, 188

Citizens Against Government Waste, 218

Citizens Against Rationing Health, 188

Citizen Trade Campaign, 55

Civilian Conservation Corps, 149

Civil Liberties Act Amendments of 1992, 11

Index

Civil rights, 46, 85, 169
Civil Rights Act of 1991, 11
Civil service, 165
Civil War (U.S.), 37
Civil Works Administration, 149
Clark, Robert C., 58
Clean Air Act of 1990, 11, 15
Clinton, Bill, 1, 5, 6, 15–16, 93, 97, 101,
 104, 129, 132, 139, 154–159, 164,
 175, 176, 178, 180, 181, 200, 201,
 203, 210, 221, 232, 248, 257, 261,
 267–268
 health-care proposal of, 183–189, 190,
 205, 208
 and Medicare, 207
Cold War, 21, 272
Collective action, 24–27, 28, 48, 194, 209,
 211, 212, 224, 227, 231. *See also*
 Interest groups
Collision-damage waivers, 67–69
Commerce Department, 179, 180
Common Cause, 26
Communism, 263
Competition, 64, 77, 118, 129, 134, 138,
 241, 242, 245–246, 247, 249, 257,
 260, 267
 foreign, 250–256
 and government agencies, 248, 250
 See also Anticompetitive group action
Complex systems, 133, 209
Computers, 55–56, 161, 255. *See also*
 Internet
Congress, 12, 15, 55, 86, 91, 92, 95, 130,
 131, 140, 141, 142, 156, 157, 158,
 165, 167, 172, 174, 176, 178, 181,
 185, 199, 213, 219
 power structure of, 202, 204
 See also House of Representatives;
 Senate
CongressDaily/A.M., 90
Congressional Budget Office (CBO), 184
Congressional Quarterly, 86, 95, 131, 140,
 185, 206, 207
Conscience of a Conservative, The
 (Goldwater), 168
Conservative Opportunity Society, 176
Conservatives, 6, 8–9, 14, 17, 65, 134,
 148, 163, 166, 168, 170, 172, 176,
 193, 203, 238
 view of government, 227, 263–265, 269
Constitution, 202, 239

Contraceptives, 109
Contract with America, 177, 264. *See also*
 Gingrich, Newt
Coolidge, Calvin, 2
Cooperatives, 136, 137, 217, 219
Corbell, Nelda, 206
Corporate Health Care Coalition, 188
Corporate welfare, 179, 218, 219, 220, 264
Corporation for Public Broadcasting, 180
Corporations, 15, 29, 48, 49, 95, 143, 270
 corporate takeovers, 75
 with Washington offices, 87
Corruption, 40, 64, 96, 97, 165, 176
Costs, 68, 73, 76, 77–78, 99, 101, 122, 130,
 136, 139, 247, 254, 255
 of campaigns, 234
 of defensiveness and uncertainty,
 106–113
 health-care, 117, 183, 186, 187, 253,
 270. *See also* Health issues,
 health care
 liability-insurance, 108, 110
 of Medicare, 207, 269
 per public-school student, 249
 systemic, 102
 total hidden, 119–121
 See also Lawyers, legal costs;
 Lobbying, expenditures;
 Social costs; *under* Interest
 groups
Council of Economic Advisers, 110
Couriers, 30–31, 114
Court decisions, 58. *See also* Lawsuits
Crime/criminals, 76, 119, 274
Crises, 22, 63, 64
Cynicism, 209

D

Dairymen, 31–32, 172
Dalton, Russell, 16
D'Amato, Alfonse M., 72, 98
Deadweight loss, 114, 139
Debt. *See* National debt
Decentralization, 241–243, 257
Defense Department, 174
Defense issues, 25
 defense spending, 8, 9, 170, 171, 172,
 173, 174, 193
Deficits, 7, 8, 153, 156, 171, 175, 208, 227,
 254, 267–268

Index

Index

J

Jacobson, Louis, 92
Japan, 16, 36–37, 64, 251, 252, 256
Japanese American Redress Entitlement
    Program, 11
Johnson administration, 58, 152, 158, 169,
    172, 183

K

Keene, Barry, 160, 161
Kennedy, John F., 154, 158, 159, 172
Kenney, Martin, 251
Korologos, Tom, 93
Kosterlitz, Julie, 188

L

Laband, David N., 76, 103, 118, 119
Ladd, Everett Carll, 16
LaPlaca, Mike, 67, 68–69, 70, 78, 91
Laws, 12, 33, 50, 58, 59, 77, 85, 90, 91, 93,
    106, 108, 161, 197, 214, 240
    banking laws, 129–130
Lawsuits, 84–85, 84(fig.), 102, 105, 106,
    107, 108, 109, 110, 113, 270
    tort litigation, 103, 112, 112(fig.), 159
Lawyers, 70, 77, 78, 79, 80, 87, 89, 90,
    93, 95, 96, 112, 161, 187, 227, 270
    in Clinton administration cabinet, 97
    legal costs, 103, 106, 108, 109, 111,
        112(fig.)
    numbers of, 83–84, 83(fig.), 85, 86,
        121
Lead abatement, 33
Leadership, 13–14, 167, 170, 186, 190,
    198–199, 200–202, 210, 244
Leath, Marvin, 8–9, 17
Legal Services Corporation, 171, 172, 180
Legal Times, 93
Liberals, 6, 8–9, 14, 15, 65, 148, 163, 164,
    166, 168, 169, 193, 244–245
    view of government, 227, 260–263,
        265, 269, 271–272
Libertarians, 238, 240
Lichtman, Steve, 107–108
Light, Paul C., 158, 159
Litigation. *See* Lawsuits
Living standards, 120
Loans. *See* Federal government, federal
    loans

Lobbying, 2, 15, 18, 33, 47, 52, 57, 59, 60,
    69, 70, 71–72, 77, 79, 80, 87, 89,
    90, 93, 96, 102, 112, 113, 118, 131,
    135, 137–138, 160, 173, 174, 187,
    188, 196, 208, 226, 227, 231, 235,
    238, 240, 243–245, 257, 270
    "astroturf" lobbying, 56
    budgets for, 92
    chiropractors' lobby, 188
    competition among lobbies, 138,
        267
    early use of term, 39
    European farm lobby, 250–251, 252
    expenditures, 103–104, 136, 161
    by former government employees,
        145
    as group vs. individual effort, 40
    insurance lobbies, 92
    lobbies as elitist, 97
    lobbyists without clients, 161
    numbers of lobbies, 41, 86–87,
        87(fig.), 103, 121, 148, 149, 160.
        See also Interest groups, num-
        bers of
    for public schools, 248–249
    as public-spirited, 49–50, 80, 97
    reforms of lobbying process, 233–234,
        236
    salaries of officers, 92
    and tax reform, 200, 201
    techniques of, 54, 206
    and trade liberalization, 252
    weakening lobbies, 252
    See also Interest groups; Special
        interests
Lobbying Handbook, The (Zorack), 54
Local governments, 162, 173, 241
Logic of Collective Action, The (Olson),
    24–27, 197
Loomis, Burdett A., 78, 87
Los Angeles, 95
Lowi, Theodore J., 223–224, 225,
    226–227, 261
Lugar, Richard, 51–52, 130

M

MacArthur, Douglas, 37
McDonald's, 217, 219, 250, 271
McFarland, Ernest W., 167
Madison, James, 2, 239

Index

Index

North American Free Trade Agreement (NAFTA), 254

O

Obstetricians, 109
Ocean Spray International, 217
OECD. *See* Organization for Economic Cooperation and Development
Office of Technology Assessment, 181
Olson, Mancur, 24–38, 46, 48, 62, 118, 126, 192, 194, 197, 198, 209, 211, 224, 225, 276–277
Openness, 256–257, 277
Opinion polls, 16, 152, 213. *See also* Public opinion
Organization for Economic Cooperation and Development (OECD), 116, 253
Ornstein, Norman J., 234, 235
Osborne, David, 247, 248
Ostrom, Brian J., 84–85

P

PACs. *See* Political action committees
Panetta, Leon, 157, 220
Parasites. *See* Economy, parasite economy; Transfer-seeking, as parasitic
Parliamentary systems, 16, 126
Peanuts, 116, 130, 138–139, 146, 180, 215, 245
Perot, Ross, 232
Perry, Pete, 141–142
Persian Gulf War, 13
Peterson, Peter G., 264
Pharmaceutical companies, 49
Pharr, Susan, 16
Philadelphia, 162
Philippines, 36
Phillips, Kevin, 244
Phoenix, Arizona, 247
Playgrounds, 107
Pluralism/hyperpluralism, 62, 64, 65, 121, 135, 143, 227
Police, 156
Political action committees (PACs), 31, 69, 70, 71, 77, 102, 136, 235
health-related, 188
Political campaigns, 88, 88(fig.). *See also* Campaign financing

Popcorn Institute, 2117
Population, 52
Postal service, 270
Poultry and Egg Export Council, 217
Poverty, national, 153–154
Power lines, 85
Presidency, 15, 158, 244
Prices, 32, 55, 63, 69, 70, 77, 106, 116, 117, 118, 130, 138, 169, 178, 183, 247
Problem solving, 5, 10, 12, 14, 18, 60, 121, 125, 148, 149, 151, 163, 193, 215, 260, 265, 270, 271, 272, 274
Productivity, 28, 29, 34, 71, 74, 119–121, 120(fig.), 154, 252. *See also* Investments, productive vs. transfer-seeking
Professionalism, 165
Programs. *See* Federal programs
Progressive Era, 58, 164–165
Progressivism, 152
Promises, 263, 265, 266
Property-rights movement, 240
Proposition 13, 161
Protectionism, 252
Public goods, 25
Public-interest groups. *See under* Interest groups
Public Interest, The, 3, 170
Public mobilization, 205
Public opinion, 182, 206. *See also* Opinion polls
Public relations firms, 87, 187
Public sector, 246–247, 248, 274
Purdue University, 116
Putnam, Robert, 16

R

Race relations, 169
Railroads, 33, 40, 150, 246, 248
RAND studies, 103, 110
Ravitch, Diane, 144–146
REA. *See* Rural Electrification Administration
Reactionary liberalism, 244
Reagan, Ronald, 3, 8, 14, 58, 95, 134, 143, 164, 166, 168, 177, 180, 201, 202, 210, 243, 267
Reagan Revolution, 170–175, 182, 185, 189, 206–207, 209, 278
Real-estate interests, 49, 89, 92, 95, 115, 117

Index

PublicAffairs is a publishing house founded in 1997. It is a tribute to the standards, values, and flair of three persons who have served as mentors to countless reporters, writers, editors, and book people of all kinds, including me.

I.F. STONE, proprietor of *I. F. Stone's Weekly*, combined a commitment to the First Amendment with entrepreneurial zeal and reporting skill and became one of the great independent journalists in American history. At the age of eighty, Izzy published *The Trial of Socrates*, which was a national bestseller. He wrote the book after he taught himself ancient Greek.

BENJAMIN C. BRADLEE was for nearly thirty years the charismatic editorial leader of *The Washington Post*. It was Ben who gave the *Post* the range and courage to pursue such historic issues as Watergate. He supported his reporters with a tenacity that made them fearless and it is no accident that so many became authors of influential, best-selling books.

ROBERT L. BERNSTEIN, the chief executive of Random House for more than a quarter century, guided one of the nation's premier publishing houses. Bob was personally responsible for many books of political dissent and argument that challenged tyranny around the globe. He is also the founder and longtime chair of Human Rights Watch, one of the most respected human rights organizations in the world.

For fifty years, the banner of Public Affairs Press was carried by its owner Morris B. Schnapper, who published Gandhi, Nasser, Toynbee, Truman, and about 1,500 other authors. In 1983, Schnapper was described by *The Washington Post* as "a redoubtable gadfly." His legacy will endure in the books to come.

Peter Osnos, *Founder and Editor-at-Large*

2146212169

Made in the USA
Lexington, KY
26 January 2010